Highly recommended reading not only for scholars and students interested in the history of modern Islamic ideas but to anybody who cares about the proper relationship between religious faith, science and politics in the Islamic world today.

Professor Torkel Brekke, Professor, author of Fundamentalism: Prophecy and Protest in an Age of Globalization *(2012)*

Uriya Shavit shows with great erudition that the modernist-apologists are not a thing of the past. The discourse of 'Abduh and Rida still inspires Arab Muslim scholars and intellectuals to formulate alternatives to both secularism and intransigent Islamism.

Professor Martin Riexinger, Aarhus Universitet, Denmark

SCIENTIFIC AND POLITICAL FREEDOM IN ISLAM

The modernist-apologetic approach to the relation between revelation and science, and revelation and politics, has been a central part of Arab discourses on the future of Muslim societies for over a century. This approach introduced historical and theological narratives and interpretative mechanisms that contextualize reason and freedom in Islamic terms to argue that, unlike with Christianity, it is possible for Muslim societies to be technologically and politically advanced without forfeiting revelation as an all-encompassing, legally binding guide.

Scientific and Political Freedom in Islam critically examines the coherence and consistency of modernist-apologetic scholars. This is done through a discussion of their general theorizing on reason and freedom, which is then followed by discussions of their commentaries on specific scientific and political issues in light of their general theorizing. Regarding the former, the focus is Darwin's theory of evolution, while the universality of the Flood, the heliocentric model, the Big Bang model and Freudianism are also discussed. Regarding the latter, the focus is Islam's desired structure of government and concept of participatory politics, while individual freedoms are also discussed. The book argues that the modernist-apologetic approach has great potential to be a force for liberalization, but also possesses inherent limitations that render its theory on the relation between revelation and freedom self-contradictory.

Introducing a significant body of new information on the reasons for the failure of secularism and democracy and the attitudes towards Darwinism in the Arab world, this book is a valuable resource for students and scholars of Islamic Studies, comparative religion, democracy studies and evolution studies.

Uriya Shavit is Associate Professor of Islamic Studies and Head of the Graduate Program in Religious Studies at Tel Aviv University. His main research interests lie in the study of modern Islamic theology, law and politics and the sociology of Muslim minorities in the West. His most recent books are *Islamism and the West*, *Shari'a* and *Muslim Minorities and Zionism in Arab Discourses*.

SCIENTIFIC AND POLITICAL FREEDOM IN ISLAM

A Critical Reading of the Modernist-Apologetic School

Uriya Shavit

LONDON AND NEW YORK

First published 2017
by Routledge
2 Park Square, Milton Park, Abingdon, Oxon OX14 4RN

and by Routledge
711 Third Avenue, New York, NY 10017

Routledge is an imprint of the Taylor & Francis Group, an informa business

British Library Cataloguing in Publication Data
A catalogue record for this book is available from the British Library

Library of Congress Cataloging in Publication Data
Names: Shavit, Uriya, author.
Title: Scientific and political freedom in islam : a critical reading of the
modernist-apologetic school / Uriya Shavit.
Description: Milton Park, Abingdon, Oxon ; New York, NY : Routledge, 2017.
| Includes bibliographical references and index.
Identifiers: LCCN 2016041414| ISBN 9781138286030 (hardback) | ISBN
9781138286047 (pbk.) | ISBN 9781315268668 (ebook)
Subjects: LCSH: Islamic modernism. | Islam and science. | Islamic civilization.
Classification: LCC BP166.14.M63 S53 2017 | DDC 297.2/6–dc23
LC record available at https://lccn.loc.gov/2016041414

ISBN: 978-1-138-28603-0 (hbk)
ISBN: 978-1-138-28604-7 (pbk)
ISBN: 978-1-315-26866-8 (ebk)

Typeset in Bembo
by Taylor & Francis Books
Printed by Ashford Colour Press Ltd.

To my parents, Zohar and Yaacov

CONTENTS

ACKNOWLEDGMENTS

I take great pleasure in paying tribute to the individuals and organizations whose support and assistance made the writing of this book possible.

The research for this book was made possible by a grant from the Edmond J. Safra Center for Ethics at Tel Aviv University. I am thankful to the head of the Center, Prof. Shai Lavi, for his support and for our interesting conversations about revelation and freedom. I am thankful also to Orit Mizrahi of Tel Aviv University's Research Authority for her patience and encouragement. I am grateful to Nitza Kanfer for her generous donation in support of my Ph.D. candidates, made in memory of her late husband, George Kanfer ZL.

Kfir Gross, my research assistant throughout this project, located dozens of important texts, proofread the Arabic transliterations and references, and, most importantly, contributed brilliant and essential insights. Carl Yonker edited the manuscript, improved it beyond recognition, and greatly contributed to its publication. Fabian Spengler compiled the index and contributed engrossing observations about the manuscript. 'Abd Natour shared with me some important texts and insights about Muhammad 'Imara. Dr. Ofir Winter, the Shalem College, read the manuscript and contributed essential corrections. I am deeply thankful for their encouragement and friendship.

I am grateful to Prof. Eyal Zisser, Vice Rector at Tel Aviv University, for his advice and support, and to Prof. Joseph Klafter, President of the University, for his encouragement, without which this study could not have been written. I am also indebted to Prof. David Thomas, University of Birmingham and editor of the *Journal of Islam and Christian-Muslim Relations*, who encouraged me to study Muslim attitudes to Darwinism. The indispensible knowledge of Marion Gliksberg, head librarian for Middle Eastern Studies at Tel Aviv University, and the assistance of Rakefet Cohen, proved, as in all my previous publications, a great asset. The graduate students in my classes on Fundamentalism in Comparative Perspective—

Muslims, Jews, Christians and Druze of different religious and political orientations—participated in some hot debates about the issues discussed in the book, and were a great inspiration for my work.

I Would like to thank James "Joe" Whiting, Acquisitions Editor, Middle Eastern, Islamic & Jewish Studies, Routledge, for his important comments, encouragement and passion for intellectual freedom; Rebecca Bomford, for her marvelous copy-editing; Emma Tyce, Editorial Assistant, who made the finalizing and publication of the book a pleasant and efficient experience; Ruth Bradley, who handled the production of the book meticulously, and John Maloney for his splendid cover design.

INTRODUCTION

At the turn of the twentieth century, Muhammad 'Abduh, the reform-minded Grand Mufti of Egypt, rejected the notion that Muslim societies need to separate religion and state, as modern Western societies did, if they wish to achieve scientific and political progress. The system of government in Islam, he argued, should not be confused with a theocratic regime, which is, in fact, the type of regime the message of the Prophet decried. In Islam, neither the political leader nor religious scholars are permitted to apply religion as a means to exercise despotic control or to curtail scientific inquiry.[1]

Almost a hundred years later, another prominent Egyptian theologian, Yusuf al-Qaradawi, relied on 'Abduh's statements to argue that it was about time for the debate on Islam as a theocratic system to come to an end once and for all. He wrote that the debate was rooted in an erroneous comparison between Islam and Christianity. Islam, he argued, safeguards scientific freedom and freedom of thought, and rejects arbitrary theocratic rule. Its democratic principles preceded those that prevail in the West, and are better than those that prevail there.[2]

'Abduh's and al-Qaradawi's words are two articulations of an approach to the relation between Islam's revelation and science and politics, which, for over a century, has been a central part of Arab discourses on the future of Muslim societies. The approach, defined in this study as modernist-apologetic, introduces historical and theological narratives and interpretive mechanisms that contextualize reason and freedom in Islamic terms to argue that it is possible for Muslim societies to join the march of dramatic advancements in the fields of science, technology and governance without forfeiting revelation as an all-encompassing, legally binding guide.

Crucial aspects of this approach had already been offered by 'Abduh's mentor, Jamal al-Din al-Afghani, and by 'Abduh's associate, Husayn al-Jisr. It was further developed and propagated by 'Abduh's student, Muhammad Rashid Rida, and

Rida's associate, 'Abd al-Rahman al-Kawakibi, and popularized by Rida's student on Western-Muslim relations, Hasan al-Banna, the founder of the Muslim Brothers movement. During the second half of the twentieth century, a number of theologians carried the torch of the approach onward through numerous publications that relied on, and further developed, the works of the early modernist-apologists. Along with al-Qaradawi, the most prolific and consistent in these efforts in contemporary times were the Egyptians Muhammad al-Ghazali and Muhammad 'Imara.

The writings on revelation, science and politics of the aforementioned theologians are critically discussed in this book. The book critically examines the core assumption of the modernist-apologists that through their interpretations of the Quran and the Prophetic traditions and contextualization of Islamic history they have satisfactorily established a way for a culture of doubt to flourish in a society inspired and regulated by revelation; for society to be, in essence, revelation-based and doubt-based at the same time. The main thesis of this book is that their approach has great potential to be a force for liberalization, but also that their approach possesses inherent limitations that render their theory on the relation between revelation and freedom self-contradictory and unlikely to pass the test of implementation.

The point of view of this study is original; its engagement with modernist-apologetic texts is not. Since the 1920s, al-Afghani, 'Abduh and their immediate disciples have received much scholarly attention. They were described as groundbreaking and influential contributors to Arab discourses on politics, law and culture. The dominant view has been that they engaged the challenges of modernity with the aim to reinvigorate stagnated, conservative Islamic thought and practice in a way that allowed for Muslim societies to revive themselves politically, scientifically and technologically. Their efforts were analyzed as an Islamic-based, modernist-inclined response to Western imperial dominance that introduced an alternative to both old and unsustainable ways of religious thinking and new Western secular ideas. The extensive body of literature authored by al-Ghazali, al-Qaradawi and 'Imara has not been subject to similar exhaustive academic research (though al-Qaradawi has enjoyed slightly more attention). But while the role of these three contemporary thinkers—a self-proclaimed one to be sure—as the emissaries and developers of an intellectual legacy that originated before they were born has not been given much scholarly attention, their pragmatic leanings, particularly regarding the accommodation of Islamic concepts and norms to modern concepts and norms, have been recognized.[3]

The study does not reject or alter this common model of a modernist trend within a nuanced spectrum of Islamic thought, but offers new perspectives as to its origins and implications. Its critical reading of modernist-apologetic works begins with the argument that their treatment of the themes of Islam and the West, and Islam and modernity, was rooted in a concern about one specific aspect of Western history. The study demonstrates that the modernist-apologists were the first Muslim theologians to recognize not only that a connection existed between the prevalence of reason and freedom and the ascendance of the West but that a connection existed between the decline of revelation in the West and the prevalence of reason and freedom there. The combination of the two conclusions had, in their minds, grave implications for the long-held status of Islamic revelation in their societies, and motivated them to put forward a defense of that status. Their defense contextualized Islamic history, theology and exegesis to make the case that Allah's final message to humanity, if correctly understood and implemented, establishes a revelation-based social order that rejects arbitrary theocratic interventions in either politics or science, and commands the free pursuit of rationalist and empirical investigations of the natural world, as well as participatory politics that check and balance the leadership.

A word of caution must be noted regarding the ambition of critically examining the latter statement. Freedom is a vague concept; it means different things to different people, and has philosophical, legal, cultural and political contexts. It can be understood narrowly and broadly. The case of rationalism, modernity, democracy and other concepts that are central to modernist-apologetic writings is less complicated, but still, a discussion of the different definitions and approaches to any of these terms could well occupy a lengthy book. This means that attempts to inquire whether the modernist-apologists have convincingly made their case about the implications of a revelation-based social order in Islam run the risk of becoming a study on whether the modernist-apologetic concept of freedom is adequately similar to that of the author's. Even if such a line of analysis is undertaken with great caution, it inevitably privileges the researcher's own norms and beliefs at the expense of the subject of his or her investigation.

This study endeavors to avoid this potential pitfall by confining its critical discussion to the terms set by the modernist-apologists themselves. Instead of invoking a normative definition as to what scientific and political freedom (as well as other pertinent concepts) are, or ought to be, and then trying to ascertain whether the modernist-apologists are "real" or "true" advocates, it examines the coherence and consistency of their approach in relation to the concepts and definitions they invoke. This is done through a critical discussion of their general theorizing on reason and freedom, which is then followed by discussions of their commentaries on specific scientific and political issues in light of their general theorizing. Regarding the former, the focus is Darwin's Theory of Evolution; the universality of the "Biblical flood," the heliocentric model, the Big Bang model and Freudianism are also discussed. Regarding the latter, the focus is Islam's desired structure of government and concept of participatory politics; individual freedoms are also discussed.

The core distinction made throughout this study between revelation-based societies and doubt-based societies calls for elaboration. "Revelation-based" as defined in this study is a society in which certain texts and ideas are established as inerrant, perfected and legally binding. Their interpretation serves as an exclusive reference for law, politics and culture. It is not legitimate to challenge their truthfulness or their position of supremacy using methods similar to those applied when examining other scientific or political conventions. A revelation-based society in which a religious establishment monopolizes the interpretation of a revelation and thus the legitimization of ideas and actions is a theocracy. The political development of Europe in medieval times saw the creation of revelation-based societies, where Emperors and Kings ruled by divine right, drawn from an interpretation of Christian revelation, and religious establishments maintained monopoly over certain social fields. In modern times several secular ideologies sought, and in some countries managed to attain, the status of ultimate, all-encompassing, and unchallengeable truths and political and legal references, including communism and fascism.

"Doubt-based" refers to a society in which no single text or idea enjoys a legally binding status of inerrancy and perfection. It is possible that in such a society certain texts and ideas are held as revealed and sacred by a majority of the population, but these texts and ideas do not serve as a reference for the legal legitimization or banning of other texts and ideas, and it is permitted to critically comment on them, and on those who interpret them, as it is on other texts and ideas. In a doubt-based society, the role of political, judicial and academic institutions is to continuously regulate the competition between different concepts of truth rather than acknowledge one concept as truth and impose it. A doubt-based society does not necessarily imply loss of faith, or a diminishing role for religion in all social spheres; it can also be established by a majority that wholeheartedly believes in the truth of a certain revelation, yet decides that revealed texts should not be given an overriding authority. Such a society applies the principle of secularism, i.e., separates political and other temporal institutions from the control of a religious establishment, as in the case of the United States.

Revelation-based society is what the modernist-apologists have vehemently defended. Doubt-based society is what they vehemently rejected. The tension created by the ascendance of Western doubt-based societies and the decline of Muslim revelation-based societies is what their approach has aimed to reconcile. An evaluation of their success in doing so is the subject of this book.

The terms revelation-based and doubt-based as introduced in this book are similar, and much inspired, but not identical, to Karl Popper's distinction between "open" and "closed" societies. Popper's celebrated association of the absence of absolute truths and the prevalence of freedom asserted the essential difference between pluralistic social orders and those based on metaphysical or meta-historical assumptions; its most important legacy is, perhaps, that it did so with humility, exposing the inherent limitations of rational scientific inquiries rather than elevating them into a new form of sanctified religion. According to Popper, in a "closed," tribal society, there is no separation between the customary or conventional regularities of social life and the regularities found in "nature." Taboos frequently regulate and dominate all aspects of life, and members of the community rarely doubt how they ought to act. In an "open society," matters are rationally reflected upon by individuals, leading to changes that are based on quests to ascertain which laws and institutions are desirable. There is an ever-widening opportunity for personal decisions, and these decisions lead to the alteration of taboos and even of political laws (which no longer carry the status of taboo).[4] The dichotomy suggested in this study between "revelation" and "doubt" societies is narrower than these definitions. A doubt-based society may or may not be rational, and may or may not be religious. It may be small or large, and its social organization may or may not be sophisticated. It is doubt-based for merely one reason: the absence of a corpus of texts and ideas that has the legal status of an absolute truth and ultimate reference that cannot be challenged, not even by applying research methods similar to those applied in the study of other, non-revealed aspects of reality.

This is a work of intellectual history. Its point of departure is that the origin of ideas, their development, their meaning and their impact are worthy of investigation as an independent and fascinating aspect of human existence, as well as a crucial influence on how cultures and politics evolve. The modernist-apologetic approach, rather than its proponents, is the focus, and a reflection of the totality of any single individual or collective corpus of writings is not intended. The scholars whose works are examined have written on a great number of issues. Some did so throughout their exceptionally prolific careers, in which they produced hundreds of articles and books. The meaning, in Islamic terms, of reason and freedom was a central theme in their writings, but was far from an exclusive theme.

Research for this book was based on a qualitative contextual reading of several hundred books and essays written by the main propagators of the modernist-apologetic approach since the late nineteenth century, as well as by their rivals. The vast majority of the works examined, including those written many decades ago, were located with little effort in Islamic-interest bookshops in Arabic-speaking countries and across Europe, as well as online, including on several websites exclusively dedicated to the works of specific scholars.

Indeed, one of my main motivations in writing this book was noticing the proliferation of articulations, old and new, of the modernist-apologetic approach on the contemporary Islamic bookshelf, both in its physical and virtual forms. This impression about the centrality of modernist-apologetic ideas in contemporary Arab discourses was further enhanced by my more than decade-long experience as a teacher of graduate seminars on the modern intellectual history of the Middle East, in which some of the students are Muslim-Arabs and some are not, and among the Muslim students, some are religious and some are not. Whenever the issue of revelation and scientific and political freedom was broached, I saw that religious Muslim participants tended to present, with great persuasion and passion, ideas of the modernist-apologists, at times without being conscious of their origins. When these ideas were debated and challenged, I could sense the intellectual and emotional distress caused among those convinced of their correctness. Through the years I have learned, in unmediated and at times almost painful ways, that the modernist-apologetic approach satisfactorily resolves, for some Muslims, a challenge to their identity and faith that other approaches fail to resolve. It is a fundamental aspect of their engagement with modern realities, and defending the arguments it establishes is, for them, something of greater importance than having the upper hand in another heated class discussion. This renders a critical reading of the approach all the more sensitive and provocative, as well as all the more important.

The book is divided into three chapters, each divided into an introduction and three sections. The first chapter examines the foundations of the modernist-apologetic quest for reason and freedom within a revelation-based framework. The first section analyzes how modernist-apologetic texts struggled to provide rationalist proofs that God exists and Muhammad was His final Prophet who brought humanity a final, inerrant revelation. The second section explores how they drew a historical and theological distinction between Islam, as a religion that is a friend of science, and Christianity, that is not, and resisted the secularization model proposed by Westerners and liberal Arabs, drawing on the arguments that the Renaissance was rooted in Islam, the Quran anticipated numerous scientific discoveries, and, most importantly, the Islamic revelation has the potential, if correctly interpreted, to accommodate any newly established scientific fact. The third section points to the analytic confusion resulting from depictions of the modernist-apologists as either liberals or fundamentalists, or from trying to quantify whether they are more similar to one or the other.

The second chapter examines the limitations of the modernist-apologetic promise for complete freedom of scientific investigation within a revelation-based framework. The first section explores modernist-apologetic literature on the theory of evolution in the late nineteenth and early twentieth centuries, and demonstrates how its commensurability and potential commensurability with the revelation were established, and how that was presented as evidence for the supremacy of the Quran over other revelations. The second section examines how contemporary modernist-apologetic literature shifted to rejecting Darwinism as a heretical Western exception that must be shunned from Muslim societies, the reasons for that dramatic transformation, and how these reasons reflect on the coherency of the modernist-apologetic commitment to scientific freedom. The third section treats contemporary Arab-liberal texts on the need for separating religion and science, and discusses why their authors viewed the early modernist-apologists as their allies.

The third chapter examines modernist-apologetic concepts of political freedom, and how the term *shura* has been applied to argue that the essence of Islam is non-theocratic and non-despotic. The first section explores the early modernist-apologetic texts that offered these ideas, and the second analyzes how contemporary modernist-apologetic authors continued and further developed this legacy, accommodating it to changing geo-strategic realities. Both sections demonstrate the failure of modernist-apologists to provide a definitive answer as to who will serve as the ultimate reference for interpretations of the revelation, and the potential implications of that failure. The third section discusses Arab-liberal renunciations of the modernist-apologetic approach to politics. It suggests that counter-approaches proposed by leading liberal voices are not as far apart from the modernist-apologetic approach as both sides in the debate tend to think.

Notes

1 Muhammad 'Abduh, *al-Islam Din al-'Ilm wal-Madaniyya* (Beirut: Manshurat Dar Maktabat al-Haya, 1989), 112–18; see this text also in: Muhammad 'Abduh, "Tabi'at al-Din al-Masihi," in Muhammad 'Imara (ed.), *al-A'mal al-Kamila lil-Imam Muhammad 'Abduh*, vol. 3 (Beirut: al-Mu'assasa al-'Arabiyya lil-Dirasat wal-Nashr, 1972), 285–90.
2 Yusuf al-Qaradawi, *Min Fiqh al-Dawla fi al-Islam* (Cairo: Dar al-Shuruq, 2001, first published 1997), 13, 30, 36–9, 49–50, 73.
3 Many of the classic and recent works that explore the intellectual life-projects of al-Afghani, 'Abduh and their early disciples are discussed, some critically, throughout the book; here, several of the more well-known studies that established the "Islamic modernists" paradigm are mentioned: Charles C. Adams, *Islam and Modernism in Egypt: A Study of the Modern Reform Movement Inaugurated by Muhammad Abduh* (New York: Russell and Russell, 1968, first published 1933); Albert Hourani, *Arabic Thought in the Liberal Age, 1798–1939* (London and New York: Oxford University Press, 1962); Malcolm H. Kerr, *Islamic Reform: The Political and Legal Theories of Muhammad 'Abduh and Rashid Rida* (Berkeley: University of California Press, 1966); Nikkie R. Keddie, *Sayyid Jamal al-Din "al-Afghani": A Political Biography* (Berkeley: University of California Press, 1972). Among the studies that established the position of al-Ghazali, al-Qaradawi and (in some) al-'Imara as modernist reformers are: Raymond William Baker, *Islam without Fear: Egypt and the New Islamists* (Cambridge, MA: Harvard University Press, 2003); Sagi Polka, "The Centrist Stream in Egypt and Its Role in the Public Discourse Surrounding the Shaping of the Country's Cultural Identity," *Middle Eastern Studies* 39:3 (July 2003), 39–64; Uriya Shavit, *Islamism and the West: From "Cultural Attack" to "Missionary Migrant"* (London and New York: Routledge, 2014), 9–25; Samuel Helfont, *Yusuf al-Qaradawi: Islam and Modernity* (Tel Aviv: Moshe Dayan Center, 2009); Bettina Gräf and Jakob Skovgaard-Petersen (eds), *Global Mufti: The Phenomenon of Yusuf al-Qaradawi* (London: Hurst & Company, 2009), a compilation of articles dealing with different aspects of al-Qaradawi's ideas and activities, including on democracy, gender, media technologies and Muslim minorities.
4 Karl R. Popper, *The Open Society and Its Enemies*, vol. 1 (London: Routledge, 1969), 171–74.

1

A QUEST FOR REASON AND FREEDOM

At the end of the nineteenth century and the beginning of the twentieth century, a group of Muslim scholars, based primarily in Egypt, reflected on the crisis of the Muslim world. Determined to defend their belief in the inerrancy of the Islamic revelation and its ability to serve as an all-encompassing guide also in modern times, they pointed to the absence of scientific and political progression in their societies as the root of that crisis, and offered a unique approach to its resolution. The scholars, associated by work and mentor-student relations, include Jamal al-Din al-Afghani (1838/9–1897), Husayn al-Jisr (1845–1909), Muhammad 'Abduh (1849–1905), Muhammad Rashid Rida (1865–1935) and 'Abd al-Rahman al-Kawakibi (1854/5–1902). Drawing a historical distinction between Christianity and Islam, and introducing mechanisms for accommodating revelation to new scientific and political concepts, their approach suggested that an Islamic society can be revelation-based without being theocratic and without forfeiting any of the blessings of reason and freedom. This approach was modernist in its recognition that certain Western scientific and political concepts can and must be absorbed into Muslim societies if those societies wish to survive and revive themselves. It was apologetic in its promise that adopting modern concepts does not constitute imitation of the West, but a return to the true message of Islam, a message that safeguards and encourages scientific and political freedoms, which had been abandoned through the ages. No single intellectual contribution has had a prevailing impact on Arab societies as much as has that of the modernist-apologists. And no set of ideas has been misconstrued to the extent that those associated with this group have been.

The modernist-apologists were not the first to recognize that something had gone wrong for the Muslim world. They were also not entirely original in identifying freedom and reason as important assets of Western societies, and in explaining them in Islamic terms. Already since the late eighteenth century, the technological superiority of Western powers had been recognized by Ottoman rulers and politicians and by the autonomous dynasty established by Muhammad 'Ali in Egypt, and efforts—at times intense—to modernize political, military, economic, judicial and academic institutions were made.

Early attempts at learning from the West paid little attention to socio-political structures and philosophies, focusing instead on technical aspects of Western power. The reasons were other than analytic blindness. In the early decades of the nineteenth century, liberalism and constitutional monarchism were but a few of the several faces of European powers, and were not the only face of any of them. The most liberal and politically stable among those powers, the British Empire, stood for Christian values, missionary zeal and Spartan education as much as for individual freedoms. France's revolutionary form of secular republicanism witnessed defeat and anarchy after a period of triumph and glory, and for a while, with the return of monarchism, seemed as no more than a tragic historical anecdote.

Already in the 1830s perspectives began to change. In 1826, Rifa'a Rafi' al-Tahtawi (1801–1873) was sent by Muhammad 'Ali to Paris as the imam of a delegation of Egyptian students who studied a variety of fields, from medicine to warfare to agriculture, in the French capital.[1] *The Quintessence of Paris*, the book al-Tahtawi authored on his impressions from his six-year sojourn in the city, described French advancements in science and technology and noted the freedoms enjoyed by the subjects of the country, who, shortly before his return to Egypt, witnessed the 1830 July Revolution and the establishment of a more restricted form of monarchism. For example, Tahtawi noted that in France the king is not above the law, freedom of religion is maintained, and any subject can speak his mind freely so long as he does not break the law.[2]

While *The Quintessence of Paris* introduced liberal political concepts to Egyptian readers, there is some exaggeration in Abu-Lughud's analysis, according to which al-Tahtawi explained French ascendance through the gradual creations of sound political systems based upon freedom and political justice, and the openness to learn from Islam.[3] While detailed, al-Tahtawi's depictions of the French political system are not the main theme of his book, and are descriptive. His interpretation of freedom is rather limited (in one place he equates it with justice, and equates justice with the rule of law and equality before the law).[4] There is nothing in his text to suggest that Egypt should adopt the political ways of France or that these are, in essence, the ways of Islam; on the contrary, he emphasized that the laws of the French are not revelation-based.[5]

Abu-Lughud's analysis is more apt for a later observer of the West, Khayr al-Din al-Tunisi (1822–1890). The reform-minded Khayr al-Din was the first president of the Tunisian legislative and executive (yet appointed) Supreme Council that was established in 1860 based on a constitution that he participated in drafting. Following a dispute with Ahmed Bey, the ruler of Tunisia, as to whether ministers should be responsible to the Bey or to the Supreme Council, he resigned in 1862. Having retired for a while from frenetic engagement in political intrigue, he had the opportunity to author *The Surest Path to Knowledge Regarding the Condition of Countries*.[6] In this book, Khayr al-Din, who encountered Western culture firsthand through his sojourn in Paris in 1852–1856, suggested Muslim societies should follow the example of the West.[7] He commented that the example of the Prophet teaches that Muslims may learn useful concepts from non-Muslims.[8] Learning from the West, however, did not imply, in his mind, blind imitation and neglect of Islam, but rather a reclaiming of a cherished past. Western concepts and achievements, as he depicted them, either have their parallels in Islam or find their roots in Muslim societies. He attributed the economic and scientific rise of the West to its interactions with Muslims in the Middle Ages.[9] He praised the freedoms prevailing in the West (including the rule of law, participatory politics and freedom of speech) as the roots of its success, and drew parallels between Islamic norms and Western freedoms (for example, that parallel to participatory politics, Islam established the communal duty to forbid what is wrong).[10] All that, he believed, had little to do with Christianity, for better or for worse; in his mind, liberal political structures emerged in the West independently of Christianity, because it separates between religious and worldly affairs.[11]

The modernist-apologists, starting most prominently with 'Abduh, took these ideas a step further. They, too, attributed the failures of Muslim societies to their neglect of rationalist scientific pursuit and political freedom. Yet they also drew a direct link between the diminishing role of religion in the West and its ascendance. They came to the conclusion that the strong position of Western societies was due to a scientific revolution that had rationalized explorations of the natural world and freed them from the arbitrary interventions of religious authorities, and to a political revolution that had made decision-making more inclusive, restricted the powers of rulers, and separated Church and state. This view was encouraged, in part, by several French and Arab liberal analyses, which they read and debated, and that convincingly made the case for the separation of religion, science and politics as being the cornerstone of national ascendance in the Christian world.

Following the English occupation of Egypt in 1882, the crisis of Islam as a comprehensive system that was able to satisfactorily address all the problems of life became all the more evident, and called for radical solutions. The recognition that the Powers that dominated the Middle East ascended whilst transforming from revelation-based to doubt-based orders produced a great sense of distress. The originators of the modernist-apologetic approach to scientific and political freedom strongly believed that there was God, that He had sent to humanity a final Prophet, and that the final Prophet provided humanity with a final revelation and with Prophetic examples, all of which are absolute truths that must serve as the premise for conduct in all aspects of life, including the scientific and the political. These truths were the bases of their education and the compasses that directed their personal lives and their conduct as intellectual and public figures. Nothing they saw in their interactions with Western texts or societies changed their absolute conviction that these long-held truths were, indeed, absolute truths. But if the experience of the West instructed that science, technology and politics were greatly advanced only after the Church lost its power to delegitimize ideas, what were the implications for Muslim societies? Perhaps that those societies, too, must become doubt-based?

This option was inconceivable for the early modernist-apologists. It clashed with their deep faith in the revelation as an inerrant, all-encompassing, universally binding guide. To give up one's identity in order to protect it from elimination made no sense. Herein lay the conundrum they faced. Western Powers had come to dominate the East as a result of a process that limited the authority of religious texts. But if Muslim societies were to do the same in order to reassert their independence, they would no longer be truly Muslim or truly independent, at least not in the sense in which the modernist-apologists understood these terms.

The solution to what seemed an unsolvable paradox was the drawing of a theological and historical distinction between Christianity and Islam that introduced theological discussions, historical narratives and interpretive mechanisms to make the case for the feasibility and desirability of an Islamic revelation-based society that was guided by reason and freedom no less, and in fact more, than the doubt-based West. The modernist-apologists Islamized modernity as a means of making a case for the possibility of modernizing Muslim societies without relinquishing revelation as the foundation of the mind and of social life. They argued that whereas Christianity is an irrational faith, the truths of Islam can and must be ascertained through reason, and thus embracing them is not a matter of blindly adhering to traditional metaphysical beliefs, but of abiding by the dictates of logical thinking. They further argued that whereas Christianity is hostile to science and to freedom, Islam encourages and protects both, and was the conveyer of empiricist methods and political liberties to the Christian world; and that whereas many modern scientific discoveries are incompatible with the Christian revelation, Islamic revelation either anticipates those discoveries, or allows for reinterpretation that ensures that revelation and science never conflict.

The promise of an Islamic revelation-based society that will be as strong as, and in fact stronger than, any doubt-based Western society is a promise to meld the best of all worlds without giving anything up: tradition and modernity, a life of virtue and an afterlife of reward, faith and reason, authenticity and reform. While this promise is far-reaching, the theses and narratives on which it rests are not radical (as opposed to the potential revolutionary implications of applying the approach to actual scientific and political issues). The modernist-apologists asserted, rather than challenged, the traditional notions of Islamic revelation as a perfected, universal message, that is appropriate for all times and places. As will be demonstrated in this chapter, the most vital mechanism they introduced for assuring the compatibility of modern concepts and Muslim revelation—the notion that the revealed passages can be accommodated to anything science proves—finds its roots in medieval Muslim orthodoxy. Thus, despite the novelty of specific arguments and conclusions the modernist-apologists made, it was difficult even for rivals who deemed their ideas outrageous to classify them as heretics.

According to a tradition narrated by 'Abdallah b. 'Umar, the Prophet said: "The best people are those living in my generation, and then those who will follow them, and then those who will follow the latter. Then there will come some people who will bear witness before taking oaths, and take oaths before bearing witness." The tradition implies that the closer Muslims were to the days of the Prophet, the better their conduct was. It is a basis for the consensus among Sunni jurists that the first three generations of Islam—the Prophet's Companions (*sahaba*), the following generation (*al-tabi'in*), and the generation after that (*tabi' al-tabi'in*), known collectively as the pious ancestors (*salaf*)—provide the example which all Muslims should follow and, thus, are the ultimate reference. The genius of the early modernist-apologists was to associate modern concepts with the times of the *salaf*. Their overarching argument was that an understanding of Islam that is true to its roots, i.e., to the days of the Prophet and the *salaf*, cherishes free scientific investigation, allows accommodation of the revelation, forbids political despotism and commands political participation. Still, as noted by Henri Lauzière, while from the late 1910s until the 1990s academic literature, first in French and later in other discourses, described al-Afghani, 'Abduh and their disciples as leaders of a *salafi* modernist trend in Islam, the term *salafiyya* hardly resonates in al-Afghani's and 'Abduh's works.[12] In contemporary popular and academic discourses, the term has been almost monopolized by the Saudi Wahhabi religious establishment and groups that identify with certain aspects of its creeds while challenging others. This is cause for much terminological confusion, all the more so because contemporary modernist-apologists also associate their views, albeit not in a prominent way, with this term.

A Prevailing Legacy

The foundational texts of the modernist-apologetic school were authored in light of a concern about an imminent collapse of the Muslim nation as a social-political reality, and the demise of Islam as an all-encompassing system. In the post-Ottoman Middle East, those concerns were actualized. The encroachment of Western ideologies and culture into Muslims lands remained strong even where their direct control over those lands waned. Islam lost its status as the basis of law and the definer of political identity in Egypt and other countries that had gained independence based on a territorial concept of nationhood.

The establishment in Egypt in 1928 of the Muslim Brothers movement by Hasan al-Banna (1906–1949), a schoolteacher, was a response to these develop-ments. Al-Banna established a grassroots mass movement with the objective of purifying Egyptian society from the promiscuous and corrupting aspects of Western culture, to reinstate Islam as an all-encompassing system governing all aspects of life, including the political, and to reestablish, gradually, the *umma* as a viable religious-political entity. While he was a political leader and a preacher and not a qualified theologian or jurist, his writings constitute an interpretation of reality through the revelation.

Al-Banna professed to have been mentored on Muslim-Western relations by Muhammad Rashid Rida.[13] His published dispatches through the 1930s and 1940s integrated and further disseminated the modernist-apologetic approach to scientific and political freedom. As will be demonstrated further in this book, he propagated the notions that the truth of Islam can be rationally ascertained; Islam differs from Christianity in safeguarding scientific freedom and rejecting theocratic rule; desired aspects of modernity, including participatory politics, are rooted in Islam; and Western renaissance is indebted to Christian interactions with Islam. Organizationally, his methods gave socio-political clout to the idea of absorbing certain aspects of modernity in Islamic fashion by applying modern means of communication and modern concepts of recruitment and contestation of power. His objective was to spur a grassroots revolution, facilitated through proselytizing in diverse social spheres, from sports clubs to cafes, and through restricted participation in political institutions that were not revelation-based.[14]

Voll distinguished between the agenda of al-Afghani, 'Abduh and the early Rida, which he described as modernist, and that of the late Rida and al-Banna, which he labeled as fundamentalist. This distinction is hardly convincing if one applies Voll's own definitions. He defined Islamic fundamentalism as a reaffirmation of foundational principles and an effort to reshape society in terms of the affirmed fundamentals through calling Muslims back to the fold of Islam, an assertive surge of Islamic feeling and reliance on Islamic fundamental principles to meet the needs and challenges of contemporary times.[15] These qualities well apply to the ambitions and strategies of al-Afghani and 'Abduh. Islamic modernism, according to Voll, is the synthesizing of modern, Western-style scientific rationalism with Islamic faith.[16] This definition is suitable also with al-Banna's theorizing, although in a way that is less obvious. Indeed, Voll conceded, as did others,[17] that al-Banna's ideas on the relation between the West and Islam and Islam and modernity bear great resemblance to those of al-Afghani and 'Abduh.[18]

While al-Banna and the Brothers have been the most effective disseminators of modernist-apologetic ideas on Islam as the religion of reason and freedom within a revelation-based premise, the impact of these ideas has extended beyond the Brothers' groups. The assumptions about the compatibility and adaptability of revelation to the beneficial aspects of modernity had become conventional wisdom in a broad spectrum of Islamic (rather than merely Islamist) intellectual circles. Several of their notional premises were integrated even by members of the Saudi *salafi* (i.e., *wahhabi*) religious establishment, who, while detesting the rationalism of the modernist-apologists and their Islamizing of Western concepts, nevertheless integrated into their writings the notion that a return to Islam true to itself will ensure the scientific and technological revival of Muslim societies, and that there is a benefit in absorbing certain Western innovations that do not contradict Islam.[19] The early modernist-apologists have been viewed favorably, as will be demonstrated in Chapters 2 and 3, by Arab liberals who call for the separation of state and religion.

One example of the extent to which premises of the approach have spread to large publics is a 2011 survey by the U.S.-based Pew Research Center on Egyptian political attitudes. It found that 71 percent of Egyptians believe that democracy is the best form of government, even as a full 62 percent are of the opinion that the laws of their country should rigorously apply the provisions of the Quran. The implication is that a sizeable portion of Egypt's population sees no inherent contradiction between the two and believes coexistence between the two is possible.[20] This opinion, rooted in modernist-apologetic conceptualizations, is anything but obvious, both in terms of the history of political theory in Muslim societies and in terms of democratic political theory. Yet the broad diffusion of modernist-apologetic literature encourages its perception as such.

During the second half of the twentieth century, three Egyptian scholars who made the reconstitution of Islam as an all-encompassing socio-political and legal system their life project shined in particular as prolific and influential standard bearers of the modernist-apologetic approach. These are Muhammad al-Ghazali (1917–1996), Yusuf al-Qaradawi (b. 1926, based in Qatar since 1961) and Muhammad 'Imara (b. 1931). Several dozen of the treatises authored by the three, and hundreds of articles, interviews and sermons given by them in the media, interpreted systematically the rise of the West and the prerequisites for Islamic revival in terms similar to those first invoked by the early modernist-apologists. Some of the ideas they presented expressly relied on the writing of the founders of the approach (and in some cases further developed these ideas). Others were inspired by them.

As young men, al-Ghazali and al-Qaradawi were disciples of al-Banna and members of the Brothers, but, for different reasons, later their official affiliation with the movement was severed. While they maintained their loyalty to al-Banna's primary concerns, i.e., the creation of Muslim societies in which Islam served as a reference regulating all aspects of life, they established themselves as respected Islamic personas in broader circles than those affiliated with the Brothers. 'Imara was never a member of the Brothers, though his political ideals greatly resemble those of the movement. Thus, the significance of the three in preserving, developing and disseminating the modernist-apologetic approach demonstrates the close association of that approach, in contemporary times, with the agenda of the Brothers, as well as its spanning of political divides.

A gulf separates the world of Jamal al-Din al-Afghani and Muhammad 'Abduh, to whom the telegraph was a fascinating new invention, and the world of Yusuf al-Qaradawi and Muhammad 'Imara, whose worldviews were shaped shortly after the last of the founding fathers of the approach, Rashid Rida, passed away, but who gained recognition across the Arab world and beyond it through satellite television programs and internet websites. The intellectual legacy created by the former in the late nineteenth century has remained so central to the scholarship of the latter at the early twenty-first century because one basic challenge to faith has not changed. As did the early modernist-apologists, contemporary modernist-apologists struggle with the decline of revelation in the scientifically and technologically far-superior West and its implications on their desired role for revelation in Islamic societies. Realizing that without the absorption and application of modern concepts and institutions the independence of Muslim societies, let alone their revival, is unrealistic, they have opted for interpreting true, authentic Islam as a system that, unlike Christianity, allows for the existence of a revelation-based social order without compromising any of the advantages of modernity.

Some Biographical Notes

As there is no shortage of biographical scholarship on most of the individuals whose works are the focus of this study, the following paragraphs will focus on describing the interpersonal relations and several foundational texts that made the modernist-apologetic approach a distinguishable intellectual chain, a torch passed from one generation to another.

After a period of study in India in the 1850s, where he became acquainted with modern sciences, and a short spell as an advisor to rulers of Afghanistan, the Persian-born al-Afghani stopped in Egypt on his way to Istanbul in 1869. There he met, for the first time, with the young Muhammad 'Abduh. During his two years in Istanbul he demonstrated his life-long talent for charming and associating with powerful individuals, and then irritating and falling from grace with the same or other powerful individuals. He then left for Egypt once again, where he remained for eight years. In Cairo, he became the unofficial mentor on religion and politics for a group of young individuals, mainly students at al-Azhar, including 'Abduh and the future leader of the nationalist liberal party al-Wafd, Sa'd Zaghlul.[21] In 1879, he was forced into exile for political subversion and returned to India, where he authored a defense on the concept of a revelation-based society, *The Refutation of the Materialists*. 'Abduh translated it into Arabic in 1886.[22] In 1883, by then in Paris, he debated the French Orientalist Ernst Renan (see below), who argued that a society cannot be Muslim and scientifically advanced at the same time. His response to this accusation constituted an ambiguous defense of the possibility for an Islamic society that is guided by reason and freedom. In 1884, he joined 'Abduh in Paris in the publication of *al-'Urwa al-Wuthqa*, a bi-monthly journal that, in half a year of existence, critically reported on imperialist policies in the Middle East and debated possible approaches for Islamic revival. In 1885, al-Afghani moved to London, where he participated in discussions on the future of Egypt. His declining years were spent as an advisor to the Iranian Shah and then to the Ottoman Sultan, where the pattern of becoming a close advisor and then falling from grace was repeated.[23]

A student at al-Azhar from 1869 to 1877, 'Abduh reflected on his mentor al-Afghani's time in Egypt as a transformative event that enlightened the minds and purified the faith of many religious scholars, including 'Abduh himself.[24] In the early 1880s, after gaining some repute as an essayist for *al-Ahram*, 'Abduh was appointed editor and then editor-in-chief of Egypt's official gazette, *al-Waqa'i' al-Misriyya*. In 1882, following his role in the 'Urabi uprising, he was sentenced to three years in exile.

'Abduh's period of exile from Egypt began—and ended—in Beirut. There, in 1882, he met with Husayn al-Jisr, a native of Tripoli and the headmaster of Beirut's al-Madrasa al-Sultaniyya.[25] An al-Azhar graduate, educator and journalist, al-Jisr's goal in life was to introduce a curriculum that combined modern sciences and religious studies as a means of fighting the appeal of missionary schools and materialist ideas.[26] He first pursued this goal in a school he opened in Tripoli in January 1879, al-Madrasa al-Wataniyya, where math, geometry, geography, philosophy,

Turkish and French were among the subjects taught. This modern curriculum met with immediate success among local parents, but the school was forced to close down under the pressures of conservative religious scholars, notables and the military, and al-Jisr moved to Beirut, where he had the opportunity to further promote his educational agenda at al-Madrasa al-Sultaniyya.[27]

The encounter between 'Abduh and al-Jisr was a milestone in the development of a distinct modernist-apologetic approach to reason and freedom. In 1888, by then back in Tripoli, al-Jisr, who was inspired by 'Abduh's teachings, published *al-Risala al-Hamidiyya*, an anti-materialist apologia that included the first methodological introduction on establishing the commensurability of Islam's revelation and modern science; 'Abduh read the book and praised it.[28] So did al-Afghani, although he was very critical of other publications by al-Jisr.[29] In 1897, 'Abduh, who returned to Egypt in 1888, published *Risalat al-Tawhid*, an apologetic rationalization of God's and Islam's truth that, according to 'Abduh, relied on the lectures he had given at al-Madrasa al-Sultaniyya, and bears some resemblance to al-Jisr's work.[30] During the 1890s, 'Abduh led reforms at al-Azhar and, in 1899, was appointed Grand Mufti of Egypt. He supported cooperation with the British occupation as a means to enhance Egyptian progression, to the extent that the occupation would be temporary.[31]

'Abduh's most extensive work as a theologian, his exegesis of the Quran, was published by his disciple Muhammad Rashid Rida in *al-Manar*. As a young man in Tripoli, Rida was a student of al-Jisr at al-Madrasa al-Wataniyya, and it was in his home that Rida first came across copies of *al-'Urwa al-Wuthqa*.[32] Rida established *al-Manar* in 1898, shortly after arriving in Cairo from Lebanon, and remained its editor and chief writer for the next thirty-seven years. 'Abduh described Rida as a loyal assistant, a man who gave a voice to his ideas, which he did not have time to write down because of his busy workload.[33] The journal became a mouthpiece for al-Afghani's and 'Abduh's ideas. Along with Quranic exegesis, it offered theological apologias, *fatwas*, and reports and analyses on important events around the world, giving special attention to the status of Muslim minorities and to Westerners' conversions to Islam. While *al-Manar* was in essence a one-man-show, reflecting Rida's personal interests and priorities, and though its circulation did not exceed several thousand copies a month, it left a profound mark on Muslim thought in the twentieth century.[34] The millions of words Rida authored and edited during his life reflected some changes of attitude and inclination, but all were directed toward one objective: making a case for Islam as a true, all-encompassing revelation that is commensurate with modern science and is the only path of salvation for corrupted humanity. One of Rida's associates in Cairo was 'Abd al-Rahman al-Kawakibi, an Aleppo-born journalist, lawyer and mayor who moved to Egypt in 1898 to escape political persecution in Istanbul. In his four remaining years, he authored articles in *al-Manar* and published two books, *Umm al-Qura* and *On the Nature of Despotism and the Harms of Enslavement*, both of which praised Islam as a religion of scientific pursuit and freedom and lamented its deterioration. His ideas bore a resemblance to ideas propagated by al-Afghani, al-Jisr, 'Abduh and Rida.[35]

The direct and close association between Muhammad al-Ghazali's, Yusuf al-Qaradawi's and Muhammad 'Imara's scholarship and that of the founding fathers of the modernist-apologetic approach is more than an implied one. The three characterized their ideas about Muslim–Western relations and the means to facilitate a resurrection of the *umma* as a continuation of the ideas presented by al-Afghani, 'Abduh and their early disciples, a vital new link that, through the articulation and adaptation of existing conceptualizations, propagates to new generations of readers the one and only interpretation of Islam that could allow Muslims to revive as a nation and as individuals. Al-Ghazali believed al-Afghani, 'Abduh and Rida to be the leaders of the wise approach to the crisis of Muslim societies, the only approach that can lead to the renaissance of Islam; he defended 'Abduh's pragmatic attitude toward the English occupation of Egypt as an act of true devotion, and described Rida as an eminent, brilliant scholar who was admired by al-Banna.[36] Al-Qaradawi suggested that the *sahwa* in the Arab world, i.e., the resurgence of religious sentiments and of movements that seek to reestablish Islam as an all-encompassing system, was not born of itself or in a void, but through the seeds planted by others, among whom are al-Afghani, 'Abduh, Rida and al-Banna.[37] 'Imara argued that the modern Western assault on the Muslim world was countered by three intellectual schools. One is the school of stagnation (*tayyar al-jumud*), which adheres to and sanctifies Islam's times of backwardness. This school is represented by, among others, some of al-Azhar's establishment and Sufi orders. Another is the school of Westernization (*tayyar al-taghrib*)—the Muslims who mistakenly believe that the school of stagnation represents true Islam, have consequently been enchanted by the achievements and triumphs of Western civilization, and have renounced the heritage of their own civilization. The third school, which 'Imara considered the only representation of true Islam and thus the only prospect for Islamic resurrection, is the reformist school (*tayyar al-tajdid*).[38] This school includes a number of orientations, including the *wahhabi* one; however, according to 'Imara, the only orientation that allows for the essential combination of a return to the roots of Islam with a rational reading of the Quran, and a balance between recognizing the uniqueness of Islamic civilization and benefiting from other civilizations, is the school developed by Jamal al-Din al-Afghani, Muhammad 'Abduh and their disciples.[39]

It took several decades for the contemporary luminaries of the modernist-apologetic approach to consolidate their positions as influential and independent voices not beholden to a particular religious or political orientation. It also took the three several decades to be seen as adherents of a distinct religio-juristic and social approach to Islam, the *wasatiyya*, in large part inspired by the teachings of al-Afghani, 'Abduh and their immediate disciples. When al-Ghazali was twenty years of age he was impressed with a sermon given by Hasan al-Banna and became a member of the Brothers.[40] The affection was mutual, and he quickly rose in the ranks of the movement, becoming a columnist in its journal and its spokesman.[41] Al-Ghazali made a name for himself as the author of apologias, which in the 1940s focused on the supremacy of Islam as an economic system in comparison to capitalism, socialism and communism.[42] In 1953, he was dismissed from the Brothers following a power-struggle with Hasan al-Hudaybi, al-Banna's successor as the movement's General Guide. His disassociation from the Brothers allowed him to continue to publish his writings in relative freedom under Nasser's and Sadat's regimes, preaching for the Islamization of society while refraining from calling for a revolution against the regime. In 1971, he was invited to serve as a professor at Umm al-Qura University in Saudi Arabia.[43] He remained in the Kingdom for seven years, where he developed a critical approach to *wahhabi* teachings, including on gender issues. Upon his return to Egypt in 1981 he was promoted to deputy-minister for *da'wa*, a position he held only for a few months. In 1985, he was appointed, at the invitation of Algeria's President, President of the scientific council of al-Amir 'Abd al-Qadir University. By then, he had already gained repute across the Arab world as a prolific author who defended the commensurability of Islam with the challenges of modernity, cautioned equally against the dangers of Western ideologies and against literalist, frozen interpretations of Islam, and presented methods for effective proselytizing. He returned to Egypt in 1989 and, in the seven years before he died, was a vocal participant in Egyptian and Arab public debates on the desired role of Islam in society.[44]

Al-Ghazali was one of the principal inspirations for a number of younger theologians, including, first and foremost, Yusuf al-Qaradawi, who, upon his teacher and friend's death, published an adulatory yet balanced biography that depicted al-Ghazali as a great fighter against those who cast doubt on the all-encompassing, binding essence of the Islamic revelation,[45] and exonerated him from any blame for his dismissal from the Brothers in 1953.[46] There are some similarities in their biographies, especially in their shared history of joining and leaving the Brothers and how this affected their status. Al-Qaradawi first became enchanted with al-Banna's teachings as a schoolboy, and as a student at al-Azhar became involved in the Brothers' activities. The writings of al-Ghazali also deeply impressed him. In early 1949, following the outlawing of the Brothers and the subsequent assassination of Egypt's Prime Minister Mahmud al-Nuqrashi by one of their members, al-Qaradawi was arrested along with a dozen other activists (including al-Ghazali). He was arrested again under Nasser's regime. In 1960, he published his first major work—*The Permissible and Prohibited in Islam*, a best-selling textbook on the foundations of Islamic law.[47] In 1961, at the time a junior scholar at al-Azhar, he moved to Qatar to teach at its newly established College for Higher Education. He did not intend to stay in the position for more than four years, but after Nasser's crackdown on the Brothers in 1965 al-Qaradawi prolonged his stay, leading to a life in exile. In Qatar, he enjoyed greater freedom than under Nasser, but such freedom came at a price. He distanced himself from the Egyptian Brothers and refrained from meddling in internal Qatari affairs while becoming, from the late 1960s, a prolific author of treatises that propagated the view that the only solution for the plight of Muslim societies was for them to return to Islam, and that such a return did not imply neglecting beneficial modern concepts but their cautious, conditional embrace. He also established himself as a leading Sunni Arab authority on religious law. A weekly show on al-Jazeera, which he has hosted since the Qatari satellite news channel was founded in 1996, further enhanced his worldwide recognition. So, too, did his masterful usage of an internet portal established under his guidance in 1997, IslamOnline.net. In 2002, he rejected an offer to become the Brothers' General Guide, aiming instead for a greater and more audacious, but less risky, role of inspiring Muslim unity at large. In 1997, he became head of the newly established European Council for Fatwa and Research (*al-Majlis al-'Urubbi lil-Ifta' wal-Buhuth*) and, in 2004, became the chair of the International Union for Muslim Scholars (*al-Itihad al-'Alami li-'Ulama al-Muslimin*), a body which aims to bring Muslim religious scholars together on the basis of scholarship and action, but largely serves as a platform for spreading his views.[48]

Muhammad 'Imara's path to prominence was different. A left-leaning activist in the 1950s, he was imprisoned in 1958 by Nasser's regime. Upon his release in 1964, he gradually substituted Marxism with Islamism. 'Imara completed his PhD in Islamic philosophy at Cairo's Dar al-'Ulum in 1975, and gained prominence first as a scholar of theology rather than as a theologian, and only later became an apologist to be reckoned with in his own right.[49] From the 1970s to the present, he has vastly contributed to the propagation of the modernist-apologetic approach in two ways. He edited and annotated compilations of the complete works of al-Afghani, 'Abduh and al-Kawakibi, contextualizing them for a new generation of readers (he also wrote a biography of al-Tahtawi and engaged with Rida's ideas; and like al-Qaradawi, he authored a biography of Muhammad al-Ghazali).[50] Along with his scholarship on the early modernist-apologists, he authored dozens of books and newspaper articles in which he reiterated and further developed their ideas. While he has not shied away from political commentary, including on the Arab-Israeli conflict, and while he has also addressed issues pertaining to religious jurisprudence, his focus has remained on producing commentary on history and theology, particularly regarding Islam's relation to Christianity and to the West.

Since the late 1990s, al-Ghazali, al-Qaradawi and, to lesser extent, also 'Imara were identified in academic literature as leaders of an independent trend within Islamic thought—the *wasatiyya*.[51] This recognition corresponded with the intensive efforts al-Qaradawi had made, since the mid-1990s, to gain recognition as the leader of a distinguishable trend in Islam. *Wasatiyya*, drawing from Q. 2:143 "We have made you a median (i.e., just) community that you will be witnesses over the people and the Messenger will be a witness over you,"[52] is associated with a pragmatic, lenient approach to religious jurisprudence that generously applies the mechanism of *maslaha* (safeguarding the primary objectives of the Lawgiver) and emphasizes the importance of gradualist, friendly proselytizing efforts; an understanding of Islam as a religion that achieves a harmonized balance between differences that other religions and ideologies fail to harmonize; and a call for Muslims to detest both the Westernization of their societies and their religious radicalization or stagnation, and instead follow the ways of the Prophet and the first three generations by renewing their religion and accommodating it to new realities.[53] The ideas associated with *wasatiyya* draw heavily on the works of the early modernist-apologists.

The usage of this label to describe this type of reformism that is an alternative to religious conservatism on the one hand and to the neglect of Islam on the other, finds its roots already in the pages of *al-Manar*, although it was not common in Rida's writing.[54]

A. Rationalizing God, His Prophet and His Revelation

Modernist-apologetic texts on scientific and political freedom accumulate to a two-pronged defense of the possibility of a revelation-based society that enjoys all the benefits of a doubt-based rationalist and modern one. It establishes that the metaphysical assumptions upon which Islam is based can be rationally proved and, moreover, that it is impossible to be rational and at the same time deny them. It also establishes that the Islamic revelation is commensurate with, and even encouraging of, all the desirable aspects of modernity, including complete freedom to pursue investigations of the natural world and reach conclusions that challenge the literal and conventional meaning of revealed passages. It is understandable why the latter effort has been given much more attention in academic studies and judged as the essential historical contribution of the modernist-apologists. Telling Muslims that there is no God but Allah, that Muhammad is His final Prophet, and the Quran is the final, divine, perfected revelation, was hardly a novelty in the annals of Islam. Still, the main objective of the formative treatises of this approach, the stepping stone upon which their defense of the concept of revelation-based society was built, was rationalizing the metaphysical premises of Islam.

Al-Afghani's *Refutation* was written in response to a letter he received in December 1880 from Muhammad Wasal, a math teacher in Hyderabad who was concerned with the spread of materialism among Muslims in India.[55] The book was intended to shock its readers with the implications of a world without God. Al-Jisr's *al-Risala al-Hamidiyya*, published according to its author in response to growing interest in Islam in England,[56] and which he considered the most important achievement of his life,[57] was in large part a rationalist discussion on the reality of a Creator and His Prophet and His revelation. So, too, was 'Abduh's *Risalat al-Tawhid*. While not the foundation of their writing or their focus, rationalist proofs for the metaphysical continued to preoccupy the contemporary standard-bearers of the modernist-apologetic approach, who have argued, largely drawing on the works of their predecessors, why no rational person can deny the existence of God or the authenticity of the Quran as His final revelation.

The prominence of rationalizing Allah, His Prophet and His revelation in modernist-apologetic writing is curious, considering that there was never a moment in any modern Arab society in which open disbelief ceased to be a taboo or was propagated by a dominant faction. Atheism has always been a negligible phenomenon. Higher criticism—in the sense of historicizing the Quran and implying that it is a man-made text, a beautiful work of literature that changed history, but no more than that—has never been incorporated into Arab-Muslim state-regulated schools and universities as a legitimate, let alone scientifically credible, approach. Materialist notions were articulated in Egypt and Syria during the late nineteenth century mainly by Christian Arab intellectuals. The Muslim critical voices that emerged in the first decades of the twentieth century—most notably, Taha Husayn and his reflections on the historical reality of Abraham and Isma'il and the reasons for the existence of seven ways of reading the Quran (*qira'at*), and 'Ali 'Abd al-Raziq and his argument that the Prophet did not convey a political message (see further in chapter 3)—never denied the existence of God, the prophecy of Muhammad or the inerrancy of the revelation. The controversies they caused were over their interpretation of the divine, not about its actual divinity. Even the darkest hour for pure, unmitigated faith in the Muslim-Arab world, seeing the rise of several socialist and even Marxist-leaning regimes in the 1950s and 1960s, did not injure the invincible status of Islam's most basic creeds. One example is the fate of an article "On the Ways to Create Our New Arab Man," published in April 1967 in the journal of the Syrian military, *Jaysh al-Sh'ab*. At the time, Syria was ruled by the Neo-Ba'th, the 'Alawite-dominated, Marxist-leaning faction of the Ba'th Party led by Salah Jadid that had seized control of the country in February 1966. The author, a junior Alawite officer, Ibrahim al-Khalas, dared to argue that Allah and religions should be acknowledged for the mummies in the museum of history that they are.[58] When word of the article spread, general strikes and demonstrations erupted in Syria's main Sunni cities, forcing the regime to retract the article and suggest it had been planted in the journal as part of an American-Israeli conspiracy.

If the demons of materialism, atheism and denial of prophecy never became a socially acceptable option, why has the modernist-apologetic approach been pre-occupied with them? One reason is that providing rationalist proofs for the reality of Allah, His Prophet and His revelation was essential for a worldview that stressed the idea that true Islam in no way negates the scientific methods that have dominated European thought since the Renaissance and have led to Western triumphs, or else the approach would contradict itself. Another reason was that in demonstrating that the foundations of the Muslim faith can be rationally proven, an apologetic argument against Christianity was affirmed. Western secularism and atheism were depicted as historical exceptions, signifying not an advance of universal nature but rebellion against one specific illogical and intolerant religious creed, Christianity, having no implications on faith in the Creator, or on Muslim faith specifically.

While atheism and materialism existed on the fringes of Arab-Muslim societies during the late nineteenth century, and have remained there throughout the twentieth century, the moment of learning of these views would have been an unsettling one for any of the modernist-apologists. In their childhoods, the reality of God was as obvious as the reality of New Zealand: they have never seen Him with their eyes, but were completely confident of His existence. The moment of being acquainted with an alternative that denied that reality was a shocking one. At stake was the certainty that there is meaning to life; that this world is followed by an eternal afterlife; and that devotion and goodness are rewarded. While always directed toward easily impressed Muslims, real and imagined, foolishly lured by the atheists, certain modernist-apologetic texts, whether at the end of the nineteenth century or at the end of the twentieth, betrayed a sense of inner distress among individuals who had realized that in a different world, the West, with which they were fascinated, and whose great material achievements they could not deny, the reality of the metaphysical was not conventional wisdom. The agony caused by this realization was much more daunting and primordial than that caused by the dominance or occupation of foreign forces and their encroachment on long-held values and traditions. It is comparable, perhaps, to the distress that a math professor will experience upon learning that in a distant and more scientifically and technologically advanced civilization two plus two equals five. So incomprehensible will be this discovery, that proving the opposite will take precedence over everything else.

The defense of the reality of the Creator occupies lengthy chapters. Yet it introduces, whether in its late nineteenth century or early twenty-first century forms, little philosophical sophistication or innovation. Modernist-apologetic reflections on the existence of Allah are not much different than those of an inquisitive schoolboy who, pondering for the first time about the fact that his father had a father who also had a father who had a father, engages with the logical impossibility of a beginning without an original source; or those of a romantic teenager who stares at the star-filled heavens and spontaneously senses the existence of a higher, metaphysical, all-knowing entity. Western philosophic discourses on the existence of God, including those that support similar notions, are sporadically mentioned, but only in the form of slogans supportive of a theistic view. This is not to say that the modernist-apologists have not made a convincing case. At their best, philosophy and theology are simple. But whether one is impressed or not, missing from modernist-apologetic rationalizations of the metaphysical is the quality of an open-minded quest for truth or serious confrontation with counter-arguments. Theirs is a project of asserting preexisting beliefs, not of exploring them. The substitute for meaningful, dialectical engagements with conflicting opinions is unequivocal statements that deny the possibility of a rational or honest disagreement with pronouncements of faith.

The first modernist-apologetic treatment of atheism, al-Afghani's *Refutation*, was different from what followed. This book, in which al-Afghani first emerged as a defender of the Islamic faith,[59] focused on utilitarian arguments about the essentiality of religion for the prosperity of nations, offering no more than a general commentary on the rationality of Islam. Herein its weakness as proof for the existence of God, because even the most compelling case for the benefits of a social order based on metaphysical faith constitutes no proof for the reality of a creator, let alone for the truth of the Muslim revelation, a matter the treatise was not directly concerned with.

Al-Afghani introduced faith in God or in a metaphysical order in general as a Hobbesian leviathan that safeguards social cohesion (however, Hobbes was not explicitly mentioned). He suggested that all religions, even in their lowest forms, are better than a philosophy that deprives humans of the virtues provided by faith.[60] According to his treatise, by reducing man to an animal that is no different than other animals, materialism releases beastly desires and aggressions.[61] It eliminates the basis for the existence of nations, and the foundations of their social organization and progression—the belief that man is the crown of creation; individuals' belief that their nation is the noblest of all nations, which encourages them to improve its conditions; and the belief that there awaits a more sublime afterlife as a reward for those who seek perfection in this life. Moreover, it eliminates the virtues of modesty, cooperation and honesty.[62] Human history, according to al-Afghani, is a story of materialist philosophy conquering minds and bringing about the downfall of nations. Its destructive effects began with the ancient Greeks, who witnessed a collapse of virtues and the loss of humaneness, leading ultimately to their capitulation to Rome, and ends with France, a country that, according to al-Afghani, was the most powerful and advanced among European nations until Voltaire and Rousseau revived materialistic teachings, denied the existence of God, presented religion as a fairytale, and encouraged promiscuity, which resulted in moral decay and social disunity. These trends, which according to al-Afghani Napoleon failed to reverse despite his best efforts, ultimately led to France's defeat by the Prussians (in 1871).[63]

In al-Jisr's and Abduh's foundational apologetic treatises, materialism was attacked further, and rationalist proofs for the existence of a Creator, rather than merely arguments about the desirability of believing in one, were introduced. As in al-Afghani's apologia, al-Jisr presented utilitarian arguments according to which life without recognition of an afterlife inevitably leads to the rule of lust, beastly desires and egoism, and, ultimately, to the end of civilization as we know it. He warned that in a world that denies the metaphysical, where people believe that nothing separates them from a plant which grows and then withers, nothing would stop them from murdering for financial gain. Indeed, he wondered, when one thinks of the corruption of some of the nations that do believe in the afterlife, it is terrifying to consider what the future holds for those nations, should they cease to believe.[64] (Years later, as the editor of the reformist newspaper *Jaridat Tarablus*, al-Jisr took great interest in the rise of the spiritualist movement in the West as proof that materialists, too, had realized that a society without belief in an existential beyond cannot function).[65]

To these justifications—which make a case for faith in God as being socially essential, but are in no way a logical proof of His existence—al-Jisr added, in a scattered and unsystematic fashion, rationalistic counter-materialist reasoning, including that there must be an original source that created matter, as it could not have been created by itself;[66] that the inability to observe something with the senses (God, the soul) does not imply that it does not exist (or else the materialists would have to concede that ether also does not exist);[67] and that the complex structure of our world, the marvelous constancy, order and harmony, implies the existence of a purposeful Creator.[68] (On the "watchmaker analogy" see Chapter 2).

As al-Jisr, 'Abduh was impressed with the constancy, order and harmony of the world, considering them to be proofs for the existence of a purposeful Creator. He insisted that when one observes the natural world, whether plants or animals, and the perfect functional operation of their abilities, one cannot but accept the facts of a Creator and an intended creation for which He is responsible:

> Does not this created world, which men of intelligence fall over themselves to investigate until they attain its secrets, in truth bear witness to its originator, the all-knowing, who has given being to every created thing and guided it? Is it possible that nothing but coincidence, the thing we call "chance," gave rise to all this order? Has chance laid down the laws upon which are built the universes mighty and lowly? Never. The artificer of all is He whom "not an atom weight in heaven and earth escapes" [Q. 34:3]. He hears and knows all.[69]

'Abduh also introduced utilitarian arguments for belief. As al-Afghani, he justified a social order based on faith in the Creator—whether as understood by Muslims or by Christians—as a force for patriotism. Addressing the death of Otto von Bismarck in 1898, he mentioned that the German Chancellor once testified that had he not believed in his religion, he would have had no motivation to serve his Kaiser. Having reached a position of affluence and power, he was driven by his personal belief that serving according to God's will, would result in the German nation having a great role in history. 'Abduh suggested that young Muslims who believed that preserving their religion is a disgrace should learn from Bismarck that believing in Allah and His revelation does not mean giving up on philosophy or on science, or the weakening of one's politics.[70] Two years later, addressing a question by a high school student in Alexandria who pondered whether faith in pre-destination was not simply a justification for laziness and a reason for the decline of Eastern, specifically Muslim societies, 'Abduh explained why the opposite was true, introducing an insight reminiscent to that suggested by Max Weber and his *Protestant Ethics* several years later. Allah, in His wisdom, created faith in predestination to help people deal with the difficulties and fears they encounter. For example, a trader who fears losses, or hazards during his travels, is energized to hit the road, prepare all that is necessary, learn what he still does not know, use his wisdom and resort to his mental strengths, if he believes that his fate has already been sealed.[71]

Rida's early treatment of God's reality emphasized the impossibility of existence without an original source, and demonstrated that by the turn of the nineteenth century the modernist-apologists had already developed some tradition of countering materialist arguments. In 1904, a reader of *al-Manar* wondered whether there is an ultimate rationalist proof for the existence of Allah, one that no one could deny. Rida answered that there are two approaches to this question: according to one, man recognizes by his very nature that God exists; according to the other, proofs for His existence should be presented, as prophets and learned men have done in the past. Rida suggested that the two approaches should be integrated. Indeed, man recognizes God by his nature, but prophets and learned men have found it necessary to present proofs in order to convince those who doubt His existence or who associate others with Him.

Polemics with people who have studied modern sciences and doubt Allah taught Rida that the following is the most compelling proof for His reality. Everyone agrees that all existing things could not have created themselves and could not have been created from nothing. Everyone also agrees that something powerful and incomprehensible is the source of all things. The materialists hold that "something" to be a "powerful matter." But when asked what that "powerful matter" is they say they do not have a clue. This implies that there is, in fact, an agreement between the materialists and the believers that an incomprehensible, powerful source is the origin of all existing things, and the only dispute is about the name of that source. Hence, there is no essential dispute between materialists and Muslims, a point which, according to Rida, supports his argument that European philosophers had never denied Allah, but rejected the God of their church because irrational characteristics, such as the Trinity, were attributed to the deity.[72]

Al-Banna's rationalization of the metaphysical, published in 1943, added another dimension that reflected a questioning approach, particularly characteristic of the era, as to the ability of science to offer a comprehensive explanation to all natural phenomena. He described materialism and the denial of God as a clear mistake and loathsome exaggeration, whereas Islam establishes the truth of the metaphysical world in a way that does not contradict rational axioms, and clarifies the relation between humans and God, and humans and the hereafter. Al-Banna suggested that the integration, in Islam, of logical thinking and faith allows for a comprehensive observation of nature that exposes the inability of humans to understand much of the natural world and leads, ultimately, to the recognition that God exists.[73]

Rational proofs for the existence of God have continued to engross the contemporary standard-bearers of the modernist-apologetic approach, albeit in a different context and with less intensity. From the 1940s to the early 1980s, communism and progressive pan-Arab socialism loomed as the new and most formidable challengers to an Islam-based social order, and much apologetic energy was invested in explaining why Islam offers humanity a more perfected social order. For modernist-apologists writing during the bipolar superpower world order, the dialectical materialism of Marxism was perceived as yet another evil materialistic force bent on eliminating Allah from the lives of Muslims and adding to the already existing pressures exerted on young Muslims by graduates of Western universities and graduates of academic institutions established by imperial powers in the Arab world. But while the challenge of materialism, as perceived by them, was potentially dangerous, particularly as it became multi-faceted and disassociated from imperialism, its denial of God was, in a sense, also less intimidating, because responses to atheism had already been formulated decades earlier, and had proven satisfactory at the time. Thus, and despite some comments suggesting that they reflected seriously on this danger, proving the existence of God was not the foundation, nor the focus, of the apologetics by al-Ghazali, al-Qaradawi and 'Imara.

Al-Qaradawi, who presented the abovementioned growing list of materialist rivals in a work from the 1960s, *The Existence of Allah*, described atheism as an epidemic spreading faster than viral diseases in a world that had become a global village, an epidemic that had infiltrated mainstream media. He noted that many young people had been confused by atheist arguments, and, given the questions posed to him on the subject in his radio broadcasts and following lectures, he came to the conclusion that the most vital battle for religious scholars had come to be the most basic one—to make the case for the existence of Allah.[74]

There was little innovation in al-Qaradawi's arguments in comparison to those of 'Abduh, al-Jisr and Rida. Invoking the core modernist-apologetic historical narrative, he suggested that atheism is rooted in the despotism and anti-scientific views of the Church, which encouraged Christians to rebel against it and renounce their religion and God. Had those Christians been aware of Allah and His true religion, they would have returned to the fold of faith.[75] According to al-Qaradawi, it is the nature of man to believe in Allah. It is a belief that comes from the bottom of the heart, a belief that does not require teaching or guidance. He quoted, in this context, Descartes and his idea that his own sense of imperfectness convinced him of the existence of a perfected entity that had infused in him this sense.[76] Atheists, argued al-Qaradawi, have no good answer as to how something could be created from nothing. To say that life on earth began through a meteor still does not answer the question of who created life on another planet.[77] Other rationalist proofs for a creator are that everything in our world is fit to fulfill its role—for example, the earth is made in a way that makes human life on it possible; and that everything, whether living or inanimate, is infused with a sense of what it needs to do in order to perform its God-given role—for example, birds are able to wander from one continent to another and return to their country of origin without erring.[78]

Al-Ghazali, equally concerned with the spread of atheist communism and with materialist thought in general, introduced in *The Bombs of Truth*—a book he composed in the 1970s—evidence against materialism which also pointed to the impossibility of a structure existing without being brought into existence by a constructor. As al-Qaradawi, he described atheism as an epidemic.[79] (In a later book, *With Allah*, he described atheism as the destruction of the heart, the corruption of the mind and an attack on social morals).[80] In the patronizing language he reserved for those who disagreed with his positions, he recalled how his patience ran out when an atheist insisted that there is no Creator. The atheist rhetorically wondered who created Allah. In response, al-Ghazali told the atheist that the question implied recognition that everything must have a Creator, and it is beyond him why an atheist can accept that the world came into existence by itself, yet cannot accept that Allah does not have a Creator. The atheist replied that because he lived in the world, he could not deny the existence of the world. Al-Ghazali responded that he was not demanding the man to deny the existence of the world but rather that he understand the basic fallacy of atheism. When he, al-Ghazali, sees a palace, he knows that an architect has built it, whereas the atheist believes that the wood and the iron and the stones and the coating came together accidentally; when he, al-Ghazali, sees an artificial satellite in the sky, he knows it was sent into space by someone intelligent in a deliberate and organized fashion, whereas the atheist believes it launched itself.[81] All in all, atheism is irrational and faith in a creator is rational, a notion al-Ghazali further supported with a lengthy, if anecdotal and misleading, discussion on Albert Einstein's theism.[82] (In his book *Illnesses and Cures* he mentioned the English astronomer James Jeans' anti-materialist views as evidence that Western science is distancing itself from materialism; he suggested Western atheism was the result of a need for liberation from an anti-rationalist religion, Christianity.)[83]

The Prophet and the Quran

Logical proofs for the existence of a Creator do not, in and of themselves, prove the truth of the Islamic message. In his aforementioned book on the reality of Allah, al-Qaradawi justified his focus on refuting atheism by arguing that it is impossible to convince people about the reality of the Prophet Muhammad and the merits of Islam, unless the primary foundation of faith, belief in God, is reasserted.[84] From the point of view of the preacher, this perhaps makes sense; logically, it does not, for if one rationally establishes that Muhammad was a true Prophet, then one establishes the existence of the one God about which the revelation Muhammad brought speaks. And if one rationally establishes that the Quran is a true, inerrant revelation, then one establishes that there is no God but Allah, and Muhammad is His final Prophet. To wit, it suffices that one rationally establishes either that Muhammad was a true Prophet or that the Quran is a revealed book to establish that the teachings of Islam and the principle of monotheism are true. However, this logic is not suggested in modernist-apologetic works.

The logical proofs presented by the modernist-apologists, early and contemporary, for the truth of the Prophet and of the revelation are that the message is strong while the messenger was weak. The humble background of Muhammad, an illiterate, was offered as evidence that he could not have composed the Quran, a marvel of literature that no human being has ever been able to match. There has never been concern on the part of the modernist-apologists with the problematic nature of relying on religious traditions, the only source on Muhammad's biography, to rationally validate religious beliefs in Muhammad's prophecy. They were also not concerned by the subjective nature of describing a text—as marvelous as it may be—as one that had never been, and could never be, matched, or with the weakness of the argument that the unmatched brilliance of a certain brilliant work testifies to its divine origin, an argument that hypothetically qualifies Mozart or Van Gogh as bearers of divine messages.

The first chapter of *al-Risala al-Hamidiyya* was dedicated to a systematic rationalistic defense of the truthfulness of Muhammad's message, a theme that recurred throughout other chapters of the book. It is intriguing that while al-Jisr's proofs regarding the truth of the prophecy preceded proofs of the reality of the Creator, he did not make the point that the former, logically, obviates the need for the other. According to al-Jisr, free inquiry and a sound mind can only lead to one conclusion—the Prophet Muhammad was the messenger of Allah and the revelation he brought is the word of Allah. Anyone who thinks differently is an extremist, a fool, and an imitator of other people.[85] Thus, freedom is the freedom to think as al-Jisr does, and wisdom is the wisdom to reach conclusions similar to his. The proofs offered by al-Jisr were grounded in core narrations about the life of the Prophet, corroborated by the Prophetic traditions and the Prophet's biographies. These include:

a The most proficient masters of the Arabic language failed to meet the Prophet's challenge and compose something that would match the eloquence and rhetoric of the Quran, whereas the most proficient theologians found the Quran to posses a quality of perfection and comprehensiveness that the human mind cannot create. This constitutes proof that the Quran is the word of Allah.[86]

b Muhammad was an illiterate man, who did not travel far from his hometown, and did not meet with knowledgeable individuals. Thus, he could not have composed something as marvelous as the Quran by himself; all the more so, considering that even the greatest philosophers, such as Aristotle, Euclid and Hippocrates, were experts in one or two fields, but none was an expert in all fields of knowledge; still all the more so, considering that even if the Prophet had not spent his life in Mecca, he would have needed decades to grasp the knowledge which he introduced as a revelation.[87]

c To prove that he was indeed the Messenger of Allah in a way that satisfied those who were not convinced by the preceding facts, and for that purpose only, the Prophet also performed miracles, changing laws of nature, such as when he split the moon. This miracle was observed not only by those near the Prophet but also by people in remote areas and thus could not have been an act of magic.[88]

'Abduh's proofs of the Quran's truth in *Risalat al-Tawhid* were reminiscent of those introduced by al-Jisr, demonstrating again the personal and intellectual encounter that encouraged the authorship of both books. As al-Jisr, he invoked the humble beginnings of the final Prophet as a decisive piece of evidence for the truthfulness of the Quran. The Prophet Muhammad, he wrote, was an illiterate orphan, born and raised among idol-worshippers. Normally, people with such a background are molded in the shape of their surroundings, all the more so if there is no book or teacher to guide them toward the right path. However, from his earliest years, Muhammad felt deeply repulsed by paganism, and remained pure in his belief and excellent in his character, as noted in Q. 93:7. Upon receiving the revelation, he had no property, army, supporters, literary talent or rhetorical skills to aid him. The only possible explanation for his rise to preeminence over other men, and for his extraordinarily intense sense of purpose, was that an awareness of the world's need to recover true belief and to turn from its corrupted morals and manners was infused in him by Allah and led him to act and, ultimately, to be victorious. Divine revelation, nothing else, illuminated the path before him and, like a captain and a warrior, led him in its heavenly authenticity. According to 'Abduh, the weakness of the Prophet was his greatest asset: when people witnessed an illiterate man correct their mistakes with arguments and evidence, and when they witnessed the inability of his rivals to compose something that would match even the shortest chapter of the Quran, they realized that his words could not have originated from within himself, or be those of another human being, and thus must be a true revelation.[89] Moreover, with time, numerous prophecies introduced by Muhammad were proven correct, for example that the Byzantine Empire shall rise again (Q. 30:2–3), or that those who believe and do good deeds will become masters of the land (Q. 24:55), providing any right-minded reader further evidence for the divinity of the Quran.[90]

Rida's final substantial work, *The Muhammadian Revelation*, reasserted the two pillars on which his mentor's rationalist proofs for the truth of the revelation relied, albeit in a less systematic manner. First, an illiterate man such as Muhammad who grew up among ignorant idol worshipers could not have composed a marvelous book such as the Quran;[91] second, the inability of anyone to compose something that matches the Quran testifies to its divine origin. Rida was convinced that lack of exposure to the marvel of the Quran was a main obstacle to mass conversion in the West. However, he did not hold this to be the only reason why Westerners stubbornly clung to their desperate, spiritually void materialistic civilization and refused to recognize the truth of Islam; a history of animosity and the poor state of Muslim societies also contributed their fair share.[92]

The unmatched marvel of the Quran has been presented also in contemporary modernist-apologetic works as one of the primary rationalist proofs for its divine origin. Much attention has been given to defending its authenticity as a revelation that had been transmitted without any distortions through the generations, suggesting an awareness had developed regarding how higher criticisms had damaged faith in Christianity.[93] The "weakness" argument, though, i.e., relying on Muhammad's humble background as rationalist proof of his Prophecy, has been marginalized. One possible reason is that in the mid-twentieth century the persona and legacy of the Prophet were broadly cited by authors of diverse orientations and backgrounds, including pan-Arab progressive socialists, to support their political agendas. Strangely, the Prophet was the subject of greater consensus than the reality of His Creator or the revelation that he brought. This being the case, the urge to defend his credentials as the true final Prophet declined.

Several examples from a rich corpus follow. In his book *The Quran Challenges*, 'Imara, relying generously on 'Abduh, rationalized the divinity of the revelation through what he described as the demonstrated and continuous inability of anyone to compose something that would match it, or match even one of its chapters.[94] In another book, he noted that the illiteracy of the Prophet, who produced a book that no one could imitate, was proof for the divinity of the revelation.[95] He offered a plethora of Islamic and Western learned sources who, so he argued, confirm the Quran's divinity, including the Scottish scholar of Islamic studies, William Montgomery Watt (1909–2006).[96] In another book he described the Quran as a marvel which is recognized as such through the application of reason.[97] Al-Ghazali compared the Quran to the sun and the moon: just as their existence and size are not affected by the way they are perceived from our planet, so too is the integrity and authenticity of the Quran as the revealed word of Allah a solid scientific fact, one that has been reasserted throughout history.[98] He further described the Quran as an unmatched wonder whose recognition as such had galvanized support for Islam.[99]

Al-Qaradawi remarked in his book *How to Engage with the Glorious Quran* that those who argue that the Quran is a historical text are not familiar with the text and with the historical situation at the time of its revelation. He quoted, typically without proper references, examples of Western enchantments with the Quran: a man who said that anyone who would find this book in the desert would recognize it as the word of God; and a professor at the University of California who said that the Quran could not have been written by a human being, and thus to deny its divinity is to imply that Muhammad is God. Words, wrote al-Qaradawi, always reveal who uttered them—whether a man or woman, young or old, happy or sad; any reader of the Quran who is a logical and sensitive person realizes that its words cannot be the words of a human being. Moreover, a reader of the Prophetic traditions will recognize that when a verse from the Quran is included in them, it enlightens them in a way that anyone who reads it, or hears it, senses that these are not the words of any man who lived before the Prophet or after the Prophet.[100] Al-Qaradawi stated that no rational person can compare the eternal Quran, to which no letter has been added and from which no letter has been removed, to the Torah, which he argued was distorted following the Babylonian Captivity, and the Gospels, which he described as inauthentic. He had no expectation that the materialists, who believe that all revelations are fabrications, would accept the truth of the Quran, but was puzzled by the reluctance of Christian missionaries, who do not deny revelations in principle, to accept the superiority, eternity and divinity of the final revelation.[101]

B. The Modernist-Apologetic Reconciling of Doubt and Revelation

Modernist-apologetic thought holds that Islam is the religion of reason and freedom, and encourages rational, scientific research, and technological innovation. It introduces Islam as a precursor and foreseer of modernity, including its methods of administration and governance, suggesting that the reason for the failures of Muslim societies is not their faith, but their neglect of it. These notions are supported by historical and theological arguments. While not systematically presented as such in any single text, they have accumulated over time to make a case for the ability of revelation-based Muslim societies to be free of arbitrary theocratic interventions. The modernist-apologists have argued that:

a   Islam and Christianity have two distinct approaches to science and politics; thus, the correlation between secularization and advancement constitutes Christian exceptionalism and is not a relevant model for Muslim societies.

b   Christian societies owe their scientific ascendance, at least in large part, to their interactions with Muslim societies at a time in history when Islam, true to itself, was scientifically advanced; in their current, advanced state, these societies are more Islamic in some respects than Muslim societies are.

c   Technological prowess that is not revelation-based is not sustainable, and thus the Islamic model of revelation-based scientific studies is superior to the Western secularized one.

d   One of the miracles of the Quran is that it introduces many scientific discoveries, technological innovations and a system of governance that were unfamiliar to humanity at the time of its revelation.

e   Contradictions between the Islamic revelation and proven scientific theories, models or facts are impossible, and the appearance of such contradictions calls for the application of allegorization which is always able to reconcile science and religion.

The weight given to each of these arguments is not the same, and their functions are different. The arguments about the Islamic origins of Western Renaissance and the Quran's concealment of modern scientific discoveries serve as evidence for the authenticity of the quest to modernize Muslim societies and as an assurance that faith is not what injured the Islamic path to development. The arguments about a distinction between Islam's and Christianity's attitude toward freedom of thought and investigation, and about the ability of Islam to accommodate any proven scientific finding, serve as evidence that the existence of a scientifically and technologically advanced revelation-based society is possible.

Islam as presented by the modernist-apologists constitutes an alternative to the daunting model of secularization—and its inevitable implications—that had challenged Muslim thinkers since the late nineteenth century. At one end of the spectrum delineated by the secularization model are revelation-based societies, doomed to backwardness due to the oppressive tendencies of religious establishments and their privileging of metaphysical predispositions over empirical, rationalist depictions of the natural world. At the other end are doubt-based societies, prosperous and advanced due to their separation of religion from the scientific and political spheres.

The modernist-apologists defined a radically different spectrum as an alternative to the abovementioned. At one end are Muslim societies that are not loyal to the true teachings of Islam and are thus backward. At the middle of the spectrum lie secularized Christian societies that have been inspired by Islam to establish scientific and political freedoms but have rejected the foundations of Islamic faith. While more Muslim than Muslim societies in this sense, their future downfall is, nevertheless, inevitable. At the other end of the spectrum is the ideal Muslim society, which Muslim societies have the ability to become. Should Muslim societies return to

Islam, true to itself as the modernist-apologists understand it, they will advance scientifically, technologically and politically, and rise once again to lead humanity because of, rather than in spite of, the revelation.

As far as apologetics are concerned, this is a sophisticated spectrum. It tells Muslims that the choice between revelation-based and doubt-based social orders is artificial and biased, and suggests that Islam has a way of providing the advantages of the latter without compromising the former. Modernity is rooted in Islam, and Islam loyal to itself comprehends all modernity's positive aspects without absorbing any of its negatives. To advance to the future, Muslims should go back to their glorious past and embark on a process of reclamation and reinterpretation, finding in their authentic self the roots and foundations of what made the West, in some respects, great. To achieve what a rival, powerful culture has achieved, Muslims must recognize their own culture as the source of those achievements. In the late nineteenth century, just as in the early twenty-first century, nothing troubled Muslims, particularly those with secondary and university-level education, more than the thought that having to choose between faith and modernity, revelation and progress, is inevitable. The tremendous appeal of the modernist-apologetic approach has been that it confidently argued why such a choice is unnecessary. To defend their independence, the modernist-apologists suggested, Muslims need not abandon their identity nor give up hope for an eternal afterlife. No other approach has offered such convincing and compelling assurances as they have.

Islam, Christianity and the Roots of the Renaissance

The historical arguments about the differences between Islam's and the Church's approaches to reason and freedom, and about the Islamic origins of Western Renaissance, turn the tables on the linkage between secularization and modernity, suggesting this linkage to be indeed valid to Western history, but only to that history. These arguments were first crystallized in direct response to allegations by a number of Western and Arab thinkers at the close of the nineteenth century and the beginning of the twentieth that Islam was the enemy of rationalism, and that Muslim societies stood no chance at progressing unless they renounced their religion or limited it to the sphere of moral guidance. The polemics involved the French scholar of the Orient, Ernst Renan (1823–1892), the French historian and politician, Gabriel Hanotaux (1853–1944), and Farah Antun (1874–1922), a Lebanese Christian-Arab journalist, who settled in Cairo in 1897.

In a lecture given at the Sorbonne, published in March 1883 in the *Journal des débats*, on the closing of the Muslim mind and the backwardness of Muslim societies, Renan suggested that Islam, in which faith rules over reason, is incompatible with scientific progress, and that the Muslims of his age are inherently hostile to science. He refuted the notion that the excellence of Muslims in the sciences in the past indicates that nothing should prevent them from restoring their former glory, as Muslims, in the future. Renan argued that children who receive an Islamic education come to believe that they posses the ultimate truth and belittle European learning and sciences, as well as other religions. While the early Arab Muslims possessed linguistic acumen, they were fatalists and far removed from any scientific and philosophical knowledge. Indeed, in medieval times there developed an Islamic superiority in these fields, but it was not a superiority of Muslim societies as such, merely the result of the relaxed and rather artificial faith of the Abbasid chief administrators, their openness to new ideas, and the integration of Greek and Persian Sasanian philosophy and sciences into the Empire.[102] Renan suggested that societies must be freed from the imposition of metaphysical assumptions—whether these are Christian or Muslim—in order to successfully investigate the natural world.[103]

Hanotaux argued, in an article published in France and translated by the Egyptian daily newspaper *al-Mu'ayyad* in 1900, and in an interview he gave to *al-Ahram* that same year, that the absence of a separation between religion and politics, and religion and science, is the main reason for the backwardness of Muslim societies in comparison to Western ones. He described Islam as a religion that encourages submission and passivity, and emphasized that the superiority of Western societies is not some God-given, essentialist gift, but the result of a historical process which did not occur in the East, at the end of which temporal regimes, to which religious authorities are subordinated, were established.[104]

A keen reader of Renan, Antun suggested in 1902 that Muslims should take note of the Christian separation between religion, politics and science, and maintain religion as a private, spiritual matter. He offered a number of explanations, including that religious authorities, believing they exclusively possess the truth, will always become oppressive if given power (he emphasized that new scientific discoveries are often oppressed, offering the example of Galileo Galilei); and that states controlled by religion are weaker, because religious authorities divide them, and legislate with their eyes toward the afterlife rather than this world.[105]

Al-Afghani's response to Renan was published, in French, in May 1883. He admitted that the pursuit of sciences had been curtailed under Islam. But he noted that this had also been the case in Christianity in the past, yet it later changed course toward science and progress, becoming free and independent; thus, the Muslim nation had the potential to achieve progress as the West has. Whereas for Renan sciences remained alienated from Islam even during the glorious days of Muslim scientific superiority, for al-Afghani the Islam of the past demonstrated a remarkable capacity to integrate sciences and to greatly develop them.[106]

Keddie observed al-Afghani's response to Renan to be an unorthodox text that indicates that by 1883 he had yet to become the unequivocal defender of Islam that he later became.[107] Kedourie went as far as to argue that the response was an endorsement of Renan's condemnation of Islam.[108] There is, however, an ambiguity in the response, which allows for a more nuanced reading. The ambiguity results, in part, from the interchangeable usage of the terms religion, society and nation. It is clear from al-Afghani's point of view that religion—any religion—is an obstacle to scientific and philosophical progress. However, it is also clear that he believed Muslim societies should be able to undergo reform without ceasing to be

Muslim. His historical analogy did not clarify whether the intended reform is one that would separate religion and state, or merely one that would make religion more tolerant.

In his response to Hanotaux, al-Jisr deplored the French Minister's sense of civilizational supremacy. In particular he protested against the notion that the absolutist power of God in Islam leads the believers to passivity and weakness, noting that in Islam, just as in Christianity, people are motivated to please God by doing good deeds. He suggested that Hanotaux's analysis misconstrued the unitary nature of God by suggesting that through the impact of Greek philosophy Christians were encouraged to endeavor to be like God.[109]

'Abduh's apologetics in his detailed responses to Hanotaux and Antun (and comment on Renan) introduced analyses that became the backbone of how future generations of Muslims narrated the history of their religion, its contribution to the Christian world, and the differences between the two. Whereas al-Afghani argued for the prospect of an Islamic reformation similar to that experienced in Christianity (without committing exactly to what that entails), 'Abduh drew a distinction. He argued that while Christianity is an irrational religion,[110] Islam is rational,[111] and places great importance on the pursuit of knowledge.[112] Whereas in Christianity the Pope held oppressive powers, including the authority to depose kings, ban princes, levy taxes and enact divine legislation, Islam did not establish the rule of religion. Islam eliminated it. Only Allah and His Prophet have control over Muslims' faith, and it is only Allah that they worship. While individual Muslims may seek the advice of experts in understanding Allah's commands, they must not accept any opinion unless supported by evidence. Thus, while Europeans could indeed only achieve progress after they separated their political and religious authorities, their experience is not relevant for Muslims.[113]

'Abduh argued that the time in history when scientists could research freely, and the Muslim world was more scientifically advanced than the Christian world, was the time in which Muslims were actually loyal to their religion. Those more advanced Muslims, who were encountered by Christians in Andalusia, enlightened Christian societies, who were at that time oppressed by the Church, with the spark of scientific knowledge that had led to the rise of Christian civilization. The Church did all that it could to extinguish the spark, and maintain the ignorance that protected its rule. However, it did not prevail in the bloody battle that ensued.[114] Meanwhile, the Muslim world witnessed the rule of despots and subsequent decline, whose origins were traced to the first infiltration of Turks to positions of leadership in the Muslim world. Nothing concerned those despots more than science, because knowledge enlightens people of their situation; so science was oppressed.[115] Thus, what Renan mistakenly defined as the persecution of science in Islam is really no more than Muslim ignorance of Islam. A Muslim return to Islam—that is, to Islam true to itself—will constitute a return to science.[116]

This historical analysis was duplicated by 'Abduh's disciple Rida, who then passed it down to al-Banna, whom he mentored on the historical dimension of

Western-Muslim relations. Both presented this narrative as part of their efforts to demonstrate that Muslims should not feel inferior to Christians, and that a return to Islam would advance, rather than set back, the material state of Muslim societies. Islam, wrote Rida in 1907, a point at which he was still more inclined to 'Abduh's tolerant approach to British occupation, liberated Muslims from imitation and submission, but submission soon returned, and freedom of thought declined; European societies have suffered from even greater oppression than Muslim societies have, but, enlightened by the sciences of Andalusia, a struggle for freedom of thought ensued, leading to their rise and to their occupying Eastern lands; now, Europeans teach Muslims their scientific methods, and Muslims should be thankful for that, because these are the methods commanded by the Quran.[117] Al-Banna explained that the analogy between the separation of church and state in Islam and in Christianity is wrong, because in Islam the authorities of religious scholars are more limited, which implies that a revival does not require the destruction of religion.[118] Islam is a religion that commands pursuit of scientific knowledge.[119] Contacts with Muslims during the Crusades and in Andalusia led to a great scientific awakening that was fiercely resisted by the Church, which ultimately lost the battle. European states developed scientifically and grew in strength. However, they removed religion from their lives, doubted the existence of God and became materialistic, promiscuous and selfish.[120]

The contemporary generation of modernist-apologetic authors further committed to this narrative. Particularly in apologias written from the late 1960s onward, they established at the core of their interpretation of modernity the ideas that Europe owes its Renaissance, in large part or even entirely, to Islam, and that Muslim societies owe their decline to the absence of true Islam that anticipated and endorses crucial aspects of modernity. There was much to encourage the preservation and continued prominence of this historical analysis. The technological chasm between the West and the Muslim world had only widened—the steam-trains, electricity and cameras that so greatly impressed nineteenth century Muslim authors paled in comparison to space travel and genetic engineering, rendering the quest to establish an Islamic contribution to humanity's advancement all the more vital. Whereas the early modernist-apologists wrote at a time when the secularization model was still a new and promising prospect, in the post-Nasserite climate authors could be confident that this model is not only undesirable but also impractical, suggesting that an Islamic validation of desired aspects of modernity should be considered not only the preferred path to scientific and technological advancement, but the only possible one. The demand to signal out the decline of religion in Christian societies as an exception was suggested both as part of the process of Islamization and as a crucial aspect of facilitating Islamization. Contemporary modernist-apologists emphasized that only if Muslims appreciate the truth about the contribution of their civilization to humanity, their societies can be purified from the damaging impact of Western ideologies.

Al-Qaradawi, for example, commented that the dark age of scientific backwardness had descended on Muslim societies not because of Islam, but because of its neglect. For a thousand years Muslims led humanity in the sciences by adhering to a religion that is rational and which regards pursuit of scientific knowledge as a communal duty.[121] He wrote that Christian encounters with Muslims during the Crusades, in Andalusia and in Sicily, led to their awakening. It was from Muslims, and not from anyone else, that Christians learned the empirical methods that allowed their Renaissance; it was the freedom and balance that they witnessed in Muslim lives that led to their religious reformation.[122] The Christian Church was oppressive. To gain liberty and to allow scientific research and technological progress, a struggle against the Church was essential, and after its defeat European peoples separated religion from the public sphere. This has no bearing on Islam, though, because Islam never witnessed a struggle between science and religion, and, from its first day, supported observation, contemplation and progress.[123]

Similarly, al-Ghazali, who identified the poor state of sciences and technology as one of the two primary problems that the Muslim world faces,[124] argued that whereas in Christian societies sciences developed in spite of a hostile Church, in Islam, when it was true to its true self, there was no struggle with science. Islam considers science a religious tool, because it teaches about the power of Allah.[125] During the first centuries after the revelation, Muslims led the world scientifically. European scientists and innovators, who developed the concept of free thinking due to their enlightening interactions with Islam, were persecuted by the Church. Ever since (and following the decline in the power of the Church), Europe has risen and the Muslim world declined, due to the decline of rationalism in its own quarters.[126] The failure to acknowledge the West's debt to Islam results from a Christian conspiracy and constitutes a distortion of human history.[127] If Muslims had remained loyal to the teachings of Islam, they would have been the pioneers in the race to conquer space. Instead, they lost touch with the true meaning of their religion.[128]

The modernist-apologetic narrative is not a fictitious account, detached from historical facts. It alludes to several important universal lessons that can and should be taught in every history class, both in the Muslim world and outside it: rational thought and empiricism are not a Western possession; there is no inherent contradiction between being religious and making important scientific contributions; and there is a correlation between scientific freedom, as well as investment in scientific education, and the level of scientific and technological advancements. This narrative is, however, also hyperbolic and narrow. Indeed, Muslim societies were, at a certain period in history, more advanced scientifically and technologically, and Western societies—in fact, humanity at large—are indebted to them for their preservation of certain works, and their development of certain scientific fields during the age in which faith in the teachings of the Church triumphed, to use Charles Freeman's expression, over Greek rationalist tradition.[129] But reducing Western Renaissance to a reflection and extension of what Muslims achieved and then lost, ignoring the complex factors and circumstances that led to the global domination of European armies and cultures, as discussed in a rich body of scholarship, is an outlandish reductionist, even naïve, reading of history.

Even if the modernist-apologetic narrative is accepted without debate, the analogy it draws is not fully developed. The achievements of Muslim scientists in the Middle Ages did not challenge fundamental religious concepts as to the origins of the universe or the origins of humankind. The pace of scientific and technological progress in modern Western societies, the ways through which these societies revolutionized the most fundamental human perceptions of the natural world since the 17th century, are historically unprecedented. Their great triumphs occurred with the application, also unique in the annals of human history, of empirical methods of experimentation that, at a certain point, were freed from the interference of metaphysical axioms and their social agents. Given that this is the case, should one not at least give consideration to the possibility that the achievements of modern Western, doubt-based societies could be only matched by other equally doubt-based societies?

The modernist-apologists have not addressed this question directly. But they have treated it indirectly through yet another historical narrative—or, more precisely, a conspiracy theory—as well through a triumphal prophecy. Their theory of a "Western cultural attack" (*al-ghazw al-thaqafi*) implied that questioning the credibility and utility of the revelation as the all-encompassing guide to life is to declare oneself an innocent—or not so innocent—victim of a vicious Western takeover of Muslim minds that was intent on doing precisely that. This theory suggests that subsequent to the defeat of the Crusaders, Western societies realized that the way to take over Muslim societies and eliminate them as a threat once and for all is to spread amongst them doubt about the truth of Islam and its place as a comprehensive system. Consequently, since the late eighteenth century, they have launched systematic and continuous cultural campaigns, mainly through missionary schools and media organs, which have resulted in many Muslims straying away from Islam, conquered without a fight. To rise once again, Muslims must first purify themselves from the ill effects of the "cultural attack." The origins of this theory are found in an article published in al-Afghani's and 'Abduh's *al-'Urwa al-Wuthqa* in Paris in 1883. It stated that Muslims who studied in the West, and imitate the West, are a spearhead for Western occupations, and suggested that the remedy for the weaknesses of the Muslim nation is a return to the fundamentals of religion.[130] Rida wrote fifteen years later about the "moral brigades," sent to the East by imperialist forces in order to corrupt it and facilitate the take over of Eastern lands while devoting only a small number of human resources.[131] Al-Banna, who wrote in 1943 about a Western "social attack," was the first to introduce the idea that a well-planned, systematic attack via cultural means was directed by the West specifically against Muslims. This attack spread doubt and atheism, leading Muslims to despise Islam and reject their traditions.[132] The theory was further developed by the contemporary modernist-apologists, and by others not belonging to their approach. By invoking it, they explained why Muslims fail in comparison to the West, why Muslims do not recognize that Islamizing their societies is the cure for their failings, and why the educational and cultural spheres, rather than the political, are where efforts should be focused.[133] Typical of conspiracy theories, one who doubts the theory of the "cultural attack" is suspected of being part of it, which is indeed an allegation contemporary modernist-apologists have made.[134]

The prophecy of decline introduced by modernist-apologetic authors declares that Western civilization is bound to collapse. That this assertion has been articulated since the early nineteenth century, and has repeatedly failed to materialize, does not deter the contemporary standard-bearers of the modernist-apologetic approach to repeat it with ever growing confidence. They argue that while Western societies developed scientifically and technologically, they are slaves to godless materialism, which has deprived them of their morals, a sense of purpose and the comfort of knowing that a rewarding afterlife exists, the result of which has been the break up of families, the proliferation of drugs, alcohol and sexual diseases, and individuals who suffer from a constant state of anguish. Such societies are in no way sustainable. The implication of this argument is that the revelation-based model is not merely an alternative to secularization, but the only possibility for societies that wish to survive. Notions of the decline of Western civilization can be traced, as noted above, to the formative treatises of al-Afghani and al-Jisr. They were repeated in analyses by Rida in al-Manar,[135] and have been presented, since the mid-1930, as a matter of fact by al-Banna, who described the West as a ship whose captain is at its wit's end in the face of a stormy sea.[136] In contemporary modernist-apologetic writings prophecies of decline have become a genre of their own. Without doubt and in spite of Western scientific and technological advances, these writings declare the death of Western civilization and the West's embrace of Islam are around the corner. According to al-Qaradawi, who dedicated the entirety of one of his books to the signs of Islam's inevitable triumph,[137] the Westerner who walked on the moon is unable to find peace of mind and happiness on the face of the earth, and only Islam can fill that void.[138] To paraphrase al-Ghazali, modern civilization separated humankind from Allah and the afterlife, utilized scientific advancements to serve the most deplorable of instincts, weakened the bonds of humanity and generated unsatisfied hearts—and only Islam can solve its problems.[139]

The Scientific Marvel of the Quran (al-I'jaz al-'Ilmi lil-Qur'an)

Along with history as evidence for the commensurability of Islam with the advances of modernity, the modernist-apologists have also provided theological evidence. This evidence centers on the concept of the scientific marvel of the Quran (al-i'jaz al-'ilmi lil-Qur'an) as well as the option of allegorizing it to accommodate contradictions between the revelation and scientific discoveries, which is another form of marvel.

The concept of scientific marvel suggests that numerous scientific facts and technological innovations that were unknown, and entirely inconceivable in the lifetime of the Prophet, are alluded to in the Quran, testifying to its divinity. The greatest achievements in science, technology and governance can be traced to the revelation, where they patiently waited for the moment that their reinterpretation would serve as yet additional proof for it being the final word of God for humankind. The point intended is not that the Quran is a textbook on the natural world; this could raise the question as to why scientific studies were at all necessary as a means to discover what the Quran already revealed. Neither did the modernist-apologists argue that scientific discoveries always have their matching verse; as explored below, they are confident that discrepancies between proven scientific facts, models and theories and the literal meaning of verses can be reconciled in a way that safeguards the integrity of both science and the revelation and this, too, constitutes a marvel. Rather, the intention in pointing to scientific and technological revolutions concealed in the Quran is to assert that the revelation is not alien to modernity and, most definitely, is not a rival of modernity; in a sense, it is a precursor of modernity.

For an outsider, most of the examples provided by the modernist-apologists for verses that miraculously anticipated future advances seem artificial and ill-founded, at times even ridiculous, and no different than how similar efforts on the part of certain Jewish Rabbis and Christian fundamentalists seem. The effect is ironic: while always introduced in the broader context of asserting the rational and scientifically inclined nature of Islam, the outlandish creativity of the marvels located in the Quran exposes the modernist-apologists as individuals who, despite their claims to the contrary, are not concerned with systematic, open-ended refutable pursuit of knowledge, but with the assertion of the revelation as the paradigmatic ultimate, all-encompassing, inerrant truth.

Al-Afghani was the first to incorporate the concept of scientific marvel in his apologetics. He noted that humanity time and again discovers and develops things that were not held to be true before, but which appear in the Quran. One example for this marvel is Q. 27:38, which tells of King Solomon asking for the throne of the Queen of Sheba to be brought to him before her arrival. According to al-Afghani, the Quran did not detail what means enabled the throne to be speedily transferred to King Solomon's realm because, at the time of its revelation, the instantaneous transfer of communiqués was incomprehensible. In the age of telegraph, they are—and the possibility mentioned in the Quran can be appreciated by those who read it. Other examples are Q. 21:30, which implies that the earth split from the sun, and 79:30, "and after that He spread the earth" (*wal-ard ba'da dhalika dahaha*). According to al-Afghani, the verb used in the latter verse has a similar root as the word used for egg, or an egg-shaped object, which is round, or close to being round. He saw in this evidence that the Quran is commensurate with the scientific fact that the earth is round, or, at the very least, that it can be allegorized to be commensurate with this scientific fact.[140]

This point, which is still a common theme in contemporary apologetics on the marvel of the Quran, was of particular importance because there are certain verses—Q. 20:53, 71:19, 88:20—that can be interpreted as implying that the earth is flat. The insistence of some late nineteenth scholars that the earth is indeed flat was perceived by the modernist-apologists as damaging to their core argument that Islam is a rationalist, science-friendly religion. Moreover, it created a parallelism between Islam and the grave faults of the Catholic Church and its insistence on erroneous concepts regarding the earth's shape.

Another example of broaching the scientific marvel of the Quran in the context of a broader apologetic argument about modernity is al-Kawakibi's book on Islam's resistance to despotism. This work by a participant in *al-Manar*'s project, discussed further in chapter 3, was more an apologia about the reconcilability of Islam, loyal to its revelation, with any desirable Western advancement, than a systematic political theory. Its treatment of science epitomized this point. Despots, wrote al-Kawakibi, are afraid of empirical studies and political philosophy, and persistently try to suppress scientific inquiries because they know all too well that ignorance causes the public to fear, and fear causes submission, whereas knowledge leads to action. Despots are even afraid of people learning what the actual meaning of the testimony "No God but Allah" is, because that implies realizing that God alone should be worshipped.[141] One of the injuries Muslim despots caused to both science and Islam is that religious scholars, fearing for their lives, were not able to freely study the Quran and establish its marvelous quality, which, to al-Kawakibi, is the most important religious issue that should be broached. This being the case, religious scholars were unable to reveal that the Quran contains thousands of verses which demonstrate its marvel, and that science has discovered in recent centuries many truths that a careful reader will find have already been mentioned explicitly, or were alluded to, in the Quran. These verses, whose true meaning was not clear upon their revelation, were meant to serve as a future demonstration of the marvel of the Quran. Al-Kawakibi offered 13 examples from the modern sciences and technology, some requiring much imagination so as to not be considered an interpretative stretch. These include Q. 41:11 and the discovery that ether is the basic material of the universe; 13:41 and 54:1 and the discovery that the moon split from the earth; 23:12 and the discovery that organic life originated from the unanimated; 105:3–4 and the impact microbes have on diseases; 25:45 and the technical possibility to "capture the shadow," i.e., photography; and 36:42 and the ability of ships to sail using steam and electricity.[142]

The predictive quality of certain verses of the Quran was integrated as evidence for the commensurability of revelation and science also in contemporary modernist-apologetic literature. Al-Qaradawi depicted science as a means to propagate the spread of religion and to assert its truths. He quoted Rida in his *Muhammadian Revelation* on a variety of astronomical and biological findings that were inconceivable at the time of revelation as evidence for the scientific marvel of the Quran, concluding that a preacher who made good use of such examples would find a way into the minds and feelings of modern, educated individuals.[143] Not only that: scientific studies and technological innovations have the potential to demonstrate the empirical and rational quality of metaphysical issues that could not have been comprehended in their entirety upon the revelation and the decades that followed. For example, early Muslim theologians thought it was impossible that man would witness in the afterlife his deeds from this life, as indicated by a literal reading of Q. 99:6 and 3:30. Then came modern science, which demonstrated that everything humans say and do can be recorded, photographed and preserved long after it happens.[144] Al-Ghazali pointed to verses that anticipated metrological phenomena and the laws of gravity (for example, Q. 35:41: "Indeed, Allah holds the heavens and the earth, lest they cease").[145] In a similar vein to other modernist-apologists, he argued that the total commensurability between science and Muhammad's revelation, and the discoveries of scientific facts concealed in the Quran but unfamiliar at the time of revelation, are evidence for the truth of the revelation.[146]

While impressed with the number of scientifically marvelous verses that support their broader agenda, contemporary modernist-apologists also noted the risks involved in this concept, something the forefathers of the approach did not do. In recent decades, works on *al-i'jaz al-'ilmi* proliferated, becoming the centerpiece of specialized institutes, books, leaflets, DVDs and internet websites.[147] The modernist-apologists do not hold that scientific marvel should be a focus of proselytizing efforts, a substitute for the pursuit of empirical studies or a precondition for the acceptance of the validity of scientific theories. Concerned with its growing centrality, they cautioned that some Muslim scholars, in their enthusiasm to locate compatibilities between verses and scientific discoveries, point to examples that are debatable.[148] Still, the modernist-apologists never introduced a systematic method outlining the conditions for demonstrating *i'jaz* and distinguishing between the obvious and the ambiguous, and some of their own examples are unconvincing as well.

Allegorizing as a Means of Reconciling Science and Revelation

The most vital aspect of the modernist-apologetic effort to establish the commensurability of a revelation-based Muslim society with modern, free, rational, empirical scientific methods is their method of applying *ta'wil*—allegorizing, or shifting from the literate meaning of a verse to a concealed meaning.[149] According to the modernist-apologists, given that the Quran is the revealed word of Allah, and thus an inerrant truth, it is not logically possible that a scientifically proven theory, model or fact that describes the natural world will contradict any of its verses. In cases where a seeming contradiction exists, a pertinent verse or verses should be allegorized so as to accommodate scientific truths. Alternatively, human powerlessness should be acknowledged. The implication is that nothing scientists have discovered, and nothing that they will discover, can potentially undermine the integrity of the Quran. Thus, religious scholars have no reason to fear modern science, and scientists can rest assured that their ability to pursue their studies will not be injured by religious scholars.

This seems a classic case of "heads I win, tails you lose." The logic is almost painfully cyclical: science cannot contradict the Quran because the Quran is the inerrant revealed word of God, and the Quran is the revealed, inerrant word of God because science cannot contradict it. But if one accepts the modernist-apologetic statement that one can rationally and beyond any doubt prove that the Quran is a revelation, one must accept *ta'wil* as sensible and essential. Otherwise, scientific facts will have to be rejected when they conflict with revealed passages, and doing so undermines the revelation itself, which is rational and speaks of the importance of pursuing knowledge.

The modernist-apologetic method of applying *ta'wil* opened the door for the integration of any desired aspect of modernity into revelation-based Muslim societies. No matter how radically a discovery challenges clear and unambiguous words, and no matter how radically new findings shake centuries-old conceptions, their potential reconciliation with the Quran, as well as with confirmed Prophetic traditions, is assured.

One reason for the relative ease with which this method was introduced and received since the late nineteenth century is that it was not revolutionary or ground-breaking; on the contrary, already in medieval Ash'ari Islamic thought it was invoked as a means to defend the revealed essence of the Quran and the integrity of confirmed Prophetic traditions, and to resist the infiltration of foreign, ostensibly non-Islamic worldviews. Abu Hamid al-Ghazali's (1058–1111) book *The Incoherence of the Philosophers* expressed his opposition to what he considered heretical, or, at the very least, erroneous, notions held by Ibn Sina and his disciples. His work legitimized allegoric interpretations of revealed verses if their literal reading clearly contradicts rational proofs. One example is his discussion on the meaning of a Prophetic tradition regarding solar and lunar eclipses and the obligation to pray when they occur. Al-Ghazali argued that there is nothing irrational in the tradition and suggested that even if an addition that is not reliable and contradicts reason ("But, if Allah reveals Himself to a thing, it submits itself to Him") was, in fact, reliable, then it should have been interpreted allegorically, because many literal meanings that are not as clear as astronomical demonstrations regarding the eclipse have been interpreted allegorically. He warned that "the greatest thing in which atheists rejoice is for the defender of religion to declare that these [astronomical demonstrations] and their like are contrary to religion."[150] Another example is in al-Ghazali's refutation of the philosophers' denial of bodily resurrection and the return of spirits to the bodies, of the existence of corporeal fire, and of the existence of paradise. He drew a distinction between the obligation to allegorically interpret verses that attribute Allah place, direction, visage, physical hand, physical eye and the possibility of transfer, because attributing such features to Allah has been rationally shown to be impossible, and the impermissibility of allegorizing verses that describe the hereafter, because what the latter promises is not impossible in terms of His power.[151]

Modernist-apologists applied al-Ghazali's spirit and ideas in a modern context, facilitating the embrace of the most radical of modern scientific revolutions and encouraging the integration of Western political concepts and structures. But because the star to which their wagon was hitched was the most formidable voice of orthodoxy, it was difficult for scholars who opposed specific conclusions they reached to accuse them of doctrinal heresy or even of excessive originality.

The first systematic introduction of allegorizing as a method of reconciling science and revelation produced by the modernist-apologists was al-Jisr's in *al-Risala al-Hamidiyya*. He argued that:

a   One must not doubt a revealed word of the Quran, or a confirmed Prophetic tradition, as doing so amounts to infidelity.

b   In cases in which a piece of conclusive rational evidence contradicts the literal meaning of a passage from the Quran or a confirmed tradition, allegorization should be applied as a means of reconciling the two. If *ta'wil* is not applied in such cases, the implication is that reason, the basis upon which the truth of the revelation is accepted, will be destroyed.

c   It is imperative not to confuse conclusive evidence with hypotheses; only the former legitimizes distancing an interpretation from the literal meaning of revealed words.[152]

An example offered by al-Jisr explains how *ta'wil* should be applied and why it is a matter of common sense. Q. 18:86 states: "When he reached the setting of the sun, he found it setting in a spring of dark mud." Understood literally, the meaning of this verse is that the sun actually sets in one or another spring upon the face of the earth. According to al-Jisr, had there not been conclusive, rational proof that this is not how the sun sets, the verse should have been accepted as is and not allegorized. But because it has been rationally and conclusively established that the sun does not set upon the face of the earth, this verse should be allegorized so as to reconcile it with known facts about the natural world.[153]

Allegorizing was al-Jisr's ultimate weapon against secularists who believe that religion is science's rival, as well as religious scholars who believe that science must bow to the literal reading of the revelation. He argued that what the materialists do not understand is that when verses are thoroughly understood, they always make sense. Thus, individuals whose knowledge of Islam is restricted to rituals may think that the existence of America cannot be acknowledged because it implies that the earth is round, and that it contradicts Islamic faith. Such arguments deride Islam, the most rationalist religion. As it has been established that the earth is indeed round, Q. 79:30 should be allegorized in a way that counters the argument that the earth is flat (the allegorizing of "spread" that al-Jisr favored was not the same as al-Afghani's egg-shape argument, but about the act of facilitating the earth for human life on it).[154]

'Abduh introduced similar ideas about allegorizing and its implications. Islam, he wrote, is based on rational investigation as a means to attain the correct faith. There is broad agreement among Muslims, save a small group, that when the literal meaning of the revelation contradicts reason, reason must be given precedence. In such cases, the germane revealed verses should be treated in one of two ways: either the human inability to grasp their true meaning should be acknowledged, or they should be allegorized, in line with the rules of the Arabic language, in a way that reconciles their meaning with what reason established.[155]

For 'Abduh, the existence of this method is the ultimate demonstration of Islam's compatibility with modern scientific methods and of the complete scientific freedom it allows. He argued that it opens every path and removes any hindrance for inquisitive philosophical minds. Scholars and students of the sciences cannot wish for greater freedom of investigation than that provided by the option of *ta'wil*. If they will not be satisfied with what it allows, nothing shall satisfy them.[156] Perhaps more than any other statement in the immense body of modernist-apologetic literature, the latter reveals the concerns that motivate the propagators of this approach and their convictions. It conveys 'Abduh's recognition that the ability to freely and rationally investigate the natural world is the most essential aspect of the West's ascendance; and his confidence and great relief thereof that he had discovered a way that makes it possible to maintain a revelation-based social and philosophical order while providing Muslim societies with similar conditions to those allowed in the West by secularization.

Following in the footsteps of their approach's founders, contemporary modernist-apologists introduced *ta'wil* as part of their reasoning for the absence and impossibility of a conflict between the Islamic revelation and proven scientific facts. Authors were satisfied that the method which met the challenges of modernity in the late nineteenth century offered a solid and useful way of resolving any conflict between the revelation and scientific inquiries pursued with full freedom in contemporary times. Al-Qaradawi invoked allegorizing as a means to ensure that conclusive rationalist proofs and revelation never conflict.[157] He presented guidelines similar to those introduced by Abu Hamid al-Ghazali and asserted by 'Abduh and al-Jisr.[158] He suggested these guidelines to be another manifestation of *wasatiyya*—in this case, a middle ground between Muslims who apply allegorizing excessively and irresponsibly, and those who apply it insufficiently where *ijtihad* is required.[159] 'Imara explained, in the context of his broader defense of Islam's rationality, that rationally proven evidence (*burhan al-'aql*) can never contradict the "literal" (*zahir*, quotation marks in the original text) meaning of a reveled word. His reference was 'Abduh and the aforementioned method according to which the appearance of contradictions should be resolved either by acknowledging the incomprehensibility of the pertinent revealed words or by resorting to allegorizing. 'Imara emphasized that this method ensures that Muslims will not need to abandon reason for the sake of the revelation, or abandon the revelation for the sake of reason—which is what happened in Western societies.[160] He also emphasized, as did 'Abduh, that allegorizing must be the exception, not the rule, and must remain loyal to the rules of Arabic.[161]

C. Liberals or Fundamentalists? The Terminological Maze

The project of the modernist-apologists can be summarized as follows. It is the response of Islamic religious scholars to their recognition that a materially superior force, superior to the point of eliminating the independence of Muslim societies, has distanced itself from religion to the extent that even the existence of the Almighty and the truth of revelation are no longer self-evident there. The aim of their response is to defend and revive the possibility of scientifically, technologically and politically free and viable revelation-based Muslim societies. The means to do so involve rationalizing the existence of God, His final Prophet and His final revelation, suggesting that Western modernity is rooted in Islam, and affirming that Islamic revelation has the unique capacity to accommodate any scientific discovery. Because the doubt-based West's challenge has remained as strong during the early twenty-first century as it was during the late nineteenth century, as has the desire of Muslim theologians to assert the truth and relevancy of Islam's revelation in the age of doubt, the core concepts of the modernist-apologetic approach have continued to captivate a third generation of thinkers with a similar passion and intensity as that of the first generation.

Humans are inclined to understand realities other than their own through analogies, and the example of studies on the modernist-apologetic approach has not differed. Investigations of different articulations of modernist-apologetic thought compared them to different and conflicting Western ideologies. Critical scholars have tended to categorize and treat modernist-apologists as either liberals or fundamentalists. Neither category does justice with the complex, synthesizing and unique nature of the modernist-apologetic approach, which is liberal and fundamentalist at the same time and, as such, is neither liberal nor fundamentalist, but a creation of its own, set against circumstances that are unique to the societies from which it originated.

Liberalism, as developed in the West, is a diverse ideological tradition relating to a common framework of thought initiated by the seventeenth-century English philosopher John Locke. Its basis lies in the perception that all men possess an inalienable right to freedom: freedom of expression, freedom of assembly and the freedom to hold property. Additionally, it maintains that the individual is at the center of the political and social sphere; the political community is sovereign and the ruler draws his or her legitimacy from it rather than from the grace of God; no faith should be imposed on a person; and scientific research and political action should be guided by human logic, empirical study and skepticism, and not by religious dogma.[162]

In its appreciation of scientific and political freedoms as the essential elements of Western advances, its insistence that metaphysical notions must be rationally demonstrated, and, most importantly, its reintroduction of a method that guarantees that the revelation can accommodate any advanced understanding of the world, the modernist-apologetic approach presents its liberal bent. However, in stark contrast to liberalism, it does not call for the liberation of societies from the potentially restrictive and imposing implications of accepting one specific revelation (or other canonical text) as the inalienable premise on which social, political and intellectual life rest, but struggles to do the exact opposite—it asserts, within a modern context and using liberal terminology, the need for a social order that is based on recognizing Islam's revelation as an inerrant, eternal, all-encompassing guide directing all aspects of existence.

Possibly the most well-known investigation of early modernist-apologetic writings, Albert Hourani's *Arabic Thought in the Liberal Age, 1798–1939*, betrays, already in its title, the analytic temptation to describe the works of al-Afghani, 'Abduh, al-Jisr, Rida and al-Kawakibi as links—vital links—of a liberal chain of thought that gradually developed in the Arabic-speaking world (as explored in the next chapter, some Arab liberals also suggest the existence of such a chain). Hourani's book was first published in 1962, when several of the intellectuals it treated were still alive. In an unusual confession for a scholar of his stature, Hourani wrote in the introduction to the 1983 edition of the book, that he was troubled by the thought that perhaps he "should have written a book of a different kind." He explained:

> When I wrote it I was mainly concerned to note the breaks with the past: new ways of thought, new words or old ones used in a new way. To some extent I may have distorted the thought of the writers I studied, at least those of the first and second generations; the "modern" element in their thought may have been smaller than I implied, and it would have been possible to write about them in a way which emphasized continuity rather than a break with the past.[163]

Hourani's musings from the 1980s as to whether the "liberal age" he coined was as liberal as he described it suggested a more restricted delineation of the conceptual progress he had defined two decades earlier, but it did not untangle the confusion his book created among generations of readers. Hourani was correct in identifying that the early modernist-apologetic works he studied had liberal elements in them and had implications for the development of liberalism in the Arab world (on some issues, such as the early modernist-apologetic treatment of the theory of evolution, it can even be said Hourani did not stress enough the novelty and implications of the approach). What Hourani's work did not fully do was distinguish between modernity as a means and the defense of a revelation-based social order as an end. He did not recognize that the founding fathers of the modernist-apologetic school were liberal and reformist only to the extent required, in their minds, to defend a privileged status for the revealed scriptures that liberal ideologies denied.

If a comparison was intended between the modernist-apologetic school and the movement known as Liberal Christianity (or Liberal Theology), it is also not analytically correct. Liberal Christianity, a movement that traces its roots to the late eighteenth century, represents an effort to preserve religious truths in the face of the challenges posed by modern science. The main caveats it addressed were higher criticism of the Bible, or rational studies that denied the divine essence of revelations by exploring them as historical texts and exposing the specific circumstances of their authorship, and discoveries in the natural world that refuted straightforward depictions in revealed passages, first and foremost Darwin's theory of evolution. Common to most liberal theologies is the notion that the truths of Christianity are not dependent on an inerrant revelation. Its most radical manifestation, Theodore Parker's (1810–1860) writings, accepted that, in light of higher criticism, neither the Old nor the New Testament should be regarded as inerrant revelations, suggested that all efforts to reconcile modern perceptions of the world and Biblical passages are doomed to failure, and presented cat as a universal spiritual call of truth, love and compassion whose existence does not depend on any singular text produced by "Jewish fishermen" (nor even on the existence of Christ).[164] Others who have not gone as far still undermined the credibility of the Bible as a definite, irrefutable source of truth. These include Theodore Munger's (1830–1910) idea that the authors of the Bible were inspired, but the Bible constitutes a history of revelation rather than revelation itself;[165] Charles Briggs's (1841–1913) assumption that revelation is a means, not an end, and that while the Bible is correct on the core issues, it also contains some errors;[166] and William Newton Clarke (1841–1912) and his thesis that the Bible itself does not claim to be inerrant and that the sacred books contained in it should not serve as the foundation of cat.[167] Darwinism was accepted by several liberal theologians (including Munger) as a theory that had been validated and thus cannot be rejected, and as a concept that is commensurate with Christian beliefs in its demonstration of the unity in creation and of gradual moral progression.[168]

While Liberal Christianity is similar to the modernist-apologetic approach in its quest to liberate believers from the shackles of literalist readings of God's words, and its struggle to demonstrate that religion can withstand the test of modernity, a wide gap separates the approaches in one crucial respect. The modernist-apologists entrenched their quest for religious reform in revelation itself, whereas the liberal Christians distanced their arguments from revelation as a source of definite authority. Whereas the rationalizing effort and the premise of the interpretative method set by the modernist-apologists asserted the divine origin and the inerrancy of the Quran, and its status as an authority that should guide all aspects of life, albeit in a way allowing for its constant accommodation, liberal Christian theologians introduced the option of Christianity without revelation at all, or undermined, to a certain extent, the unalienable status of Biblical passages as revealed words. As will be demonstrated in the next chapters, this difference is not one of splitting hairs.

The categorization of modernist-apologetic authors as fundamentalists is also a mistake. Originally, fundamentalism is an American Protestant movement that developed in the early twentieth century as a backlash against liberal theology and perceived challenges to the Christian revelation in school curriculums. Already in the nineteenth century, the defense of the inerrancy of the Bible and its literalist reading became a primary religious concern. Sandeen cautions against seeing the doctrine of inerrancy as an essential aspect of Christianity; he suggests it developed in order to support an insistence on a literalist reading of the Bible. That insistence was encouraged because in the age of facts, empiricism, rationalism and scientific revolution that American and other Western societies had witnessed, some religious leaders came to be convinced that allegorizing revealed passages would not be deemed or seen as credible.[169] The pinnacle of these sentiments was the 1878 Niagara Bible Conference that established the verbal, plenary inspiration of the scriptures along with thirteen other creeds.[170]

The reemergence, following the end of the Great War, of the crusade for inerrancy and literalism as a mass movement was concentrated in the southern states of the Union. It corresponded with a number of developments—negative views of

Germany (the homeland of higher criticism), the fear of communism, and the resentment of rural populaces towards East Coast professors whom they believed to be arrogant instructors who distorted the pure faith of their students. In the post-war years, amid news of the gratuitous destruction and misery brought about by the actions of human beings, anxiety over the implications of life without God and revelation grew. Darwinism was interpreted by some Christians as an atheist plot that legitimized the rule of the strong and disregard of morals and virtues. As such, the fight against its teaching in public institutions became the center of their campaigns, serving as a great energizing and unifying force.[171]

The term fundamentalism was coined in the 1920s. It draws from a series of 90 articles, initiated by Californian businessman Lyman Stewart, and published between 1910 and 1915. The articles confirmed what their authors believed to be the fundamentals of Christian religion, refuted higher criticism, and proved the inerrancy and divine-inspiration of the scriptures based on rationalist argumentations such as the fulfillment of prophecies and the perfection of the text. Compiled in volume-sets, Stewart financed the distribution of more than three million copies among religious communities across the United States.[172] The post-war rise of the fundamentalists culminated in 1925 in Tennessee, after the State Legislature enacted a law (the Butler Act) that forbade denying the Bible's account of the origin of man. John Scopes, a high school biology teacher, defied the law in order to put the matter to the test. The trial that ensued, known as the Scopes Monkey Trial, was a media circus that ended with Scopes' symbolic conviction, and exposed the depth of disagreement in American society about the authority of the Bible. It divided the nation between fundamentalist literalists, who insisted that scriptural passages should override the judgments of scientists, and modern Christians and secularists, who fought to maintain a separation between science and religion.[173]

While the public appeal and energy of American fundamentalism declined in the immediate aftermath of the Scopes Monkey Trial, the movement did not disappear, and from the 1980s has become a formidable social and political force in the United States. At that time, the term fundamentalism started to become common in academic literature and popular discourses that depicted what seemed to some analysts a surprising historical occurrence: the surge, across different societies, of religious movements that resist secularism and liberal theologies, and, drawing on notions of authenticity, assert religious creeds through revivalist and passionate rhetoric. Several studies examined the fundamentalist phenomenon on a universal comparative basis, the most comprehensive effort being a five-volume compilation of articles edited by Marty and Appleby and published between 1991 and 1995. The diversity of the movements studied in these volumes necessitated a broad and fluid definition and obscured its comparative analytic utility.[174] The generous application of the term did not pass on analyses of articulations of the modernist-apologetic agenda. The term was attributed to the early modernist-apologists, for example, in Davidson's study *Islamic Fundamentalism*, in which al-Afghani is first on the list of Islamic fundamentalist personalities (al-Banna is second),[175] and was used in numerous studies to describe contemporary Muslim Brothers and affiliated movements and intellectuals, including al-Ghazali and al-Qaradawi.[176]

In one crucial sense, the modernist-apologetic approach to science and politics is indeed similar to American fundamentalism. Both respectively defend the inerrancy of revelations and insist on using them as authoritative guides in modern times; both respectively distinguish correct readings of revealed texts from the erroneous readings of others of the same religion. Yet here the similarities end, and an essential difference emerges. Whereas American fundamentalism signifies a struggle to ban any scientific discoveries, models and theories that conflict with the literal interpretation of revealed passages, the modernist-apologetic approach constitutes an effort to demonstrate how each and every verse of the revelation can be interpreted in a way that accommodates modern concepts. In American fundamentalism, the claim for scriptural authenticity is intended to eliminate any new concepts that can challenge the authority of the revelation; in modernist-apologetic literature, the claim for scriptural authenticity is intended to facilitate the integration of modern scientific and political concepts.

The agenda of the American fundamentalists has centered on educational institutions and on debating liberal co-religionists. Since the inception of their movement, they have struggled to ensure that their children would not be exposed to ideas that defy the creeds of Christianity as they understand them. It has not been their declared intention to change the constitutional separation between church and state in America, although it can be argued that their success would have inevitably led to this result. The ambition of the modernist-apologists has been far greater. The different articulations of their approach sought to mold a revelation-based political, social, cultural and academic order in accordance with their specific understanding of the revelation.

Terminologies carry connotations, and connotations affect perceptions. Labeling the project of al-Afghani and 'Abduh as liberal obscures its quest to preserve the place of revelation as an inerrant guide, regulating all aspects of life, and to preserve religion as the exclusive framework that defines social identity. Understanding the discourse of present day modernist-apologetic theologians as fundamentalist belittles the centrality of efforts to integrate modern sciences and democratic political institutions into Muslim societies in their discourse. Both encourage futile searches for double-speech where it does not exist; both encourag attempts at exposing the "concealed" intention of elusive works that, from the point of view of their writers, make perfect and consistent sense, putting aright, as they see it, divine conceptual structures that had been distorted through the years.

The most unfortunate result of reading modernist-apologetic texts as either liberal or fundamentalist is a lack of appreciation for the originality of this approach, the singularity of its revivalist call for reform, and the reasons for its continuous broad appeal. Through its contextualization of rationalist investigations as to the truth of Allah, His Prophet, and His revelation, its interpretation of the history of Muslim-Christian relations and the role Islam had in Western Renaissance, and its reintroduction of a hermeneutical method that assures the potential reconciliation of any proven scientific fact with the revelation, this approach made a case for the possibility of a revelation-based society that enjoys all the advantages of a doubt-based one. At the core of modernist-apologetic thought is the promise that individuals can be free from arbitrary theocratic interventions without forsaking the comfort and confidence produced by living in a society where the existence of God and of an afterlife rewarding the righteous remain unchallenged. Any attempt to quantify whether this approach to scientific and political freedom belongs more to old ways of thinking or to new ones misses the novelty of the modernist-apologetic project: the argument that one need not choose, that modernity is tradition, revelation is doubt, and all the advances that the West achieved through its doubt-based path, and more, can be integrated into Muslim societies without relinquishing what is most dear and cherished. The next two chapters examine the consistency and coherency of that promise.

Notes

1 For a concise biography of al-Tahtawi: Muhammad 'Imara, *Rifa'a al-Tahtawi: Ra'id al-Tanwir fi al-'Asr al-Hadith* (Cairo: Dar al-Shuruq, 2009), 35–138; Albert Hourani, *Arabic Thought in the Liberal Age, 1798–1939* (London and New York: Oxford University Press, 1962), 68–84; Sati Khaldun al-Husri, *Three Reformers: A Study in Modern Arabic Political Thought* (Beirut: Khayats, 1966), 11–31.

2 Rifa'a Rafi' al-Tahtawi, *Takhlis al-Ibriz fi Talkhis Bariz* (n.d., published by the United Arab Republic—The Egyptian Region, first published in 1834), 140, 150, 153.

3 Ibrahim A. Abu-Lughud, *Arab Rediscovery of Europe: A Study of Cultural Encounter* (Princeton, NJ: Princeton University Press, 1963), 147.

4 Al-Tahtawi, *Takhlis al-Ibriz fi Talkhis Bariz*, 148.

5 Ibid., 153.

6 On the political reforms in Tunisia in the mid-nineteenth century see: Nikula Ziada, *Tunis fi 'Ahd al-Himayya 1881–1934* (n.p. 1963), 59–94; for a concise biography of Khayr al-Din: Hourani, *Arabic Thought in the Liberal Age, 1798–1939*, 84–95; al-Husri, *Three Reformers: A Study in Modern Arabic Political Thought*, 33–53.

7 Khayr al-Din al-Tunisi, *Aqwam al-Masalik fi Ma'rifat Ahwal al-Mamalik* (Al-Dar al-Tunisiyya lil-Nashr, n.d., first published 1867), 228.

8 Ibid., 91.

9 Ibid., 130–36, 169–70.

10 Ibid., 206–27.

11 Ibid., 97.

12 Henri Lauzière, "The Construction of *Salafiyya*: Reconsidering Salafism from the Perspective of Conceptual History," *International Journal of Middle Eastern Studies*, 42:3 (August 2010), 373–76.

13 Hasan al-Banna, *Mudhakkirat al-Da'wa wal-Da'iya* (Cairo: Dar al-Kitab, n.d.), 49–50; Richard P. Mitchell, *The Society of the Muslim Brothers* (New York, Oxford and Toronto: Oxford University Press, 1993), 5.

14 Hasan al-Banna, "Risalat al-Minhaj" (September 1938), in *Majmu'at Rasa'il al-Imam al-Shaid Hasan al-Banna* (Cairo: Dar al-Tawzi' wal-Nashr al-Islamiyya, 2006), 252–56; "Risalat al-Mu'atamar al-Khamis" (February 1939), in Ibid., 336–37, 341–42, For a detailed analysis of the Brothers' organizational frameworks: Mitchell, *The Society of the Muslim Brothers*, 163–84; on the Brothers' activist essence see also: Nazih A. Ayubi, *Political Islam: Religion and Politics in the Arab World* (London: Routledge, 1991), 132.

15 John O. Voll, "Fundamentalism in the Sunni Arab World: Egypt and the Sudan," in Martin E. Marty and R. Scott Appleby (eds), *Fundamentalisms Observed*, part of the

Fundamentalism Project, vol. 1 (Chicago, IL and London: University of Chicago Press, 1991), 347.

16 Ibid., 355.

17 For example, Ibrahim M. Abu Rabi, *Intellectual Origins of Islamic Resurgence in the Modern Arab World* (Albany: State University of New York Press, 1996), 79–84.

18 Voll, "Fundamentalism in the Sunni Arab World: Egypt and the Sudan," 366.

19 For example, Muhammad b. Salih al-'Uthaymin, "Hukm man Yad'a anna Sabab Takhaluf al-Muslimin Huwa Tamasukuhum bi-Dinihim," in *Fatawa al-Balad al-Haram* (Cairo: al-Maktaba al-Tawfiqiyya, n.d.), 1069–71; 'Abdallah b. Salih Fawzan, "Mawqifuna min al-Hadhara al-Gharbiyya," in ibid., 1072–73.

20 Pew Research Center, "Egyptians Embrace Revolt Leaders, Religious Parties and Military, As Well," *Global Attitudes Project*, April 25, 2011, accessed September 1, 2015: http://pewglobal.org/files/2011/04/Pew-Global-Attitudes-Egypt-Report-FINAL-April-25-2011.pdf.

21 Nikkie R. Keddie, *Sayyid Jamal ad-Din "al-Afghani": A Political Biography* (Berkeley: University of California Press, 1972), 87.

22 Jamal al-Din al-Afghani, *al-Radd 'ala al-Dahriyyin* (Cairo: Dar al-Karnak, n.d.).

23 For a concise biography of al-Afghani: Hourani, *Arabic Thought in the Liberal Age, 1798–1939*, 108–129; Nikki R. Keddie, *An Islamic Response to Imperialism: Political and Religious Writings of Sayyid Jamal al-Din "al-Afghani"* (Berkeley and Los Angeles: University of California Press, 1968), 11–35.

24 Muhammad 'Abduh, "Kitab Ta'rikh al-Ahdath al-'Urabiyya," in Muhammad 'Imara (ed.), *al-A'mal al-Kamila lil-Imam Muhammad 'Abduh*, vol. 1 (Beirut: al-Mu'assasa al-'Arabiyya lil-Dirasat wal-Nashr, 1972), 481–82. On al-Afghani's great impact on the young 'Abduh in the 1870s see also: 'Abbas Mahmud al-'Aqqad, *al-Ustadh al-Imam Muhammad 'Abduh* (Cairo: Maktabat Misr, 1960), 122–33.

25 Johannes Ebert, *Religion und Reform in der Arabischen Provinz* (Frankfurt am Main: Peter Lang, 1991), 84–85.

26 'Ismat Nasar, "taqdim," in Husayn al-Jisr, *al-Risala al-Hamidiyya fi Haqiqat al-Diyana al-Islamiyya wa-Haqqiyyat al-Shari'a al-Muhammadiyya* (Cairo and Beirut: Dar al-Kitab al-Misri, Dar al-Kitab al-Lubnani, 2012, first published 1888), 27–34.

27 Ebert, *Religion und Reform in der Arabischen Provinz*, 79–86.

28 'Ismat Nasar, "taqdim," in Husayn al-Jisr, *al-Risala al-Hamidiyya fi Haqiqat al-Diyana al-Islamiyya wa-Haqqiyyat al-Shari'a al-Muhammadiyya*, 38.

29 Ebert, *Religion und Reform in der Arabischen Provinz*, 93.

30 Muhammad 'Abduh, author's preface in *The Theology of Unity*, translated by Ishaq Musa'ad and Kenneth Cragg (London: George Allen & Unwin, 1966), 27–8; for the Arabic version: "Risalat al-Tawhid," in Muhammad 'Imara (ed.), *al-A'mal al-Kamila lil-Imam Muhmmad 'Abduh*, vol. 3 (Beirut: al-Mu'assasa al-'Arabiyya lil-Dirasat wal-Nashr, 1972), 353–54; on 'Abduh's time at the school also: 'Abd al-Halim al-Jundi, *al-Imam Muhammad 'Abduh* (Cairo: Dar al-Ma'arif, 1979), 7–85.

31 On 'Abduh's biography: Hourani, *Arabic Thought in the Liberal Age, 1798–1939*, 130–160; 'Abd al-Aziz Ahmad Ayyad, *The Politics of Reformist Islam: Muhammad 'Abduh and Hasan al-Banna* (Ann Arbor, MI: University Microfilms International, 1991), 1–27; al-Jundi, *al-Imam Muhammad 'Abduh*, 7–85.

32 'Ismat Nasar, "taqdim," 35; Ebert, *Religion und Reform in der Arabischen Provinz*, 167.

33 Muhammad 'Abduh, "al-Shaykh Rashid Rida," in Muhammad 'Imara (ed.), *al-A'mal al-Kamila lil-Imam Muhmmad 'Abduh*, vol. 3 (Beirut: al-Mu'assasa al-'Arabiyya lil-Dirasat wal-Nashr, 1972), 131–32.

34 On Rida's early life and the founding, objectives, and the impact of *al-Manar*, see Hourani, *Arabic Thought in the Liberal Age, 1798–1939*, 222–44; Umar Ryad, *Islamic Reformism and Christianity: A Critical Reading of the Works of Muhammad Rashid Rida and His Associates (1898–1935)* (Leiden: Brill, 2009), 2–9; Yusuf Ibish, *Rihlat al-Imam Muhammad Rashid Rida* (Beirut: al-Mu'assasa al-'Arabiyya lil-Dirasat wal-Nashr, 1971),

5–8; Ahmad al-Sharbasi, *Rashid Rida: Sahib al-Manar, 'Asruhu wa-Hayatuhu wa-Masadir Thaqafatihi* (n.p., 1970), 101–44.

35 For a concise biography of al-Kawakibi: Muhammad 'Imara, "Hayatuhu," in Muhammad 'Imara (ed.), *al-A'mal al-Kamila li-'Abd al-Rahman al-Kawakibi* (al-Hay'a al-Misriyya al-'ama lil-Ta'lif wal-Nashr, n.d.), 14–32; al-Husri, *Three Reformers: A Study in Modern Arabic Political Thought*, 55–112, Itzchak Weismann, *Abd al-Rahman al-Kawakibi: Islamic Reform and Arab Revival* (London: Oneworld Publications, 2015).

36 Muhammad al-Ghazali, *'Ilal wa-Adwiya* (Doha: 1984), 122–25.

37 Yusuf al-Qaradawi, *Ummatuna bayna Qarnayn* (Cairo: Dar Al-Shuruq, 2002, first published 2000), 104–5.

38 Muhammad 'Imara, *al-Istiqlal al-Hadari* (October 6th City: Nahdat Misr lil-Tiba'a wal-Nashr wal-Tawzi', 2007), 14–17, 139.

39 Ibid., 39–41, 60, 118–22.

40 Yusuf al-Qaradawi, *al-Shaykh al-Ghazali Kama 'Araftuhu: Rihlat Nisf Qarn* (al-Mansurah: Dar al-Wafa' lil-Tiba'ah wal-Nashr wal-Tawzi', 1995), 25–28.

41 Mahmud 'Abduh, *Muhammad al-Ghazali: Da'iya al-Nahda al-Islamiyya* (Beirut: Markaz al-Hadara li-Tanmiyyat al-Fikr al-Islami, 2009), 20.

42 Muhammad al-Ghazali, *al-Islam wal-Awda' al-Iqtisadiyya* (Cairo: Dar al-Kitab al-'Arabi, third printing, 1952, first published 1947); *al-Islam wal-Manahij al-Ishtirakiyya* (Cairo: Dar al-Kutub al-Haditha, fourth printing, 1960, first published 1949); *al-Islam al-Muftara 'alayhi: bayna al-Shuyu'iyyin wal-Ra'smaliyyin* (Cairo: Maktabat Wahaba, fifth printing, 1960, first published 1950).

43 'Abd al-'Aziz al-Khadar, *al-Sa'udiyya Sirat Dawla wa-Mujtama'* (Beirut: Arab Network for Research and Publishing, 2010), 236.

44 Khalid Muhsin (ed.), *Misr bayna al-Dawla al-Islamiyya wal-Dawla al-'Almaniyya* (Cairo: Markaz al-I'lam al-'Arabi, 1992), 12–13, 150–52;

45 Al-Qaradawi, *al-Shaykh al-Ghazali Kama 'Araftuhu*, 68–70.

46 Ibid., 38–43.

47 Yusuf al-Qaradawi, *al-Halal wal-Haram fi al-Islam* (Cairo: Maktabat Wahaba, 2004, first published August 1960).

48 On al-Qaradawi's biography: Jakob Skovgaard-Petersen, "Yusuf al-Qaradawi and al-Azhar," in Bettina Gräf and Jakob Skovgaard-Petersen (eds), *Global Mufti: The Phenomenon of Yusuf al-Qaradawi* (London: Hurst & Company, 2009), 27–53; Husam Tammam, "Yusuf Qaradawi and the Muslim Brothers: The Nature of a Special Relationship," in ibid., 55–83; Samuel Helfont, *Yusuf al-Qaradawi: Islam and Modernity* (Tel Aviv: Moshe Dayan Center, 2009), 35–38; Akram Kassab, *al-Manhaj al-Da'wi 'ind al-Qaradawi* (Cairo: Maktabat Wahaba, 2006), 281–84; Yusuf al-Qaradawi, *Nahnu wal-Gharb: As'ila Sha'ika wa-Ajwiba Hasima* (Cairo: Dar al-Tawzi' wal-Nashr al-Islamiyya, 2006), 124–25. On the goals of the International Union for Muslim Scholars see on its website: www.iumsonline.net/ar/default.asp?MenuID=2.

49 See 'Imara's biography on his personal website: http://www.dr-emara.com (accessed July 10, 2015); Anke Von Kügelgen, "A Call for Rationalism: 'Arab Averroists' in the Twentieth Century," *Alif: Journal of Comparative Poetics*, 16 (January 1996), 109–10; Mona Abaza, "Two Intellectuals: The Malaysian S. N. Al-Attas and the Egyptian Muhammad Immara, and the Islamization of Knowledge Debate," *Asian Journal of Social Science*, 30:2 (2002), 359–60.

50 Muhammad 'Imara, *al-Shaykh Muhammad al-Ghazali: al-Mawqi' al-Fikri wal-Ma'arik al-Fikriyya* (Cairo: Dar al-Salam, 2009).

51 Raymond William Baker, "Invidious Comparisons: Realism, Postmodern Globalism, and Centrist Islamic Movements in Egypt," in John L. Esposito (ed.), *Political Islam: Revolution, Radicalism or Reform?* (Boulder, Co and London: Lynne Rienner Publishers, 1997), 125; Raymond William Baker, *Islam without Fear: Egypt and the New Islamists* (Cambridge, MA: Harvard University Press, 2003); Nabil 'Abd al-Fattah, *Taqrir al-Hala al-Diniyya fi Misr*, vol. 2 (Cairo: Markaz al-Dirasat al-Siyasiyya wal-Istratijiyya bil-Ahram, 1998), 353–56; Sagi Polka, "The Centrist Stream in Egypt and its Role in

the Public Discourse Surrounding the Shaping of the Country's Cultural Identity," *Middle Eastern Studies*, 39:3 (July 2003), 41. In both of Baker's studies, as well as in 'Abd al-Fattah's, 'Imara is not identified as one of the main *wasati* authors.

52   All translations of Quran verses in this book are from Saheeh International, *The Qur'an* (Jeddah: al-Muntada al-Islami, 2004).

53   Uriya Shavit, *Shari'a and Muslim Minorities: The Wasati and Salafi Approaches to Fiqh al-Aqalliyyat al-Muslima* (Oxford: Oxford University Press, 2015), 16–49.

54   Rida used the term *wasatiyya* to describe balanced reformism that is an alternative to blind *taqlid*, which is not capable of absorbing modernity, and to Muslims who reject *Shari'a* as incapable of accommodating modernity. However, the term was not common to his writings: "Kitab Yusr al-Islam wa-Usul al-Shari'a," *al-Manar* 29:1 (March 22, 1928), 63–70. Al-Qaradawi considered Rida to be one of the intellectual fathers of *wasatiyya*: Yusuf al-Qaradawi, *Fiqh al-Wasatiyya al-Islamiyya wal-Tajdid: Ma'alim wa-Manarat* (Cairo: Dar al-Shuruq, 2010), 106–68.

55   See 'Abduh's introduction in al-Afghani, *al-Radd 'ala al-Dahriyyin*, 33–35.

56   Husayn al-Jisr, *al-Risala al-Hamidiyya fi Haqiqat al-Diyana al-Islamiyya wa-Haqqiyyat al-Shari'a al-Muhammadiyya* (Cairo and Beirut: Dar al-Kitab al-Misri, Dar al-Kitab al-Lubnani, 2012, originally published 1888), 4–5.

57   Ebert, *Religion und Reform in der Arabischen Provinz*, 86.

58   Ibrahim Khalas, "al-Tariq li-Khalq Insanuna al-'Arabi al-Jadid," *Jaysh al-Sha'b*, no. 794 (April 25, 1967), 34.

59   Keddie, *An Islamic Response to Imperialism*, 22.

60   Al-Afghani, *al-Radd 'ala al-Dahriyyin*, 94–105.

61   Ibid., 64.

62   Ibid., 51–63.

63   Ibid., 75–92.

64   Al-Jisr, *al-Risala al-Hamidiyya*, 351–53.

65   Ebert, *Religion und Reform in der Arabischen Provinz*, 156–57.

66   Al-Jisr, *al-Risala al-Hamidiyya*, 158.

67   Ibid., 329.

68   Ibid., 172–74, 206–09, 263–64.

69   Muhammad 'Abduh, *The Theology of Unity*, 49 (in Arabic "Risalat al-Tawhid," 374).

70   Muhammad 'Abduh, "Bismarck wal-Din," in Muhammad 'Imara (ed.), *al-A'mal al-Kamila lil-Imam Muhammad 'Abduh*, vol. 3 (Beirut: al-Mu'assasa al-'Arabiyya lil-Dirasat wal-Nashr, 1972), 489–91.

71   Muhammad 'Abduh, "al-Qada' wal-Qadr," in ibid., 481–83.

72   *Al-Manar*, "al-Dalil 'ala Wujud Allah Ta'ala," 7:4 (May 2, 1904), 138–40.

73   Al-Banna, "Risalat al-Mu'atamar al-Khamis," 361–66; "Da'watuna fi Tawr Jadid" (August 1942), in *Majmu'at Rasa'il al-Imam al-Shaid Hasan al-Banna* (Cairo: Dar al-Tawzi' wal-Nashr al-Islamiyyah, 2006), 481–82.

74   Yusuf al-Qaradawi, *Wujud Allah* (Casablanca: Dar al-Ma'rafa, n.d.), 5–7, 15.

75   Ibid., 3–5, 13.

76   Ibid., 17.

77   Ibid., 27–28.

78   Ibid., 32–58.

79   Muhammad al-Ghazali, *Qadha'if al-Haqq* (Damascus: Dar al-Kalam, 1991), 208.

80   Muhammad al-Ghazali, *Ma'a Allah: Dirasat fi al-Da'wa wal-Du'a* (al-Jiza: Nahdat Misr lil-Tiba'a wal-Nashr wal-Tawzi', 2005), 184.

81   Al-Ghazali, *Qadha'if al-Haqq*, 197–203.

82   Ibid., 207–211. 'Imara was just as convinced that Einstein's theorizing resulted in a decline of the materialist trend in the West: *Ma'rakat al-Mustalahat: bayna al-Gharb wal-Islam* (Nahdat Misr lil-Tiba'a wal-Nashr wal-Tawzi', n.d.), 53.

83   Al-Ghazali, *'Ilal wa-Adwiya*, 185–86.

84   Al-Qaradawi, *Wujud Allah*, 7–8.

85   Al-Jisr, *al-Risala al-Hamidiyya*, 23.

86   Ibid., 26–29.
87   Ibid., 126–27, 356–57.
88   Ibid., 35–38, 375.
89   'Abduh, *The Theology of Unity,* 112–19 (in Arabic, "Risalat al-Tawhid," 429–36).
90   'Abduh, *The Theology of Unity,* 120 (in Arabic, "Risalat al-Tawhid," 436). And also see his response to Farah Antun's argument that Islam limits scientific freedom: Muhammad 'Abduh, *Al-Islam Din al-'Ilm wal-Madaniyya* (Beirut: Manshurat Dar Maktabat al-Haya, 1989), 108.
91   Muhammad Rashid Rida, *al-Wahy al-Muhammadi* (Beirut: Mu'asassat 'Izz al-Din, 1986), 100.
92   Ibid., 61–68.
93   For example, al-Ghazali, *Ma'a Allah: Dirasat fi al-Da'wa wal-Du'a,* 275; Muhammad 'Imara, *Shubuhat Hawla al-Islam* (Nahdat Misr, 2002), 6–17.
94   Muhammad 'Imara, *al-Qur'an Yatahada* (Cairo: Maktabat al-Imam al-Bukhari lil-Nashr wal-Tawzi', 2009), 5–8.
95   Muhammad 'Imara, *al-Islam wa-Huquq al-Insan – Darurat, La Huquq* (Jedda: Maktabat Bustan al-Marfa, 2004–5).
96   'Imara, *al-Quran Yatahada,* 11.
97   Muhammad 'Imara, *Ma'rakat al-Mustalahat,* 159.
98   Muhammad al-Ghazali, *Nazarat fi al-Qur'an* (Nahdat Misr lil-Tiba'a wal-Nashr wal-Tawzi', 2005), 22–23.
99   Ibid., 25.
100   Yusuf al-Qaradawi, *Kayfa Nata'amalu ma'a al-Qur'an al-'Azim* (Cairo: Dar al-Shuruq, 2000), 23.
101   Ibid., 25–28.
102   For an Arabic translation of his ideas on "Islam and Science" and commentary on these ideas by Muhammad al-Haddad: "al-Nass al-Haqiqi wal-Kamil lil-Munazara bayna Raynan wal-Afghani," n.d., accessed October 21, 2015: http://nachaz.org/index.php/fr/textes-a-l-appui/histoire/53-2012-07-18-01-32-26.html. For an analysis: Albert Hourani, *Arabic Thought in the Liberal Age,* 120–21.
103   Ernest Renan, "Ta'qib Raynan 'ala Radd al-Afghani," n.d., accessed October 21, 2015: http://nachaz.org/index.php/fr/textes-a-l-appui/histoire/53-2012-07-18-01-32-26.html.
104   For the texts of the article and an interview in which he expressed these views: "Maqal Misye Hanotaux, Wazir Kharijiyyat Faransa," in 'Abduh, *al-Islam Din al-'Ilm wal-Madaniyya,* 23–39; "Hadith Hanotaux ma'a Sahib Jaridat al-Ahram," in ibid., 49–59.
105   Farah Antun, *Ibn Rushd wa-Falsafatuhu* (Alexandria: Idarat al-Jami'a, January 1903), 151–60. Antun opened his work with a dedication to the "new plant," a plant thriving, as he put it, of Muslim and Christian thinkers who have realized the damage caused by not separating religion from state, as such a separation (which still recognizes the sanctity of religion) is essential in order to match the civilizational achievements of Europe and maintain their honor. For an analysis of his ideas in this book see also: Hourani, *Arabic Thought in the Liberal Age, 1798–1939,* 253–56.
106   Jamal al-Din al-Afghani, "al-Radd 'ala Raynan," accessed October 21, 2015: http://nachaz.org/index.php/fr/textes-a-l-appui/histoire/53-2012-07-18-01-32-26.html; Hourani, *Arabic Thought in the Liberal Age 1798–1939,* 121–23.
107   Keddie, *An Islamic Response to Imperialism,* 22.
108   Elie Kedourie, *Afghani and Abduh: An Essay on Religious Unbelief and Political Activism in Modern Islam* (London: Frank Cass, 1966), 43–45.
109   Ebert, *Religion und Reform in der Arabischen Provinz,* 120–21.
110   Muhammad 'Abduh, "Tabi'at al-Din al-Masihi" (part of his response to Farah Antun), in Muhammad 'Imara (ed.), *al-A'mal al-Kamila lil-Imam Muhammad 'Abduh,* vol. 3 (Beirut: al-Mu'assasa al-'Arabiyya lil-Dirasat wal-Nashr, 1972), 260–62.
111   Ibid., 282; "al-Asl al-Awwal lil-Islam" (part of his response to Farah Antun), also in 'Abduh, *al-Islam Din al-'Ilm wal-Madaniyya,* 109–10.

112   Ibid., 90 (his response to Hanotaux's interview in *al-Ahram*).

113   Ibid., 97 (response to Hanoutaux's interview), 112–15 (response to Farah Antun).

114   Ibid., 63–64 (response to Hanoutaux's article); Muhammad 'Abduh, "Tabi'at al-Din al-Masihi," 265–74.

115   'Abduh, *al-Islam Din al-'Ilm wal-Madaniyya*, 157–61.

116   Ibid., 193.

117   *Al-Manar*, "Manafi' al-'Urubbiyyin wa-Madharuhum fi al-Sharq," 10:3 (May 12, 1907), 192–99.

118   Hasan al-Banna, "Risalat nahwa al-Nur" (October 1936), in *Majmu'at Rasa'il al-Imam al-Shahid Hasan al-Banna* (Cairo: Dar al-Tawzi' wal-Nashr al-Islamiyya, 2006), 172.

119   Ibid., 166–67.

120   Hasan al-Banna, "Risalat bayna al-Ams wal-Yawm" (1943), in *Majmu'at Rasa'il al-Imam al-Shahid Hasan al-Banna* (Cairo: Dar al-Tawzi' wal-Nashr al-Islamiyya, 2006), 520–21.

121   Al-Qaradawi, *Ummatuna bayna Qarnayn*, 135–39.

122   Yusuf al-Qaradawi, *Ta'rikhuna al-Muftara 'alayhi* (Cairo: Dar al-Shuruq, 2008), 104–23. The concluding remarks of this analysis, somewhat contrary to the spirit of the lengthy discussion, suggest that interactions with Muslims were one of the main reasons, but not the only reason, for the Renaissance (123).

123   Yusuf al-Qaradawi, *Min Ajl Sahwa Rashida* (Cairo: Dar al-Shuruq, 1988, accessed August 2, 2012: http://www.mlazna.com), 95–96.

124   Muhammad al-Ghazali, "Hadha Dinuna," *al-Sha'b*, no. 538, March 20, 1990, 12.

125   Muhammad al-Ghazali, *Zalam min al-Gharb* (Cairo: Dar al-Kitab, n.d.), 252–57.

126   Muhammad al-Ghazali, "Hadha Dinuna," *al-Sha'b*, no. 771, August 31, 1993, 12. 'Imara offered a similar narrative, however, suggesting that what Europeans had learned from their interactions with Muslims during the Crusades and in Andalusia was one of the reasons (rather than the only reason) for the Renaissance: 'Imara, *al-Istiqlal al-Hadari*, 128–29.

127   Muhammad al-Ghazali, "Hadha Dinuna," *al-Sha'b*, no. 491, April 24, 1989, 12.

128   Al-Ghazali, *'Ilal wa-Adwiya*, 34.

129   Charles Freeman, *The Closing of the Western Mind: The Rise of Faith and the Fall of Reason* (New York: Vintage Books, 2005), 5. For recent concise and detailed overviews of Muslim contributions to the advance of sciences in Europe: Michael Hamilton Morgan, *Lost History: The Enduring Legacy of Muslim Scientists, Thinkers and Artists* (Washington, DC: National Geographic, 2007); John Freely, *Light from the East: How the Science of Medieval Islam Helped to Shape the Western World* (London: I. B. Tauris, 2015).

130   *Al-Qism al-Thani min al-'Urwa al-Wuthqa* (Paris, 28 March 1884), 70–73.

131   *Al-Manar*, "al-Juyush al-Gharbiyya al-Ma'nawiyya: fi al-Futuhat al-Sharquiyya," 1:17 (July 13, 1898), 299–308.

132   Hasan al-Banna, "Risalat bayna al-Ams wal-Yawm," 522–25.

133   For a detailed discussion on this theory in contemporary modernist-apologetic thought, and the functions it serves: Uriya Shavit, *Islamism and the West: From "Cultural Attack" to "Missionary Migrant"* (London and New York: Routledge, 2014), 26–68.

134   Ibid., 76–77.

135   *Al-Manar*, "al-Ilhad fi al-Madaris al-'Almaniyya," 14:7 (July 26, 1911), 544–48; "al-Rihla al-'Urubiyyya" (part 6), 23(2):8 (October 20, 1922), 635–40. The latter article contains a depiction of a meeting between Herbert Spencer and Muhammad 'Abduh in 1903, in which Spencer expressed concern about the hegemony of materialistic ideas in Europe and the decline of morals and virtues. See also: "Hadith bayna al-Filusuf al-Inglizi Spencer wa-bayna al-Ustadh al-Imam," in Muhammad 'Imara (ed.), *al-A'mal al-Kamila lil-Imam Muhmmad 'Abduh*, vol. 3, 492–94.

136   Hasan al-Banna, "Risalat nahwa al-Nur," 159; for his views on the decline of the West also: *al-Salam fi al-Islam* (Manshurat al-'Asr al-Hadith, June 1971, first published in al-Shihab, December 13, 1947), 7–18.

137   Yusuf al-Qaradawi, *al-Mubashshirat bi-Intisar al-Islam* (Beirut: Mu'assasat al-Risala, 2000).
138   Yusuf al-Qaradawi, *Hajat al-Bashriyya ila al-Risala al-Hadariyya li-Ummatina* (Cairo: Maktabat Wahaba, 2004), 5.
139   Muhammad al-Ghazali, *Mustaqbal al-Islam Kharij Ardihi: Kayfa Nufakkiru fihi?* (Cairo: Dar al-Shuruq 1997, first published 1984), 5–6.
140   Jamal al-Din al-Afghani, "al-Siyasa wal-'Ulum fi al-Qur'an," in Muhammad Imara (ed.), *al-A'mal al-Kamila li-Jamal al-Din al-Afghani* (n.d.), 266–270.
141   'Abd al-Rahman al-Kawakibi, "Kitab Taba'i al-Isti'bad wa Masari' al-Istibdad," in Muhammad 'Imara (ed.), *al-A'mal al-Kamila li-'Abd al-Rahman al-Kawakibi* (al-Hay'a al-Misriyya al-'ama lil-Ta'lif wal-Nashr, n.d.), 356–58.
142   Ibid., 352–53.
143   Yusuf al-Qaradawi, *Thaqafat al-Da'iya* (Cairo: Maktabat Wahaba, 10th printing, 1996), 12, 117–18.
144   Ibid., 114.
145   Muhammad al-Ghazali, *Nazarat fi al-Quran*, 116–22.
146   Ibid., 113–15.
147   To note but a few recent out of numerous examples: Zakir Naik, *The Quran and Modern Science: Compatible or Incompatible?* (Riyadh: Maktabat Dar-us-Salam, 2007); Maurice Bucaille, *The Quran and Modern Science* (UKIM Dawah Centre International, 2014, first published 1993); Islamwise, *Science and Islam* (n.d.); Magdy Abdel Baki, *True Religion—Unequivocal Evidence* (Engineering House Press, n.d.). Among the discoveries predicted by the Quran mentioned in these works as testimony of its authenticity as a revelation are the spherical shape of the earth, the rotation of the sun, that the sun will extinguish after a certain period, the expansion of the universe, the darkness in the depth of the ocean, that surface tension prevents the waters of neighboring seas from mixing, that space will be conquered by humans, that every living thing is made of water, the lifestyle and communication of ants, and that the first sense to develop in a human embryo is hearing.
148   Yusuf al-Qaradawi, *Kayfa Nata'amalu ma'a al-Qur'an al-'Azim*, 396–99. One of the examples al-Qaradawi offers of excessive unsubstantiated demonstration of a marvel is the law of gravity – an example provided by none other than al-Ghazali. Al-Ghazali, for his part, expressed concern (somewhat contradicting his own efforts in this field) about recent establishments of institutions dedicated to studying the scientific marvel of the Quran, some of which, so he found, locate evidence for *i'jaz* where it does not exist: Muhammad al-Ghazali, *Kayfa Nata'amalu ma'a al-Qur'an?* (al-Jiza: Nahdat Misr lil-Tiba'a wal-Nashr wal-Tawzi', seventh printing, July 2005), 138. In this discussion he doubts the validity of the term "scientific marvel" itself (138–43).
149   For this definition: 'Abas Amir, *al-Ma'na al-Qur'ani bayna al-Tafsir wal-Ta'wil* (Beirut: Mu'ssasat al-Intishar al-'Arabi, 2008), 98.
150   Abu Hamid al-Ghazali, *The Incoherence of the Philosophers*, Translated by Michael Marmura (Provo, Utah: Brigham Young University, 2000), 6–7.
151   Ibid., 214–15; on al-Ghazali's theory of allegorizing revealed verses: Martin Whittingham, *al-Ghazali and the Qur'an: One Book, Many Meanings* (London and New York: Routledge, 2007), 28–115; Iysa A. Bello, *The Medieval Islamic Controversy between Philosophy and Orthodoxy: Ijma' and Ta'wil in the Conflict between al-Ghazali and Ibn Rushd* (Leiden: E. J. Brill, 1989), 52–65.
152   Al-Jisr, *al-Risala al-Hamidiyya*, 278–79, 292–93.
153   Ibid., 279.
154   Ibid., 355–57.
155   'Abduh, *al-Islam Din al-'Ilm wal-Madaniyya*, 109–10.
156   Ibid., 110.
157   Yusuf al-Qaradawi, *Khitabuna al-Islami fi 'Asr al-'Awlama* (Cairo: Dar al-Shuruq, 2009, first printed 2004), 76.

158 Al-Qaradawi, *Kayfa Nata'amalu ma'a al-Qur'an al-'Azim*, 284–87; *al-Sahwa al-Islamiyya min al-Murahaqa ila al-Rushd* (Cairo: Dar al-Shuruq, 2008, first printed 2002), 266.

159 Al-Qaradawi, *Kayfa Nata'amalu ma'a al-Qur'an al-'Azim*, 288–309; *al-Sahwa al-Islamiyya min al-Murahaqa ila al-Rushd*, 266.

160 Muhammad 'Imara, *al-Qur'an Yatahada* (Cairo: Maktabat al-Imam al-Bukhari lil-Nashr wal-Tawzi', 2009), 160.

161 'Imara, *Ma'rakat al-Mustalahat*, 173.

162 D. J. Manning, *Liberalism* (London: J. M. Dent, 1976), 9–56.

163 Albert Hourani, *Arabic Thought in the Liberal Age, 1798–1939* (Cambridge: Cambridge University Press, 1983), viii–ix.

164 Theodore Parker, *A Discourse of the Transient and Permanent in Christianity*, published by Electronic Texts in American Studies, University of Nebraska, January 16, 2007, accessed October 27, 2014: http://digitalcommons.unl.edu/etas/14/; Conrad Wright, "Introduction," in *Three Prophets of Religious Liberalism: Channing, Emerson, Parker* (Boston: Beacon Press, 1961), 3–46; Garry Dorrien, *The Making of American Liberal Theology: Imagining Progressive Religion, 1805–1900* (Louisville, KY: Westminster John Knox Press, 2001), 80–108; Henry Steele Commager, *The Search for a Usable Past and Other Essays in Historiography* (New York: Alfred A. Knopf, 1967), 143–50; Richard A. Grusin, *Transcendentalist Hermeneutics: Institutional Authority and the Higher Criticism of the Bible* (Durban and London, Duke University Press, 1991), 122–29.

165 Dorrien, *The Making of American Liberal Theology: Imagining Progressive Religion, 1805–1900*, 282–301.

166 Ibid., 350–61.

167 Garry Dorrien, *The Making of American Liberal Theology: Idealism, Realism and Modernity 1900–1950* (Louisville, KY: Westminster John Knox Press, 2003), 34–36.

168 Dorrien, *The Making of American Liberal Theology: Imagining Progressive Religion, 1805–1900*, 299–301.

169 Ernest R. Sandeen, *The Roots of Fundamentalism: British and American Millenarianism 1800–1930* (Chicago: University of Chicago Press, 1970), 104–8.

170 Ibid., 134–36; Stewart G. Cole, *The History of Fundamentalism* (Westport, CT: Greenwood Press, 1971), 34.

171 Norman F. Furniss, *The Fundamentalist Controversy, 1918–1931* (Hamdan, CT: Archon Books, 1963), 17–40.

172 Cole, *The History of Fundamentalism*, 53–5; Sandeen, *The Roots of Fundamentalism: British and American Millenarianism 1800–1930*, 189–205.

173 Ibid., 4–10, 84–90; Randy Moore, "Creationism in the United States" (part 1), *The American Biology Teacher*, 60:7 (September 1998), 488–93.

174 Martin E. Marty and R. Scott Appleby defined fundamentalists as individuals who, convinced of the conspiring nature of secularists and liberal religionists, adopted a set of strategies for fighting back against what is perceived as a concerted effort by secular states or elements within them to push people of religious consciousness and conscience to the margins of society: "Introduction," in Martin E. Marty and R. Scott Appleby (eds), *Fundamentalisms Comprehended*, part of the Fundamentalism Project, vol. 5 (Chicago and London: University of Chicago Press, 1995), 1. Other examples of studies offering comparative perspectives: S. N. Eisenstadt, *Fundamentalism, Sectarianism and Revolution: The Jacobin Dimension of Modernity* (Cambridge: Cambridge University Press, 1999); Lawrence J. Silberstein, *Jewish Fundamentalism in Comparative Perspective: Religion, Ideology and the Crisis of Modernity* (New York: New York University, 1993).

175 Lawrence Davidson, *Islamic Fundamentalism: An Introduction* (Westport, CT and London: Greenwood Press, 2003), 95–96.

176 For an example on al-Ghazali and al-Qaradawi: Ahmad S. Moussalli, *Moderate and Radical Islamic Fundamentalism: the Quest for Modernity, Legitimacy, and the Islamic State* (Gainesville: University Press of Florida, 1999), 8. For examples of the usage of the term in describing the Muslim Brothers and other movements that call for the

reinstitution of Islam as a comprehensive system of life: Beverley Milton-Edwards, *Islamic Fundamentalism since 1945* (London and New York: Routledge, 2004), 3; M. A. Faksh, "Islamic Fundamentalist Thought: An Analysis of Major Theoretical Formulations," in Bryan S. Turner (ed.), *Islam: Critical Concepts in Sociology, vol. IV: Islam and Social Movements* (London and New York: Routledge, 2003), 165; Johannes J. G. Jansen, *The Dual Nature of Islamic Fundamentalism* (Ithaca: Cornell University Press, 1997), 49; Anthony Hyman, "Muslim Fundamentalism," *Conflict Studies*, No. 174 (London: Institute for the Study of Conflict, 1985), 4; Gudrun Krämer, "Good Counsel to the King: The Islamist Opposition in Saudi Arabia, Jordan and Morocco," in Joseph Kostiner (ed.), *Middle East Monarchies: The Challenge of Modernity* (Boulder, CO and London: Lynne Rienner Publishers, 2000), 257.

2

ISLAM AND SCIENCE

In 1990, in his weekly column in an Egyptian newspaper, Muhammad al-Ghazali wrote that he and his colleagues had noted a multifaceted conspiracy to lead people astray from recognizing the existence of Allah while learning modern sciences. This conspiracy, which he believed reveals ignorance rather than knowledge, is the result of materialist science that was developed by people who were the least respectful of religion because the religion they were familiar with—Christianity—was the least respectful of the human mind.

According to al-Ghazali, one example of false science that promotes atheism is a peculiar theory about the beginning of creation. This theory argues that fifty million years ago a massive explosion occurred which discharged massive quantities of gases and atoms that began to spread here and there and everywhere. As the years went by, those gases and atoms came into contact with one another, thus forming the stars, the sun and the Earth. If we are to believe this theory, al-Ghazali posited, then the sun did not precede the moon, night did not precede day, and our planet was created by accident. Such notions, he argued, cannot be accepted; in Q. 20:53, Moses' words to Pharaoh are that Allah created the earth. The suggestion that an explosion occurred just by itself, and that this explosion ultimately resulted in planets that are organized and move in a precise orbit, is nothing but folly in the name of science. It is a disobedient and rebellious denial of Allah, which modern science must reject, choosing instead to examine, in a humble way, the deeds of the Creator, as was the way of early Muslims.[1]

A few years before suggesting the Big Bang model to be a form of heresy, al-Ghazali wrote about the great shame he felt when reading about senior religious scholars who reject the heliocentric model. He emphasized that learning sciences in a serious way is an important aspect of the Islamic religion.[2] At the time he shared his observations about the Big Bang model, it had already been established for over half a century as the dominant cosmological model explaining the origins of the universe and its evolution. Empirical evidence gathered since the late 1920s consistently supported it and one could not find a university astrophysics department whose professors denied this model's scientific essentiality. Consequently, across religious orientations, the Big Bang model was encouraged as a testimony to the truth of divine revelations. In 1951, the Catholic Church deemed it to be compatible with its creed and, moreover, proof for the existence of the Creator, a notion popularized by some Christian apologists.[3] Some Muslim scholars argued that the theory is compatible with the Quran, and, moreover, proves its authenticity as a revelation. Muhammad Asad (1900–1992), one of the more well-known European converts to Islam, a scholar and diplomat, interpreted Q. 21:30 ("Do not the unbelievers see that the heavens and the earth were joined together before We clove them asunder?") as anticipating the modern scientific view of the universe in his 1980 exegesis.[4] Three decades later, Zakir Naik, a popular apologist of Islam as a perfect social system, and of the Quran's scientific marvel, invoked the same verse to demonstrate that the Quran is commensurate with a theory, which, so he emphasized, "is supported by observational and experimental data gathered by astronomers and astrophysicists for decades." He concluded: "The Striking convergence between the Quranic verse and the 'Big Bang' is inescapable! How could a book, which first appeared in the deserts of Arabia 1400 years ago, contain this profound scientific truth?"[5]

Al-Ghazali chose a different view. Something, or someone, convinced him at some point that the Big Bang model is unacceptable theologically and absurd scientifically. Having reached the conclusion that the model contradicts the revelation, and that it does not make any scientific sense, he was confident that the Quran should not be reinterpreted to accommodate it, and declared it an illegitimate, anti-religious lie that must be abandoned.

The Big Bang was not the only major scientific model al-Ghazali wanted to see eschewed by schools and universities. Writing in 1992 on the implications of Islamizing the sciences, he promised that such a process would not eliminate modern empirical disciplines that are based on solid experimentations and logical inquiries, including geology, biology, psychology and astrophysics. However, al-Ghazali made several exceptions: Freud's ideas on the subconscious, which he thought gave no consideration to morals, and Darwin's "fairytale" theories. An overview of his to-be-censored list suggests that in a society that follows the guidance of this leading contemporary modernist-apologetic voice, high schools and universities will have to neglect teaching the most basic theories in the modern life, exact and social sciences—not to mention the radical revision of history textbooks that will be required in order to correct what al-Ghazali perceives to be misconceptions created by the West about Muslim contributions to humanity.[6]

The Problematic of Certainty and the Boundaries of Legitimacy

From its inception, propagators of the modernist-apologetic approach have repeatedly asserted their commitment to a central tenet of their revivalist agenda: in

Muslim societies loyal to the true spirit of Islam, scientists will be free from the kind of arbitrary interventions of the religious establishment that injured the advancement of knowledge in the medieval West, and empirical discoveries will always be welcomed as commensurate with the revelation. Read in the light of such a commitment, al-Ghazali's comments on the Big Bang model and other scientific theories seem to refute and contradict this tenet: he appears as a theologian who passionately preaches the importance of scientific excellence and progress, a respected pundit who promises a religious revolution that would safeguard the freedom of research. Yet, at the same time, he belittles and degrades the most revolutionary contributions of inquisitive geniuses whose works he does not have the training to judge, and calls to eliminate fundamental scientific theories from public life. As will be explored below, such vulgar, know-it-all judgments are not uncommon in contemporary modernist-apologetic texts, and occur more frequently in contemporary discourse than in early articulations of this approach.

Al-Ghazali's remarks expose an inherent dissonance in the modernist-apologetic concept of scientific freedom. The great sophistication and appeal of the modernist-apologetic approach regarding science has been its promise that any potential contradiction between tradition and modernity, between science and revelation, is reconcilable, and that it is thus possible to provide the intellectual benefits of a doubt-based society without compromising the spiritual security of a revelation-based existence. The modernist-apologists established two interrelated arguments that, combined, were presented as guarantors of free examinations of the natural world. The restrictive quality of the cyclical argument that belief in Islam's truth should be ascertained only through free logical inquiry and logical inquiry can lead only to belief in Islam's truth was indirectly defended already in the works of 'Abduh and al-Jisr. Both promoted the notion that the miraculous nature of the Quran and the option of allegorizing it to accommodate *proven* scientific theories, models and facts make it possible for Muslims to enjoy the full freedom of scientific investigation without having to concede the emotionally reassuring confines of absolute faith in a Creator, a Prophet and a revelation.

Alas, this structure is dependent on determining the status of scientific ideas as proven, disproven and yet-to-be-proven scientific ideas. Thus, if one follows the modernist-apologetic line of thinking, absolute scientific freedom is not guaranteed at all; rather, the freedom that exists is that allowed by the criteria set in order to determine *what* qualifies a theory, model or fact as absolutely scientifically proven, and *who* has the authority to determine it qualifies as such. It follows from this that the clear-cut modernist-apologetic differentiation between (a) a religion that cannot accommodate seemingly challenging scientific theories and, thus, is the enemy of science and theocratic in nature (Christianity), and, (b) a religion that, when true to its foundations, can accommodate such theories and does not hinder scientific progress (Islam), is tenuous. Indeed, the modernist-apologetic concept of allegorizing allows room, potentially even much room, for the religious legitimization of any scientific finding, model or theory, even if such findings seem to contradict revealed passages. But whether or not the room allowed provides scientists with freedom from theocratic interference entirely depends on the nature of the authority that determines the status of scientific notions. If that role is reserved for theologians, or for politicians, judges and even scientists who ground their decisions in theological argumentations, then scientific studies become hostage to theological considerations.

Reading his articles there is no doubt that al-Ghazali is certain scientific truths exist and that their status as such cannot be challenged, and that he is confident of his qualification to judge which scientific theories are religiously legitimate and which are not. But if he were to shift from the realm of opinion columns to the implementation of his ideas in a future ideal Islamized society, in which the state comprehensively Islamizes the sciences, matters would become more complicated and challenging. The reality, as implied by his censorship wish list, is that the status of scientific theories, and, subsequently, their religious legitimacy, *are* contested among scientists, among theologians, and between scientists and theologians. This suggests that the implementation of the modernist-apologetic concept in a meaningful, universally binding way would require a mechanism tasked with passing judgment on conflicting opinions as to what has been proven, what is yet to be proven and what has been disproven by science. Otherwise, the Islamized society will not be protected from blasphemous theories masked as factual descriptions of the natural world. What will be the structure and composition of that authority? Who will be its members? How will they be selected? What will be the punishment for those who disobey it? Al-Ghazali is silent on the question of interpretive authority. His texts suggest there cannot be confusion as to the precise scientific status of theories, models and facts—a suggestion that runs counter to the circumstance against which his protests were articulated.

The neglect of the problem of scientific certainty and interpretative authority characterizes modernist-apologetic writing in general. Throughout a century and a half of scholarship, none of the luminaries of this approach addressed this problem. The philosophical challenges to the existence of scientific certainties, old and new, were not broached by the modernist-apologists. Neither did they recognize scientific polemics as a historically integral part of the evolution and perfection of scientific quests. The narrative provided on the relations between modern science and religion depicted Christian establishments as resisting proven scientific facts due to their singular stubbornness and anti-rationalist views. This narrative left no room for a more nuanced account of the contentious way in which scientific revolutions actually occur within scientific communities. Not incidentally, contemporary modernist-apologetic works on science making occasional references to Western scientists and philosophers ignored the most influential work published in the twentieth century on the history of science—Thomas Kuhn's *The Structure of Scientific Revolutions*, in which he demonstrated that scientific knowledge does not develop in a gradualist, consistent way, but through competition between paradigms.[7]

The assumption implied in treatments of the exact, life, and social sciences by modernist-apologists has been threefold: that at any given time scientific notions can be clearly and unambiguously established as proven, disproven or yet-to-be-proven; that they, as theologians, are qualified to accurately determine which of the three is correct; and that their judgments will not be disputed by any rationalist, yet faithful, mind. The scientifically proven has been identified in the revealed texts, demonstrating their marvel; or, in cases where it was not identified, revealed texts were allegorized to accommodate it. The yet-to-be-proven was described as requiring additional studies before its legitimacy could be decided; alternatively, the potential of the revelation to accommodate it was established, cautiously. The disproven, if perceived as religiously dangerous, was delegitimized.

One early, and revealing, example of the assumption that the scientific status of theories, models and facts can be carefully ascertained is 'Abduh's treatment of evidence regarding the Flood. The story of Noah's ark is narrated in two chapters of the Quran—Hud (11) and Noah (71). Q. 11:43 and 71:26 suggest that the Flood was universal, eliminating all of humanity rather than a certain people in a particular region. So does Q. 37:77, which states that Noah's descendents were the only ones left on the face of the earth. In 1900, a Palestinian from Nablus, 'Abdallah Qadumi, sent 'Abduh a query about the compatibility of scientific evidence demonstrating that the Flood was not universal with the Quran.

The issue was not new; it had preoccupied Christian scientists from the mid-seventeenth century. At that delicate historical junction, to quote Cohn, "science was becoming an autonomous activity, with its criteria of truth," but almost every scientist was convinced that it could, and must, be reconciled with religion. Investigations of the natural world were perceived as a means to demonstrate the truth of the revelation, including the occurrence of a universal Flood.[8] Marine fossils, comets and calculations of the ocean's water capacity were introduced and debated. Read in historical perspective, these studies reveal how the desire to assert the truth of revelation can serve as an important incentive to shed new light on the workings of the natural world. But, as Allen almost painfully demonstrated, it also reveals that pure faith can blind even the most astute of minds from observing factual evidence in front of their own eyes.[9] During the nineteenth century, as the study of geology developed, notions of a scientifically proven global deluge were refuted, but the debate continued.

In his response to Qadumi, 'Abduh wrote that many scientists accepted the view shared by Muslims, Jews and Christians, that the Flood was universal and, as evidence, pointed to fossils of shells and fish on mountaintops. However, some contemporary scientists argued that the Flood was not universal, introducing evidence whose discussion, 'Abduh argued, required more space than he could allow. According to 'Abduh, scientific findings permit allegorizing revealed passages and reliable Prophetic traditions that contradict them only if they are decisively and logically proven. As no such decisive proof regarding the non-universality of the Flood was presented, it is not permitted to accept or to teach others that the Flood was a local event.[10]

The response by 'Abduh is a rare application of his theory of hermeneutics. It implies that:

a   Scientific findings should be evaluated against the revelation;
b   Proven scientific facts legitimize the allegorizing of conflicting revealed passages;
c   The non-universality of the Flood has not been sufficiently proven, and thus it is illegitimate to adapt the Quran to this thesis.

What is missing in this decision, as in 'Abduh's more theoretical writing on the relation between science and revelation in general, is a clear conception as to how the yet-to-be-proven scientifically is to be distinguished from the proven and dis-proven. What precisely is the methodology that determines what has been satis-factorily proven and thus justifies allegorizing? What weight of evidence is required to transform the yet-to-be-proven to the status of proven or disproven? 'Abduh did not explain what qualified him, a highly educated theologian and religious jurist but no scientist, to pass judgment on a polemic pertaining to fossils, the layers of the earth and the composition of comets. Given his unequivocal opinion that the time was not ripe for allegorizing the verses germane to the universality of the Flood, and that true believers should not do so, one also wonders what did he, the Mufti of Egypt, thought should be done about Muslim scholars and educators who would beg to differ on the point and teach the non-universality of the Flood.

To realize that the existence of scientific certainties cannot be taken for granted, the modernist-apologists did not need to dive deeply into textbooks on the history or philosophy of science. Whether in the late nineteenth or early twenty-first century, whether dealing with Noah's ark or with the Big Bang theory, it sufficed that they reflected on their disagreements with scientists of their day (who accepted and taught certain theories which they rejected) or on their disagreements with other religious scholars (who deemed certain theories and facts which the modernist-apologists accepted to be blasphemous) to encourage, in fact to force, the recog-nition that some structured method of deciding which scientific theories are proven and legitimate would have to be practiced, if the Islamizing of the sciences in a revived, Islamized society is ever to be as comprehensive and binding as they desired. One cannot escape the thought that the challenge of scientific certainty and the implications of theological interpretive authority on scientific freedom have been neglected in modernist-apologetic literature not so much because they could not have been recognized, but because recognizing them would have forced an admission that the modernist-apologetic concept of scientific freedom is potentially more restrictive and arbitrary than they were willing to concede.

The Heliocentric Model as Hermeneutics

The problem of revealed authority and rational certainty is not unique to Arab-Muslim modernist-apologetic deliberations on scientific freedom. It complicates any concept of scientific freedom that draws on a promise of reconciling revealed words with *proven* scientific facts. Ultimately, the question will be the same: who should have the final say as to what constitute proven scientific facts that legitimize allegorizing God's words?

In one of his apologias on the reconcilability of Islam and science, al-Ghazali described the trial of Galileo Galilei as an epitome of the Church's animosity toward science. He argued that there was no reason for the Church's rejection of the heliocentric model beyond its stubborn resentment of empirical investigations of the natural world, because Galileo presented facts, and these facts did not contradict the Bible.[11] But the matter was actually more complicated than an obstinate Church, insisting on falsehoods, and a defiant scientist, insisting on truths. Galileo's long struggle to have his discoveries gain legitimacy demonstrates how risky any attempt to reconcile science and theology just is to both scientists and theologians.

The Holy See rejected the heliocentric model, in part because it appeared to contradict Joshua 10:12: "Sun, stand still over Gibeon." If Copernicus was correct, how can one explain that a man demanded God tell the sun that had not been moving to stand still?[12] Moreover, a denial of the geocentric model injured the cosmological notions of the Church as to the precise positions of Paradise and Hell.[13] Clerics felt confident opposing the accommodation of their creed to heliocentrism because it was still perceived as no more than a speculation in the seventeenth century. Galileo's teachings were based on observations he had made while using telescopes to gaze at the heavens at a time when most scholars believed that only direct vision had the ability to grasp the actual reality (some objections were based on the poor functioning of lenses then in use).[14] A core decree issued by the Council of Trent (1545–1563) was that no one should dare interpret the Holy Scriptures in a manner contrary to the Church's interpretation; to preach Copernicus' ideas when they were still rejected by the Church, as Galileo insisted on doing, was more than a challenge to the literal meaning of the Bible—it was a challenge to the Church's authority as the ultimate arbitrator between truth and falsehood.

Galileo never intended to clash with Rome. Neither was his faith in the inerrancy of the Bible shaken. But he was also passionately committed to presenting the results of his observations, fully conscious of their importance to the advancement of human knowledge and the possible implications for doing so.[15] In 1615, already under investigation for his Copernican views by the Inquisition, Galileo introduced, in the form of a letter to the Grand Duchess (of Tuscany), Christina, a broad theory of hermeneutics intended to resolve not only the conflict over the heliocentric model but all future conflicts between science and the Church. Many of the ideas presented by Arab-Muslim modernist-apologists three centuries later read as though they had been inspired by this letter, although there is no evidence any were familiar with it, and it is unlikely that they were. In the letter, Galileo stressed his—and Copernicus'—religious devotion. He explained that while the Bible is inerrant, depictions of natural phenomena are not its main purpose, and where such depictions appear often simple language was used in order to avoid confusing common people. The study of the physical world should therefore not be based on the revelation, and nothing that is demonstrated through observation should be called into question because it contradicts Biblical passages. God wishes for people to use the senses, reason and intellect with which He has endowed them. Given that two truths—the revelation and the facts of the natural world—cannot contradict one another, in instances when a revealed word contradicts a demonstrated conclusion about the natural world, the former must be reinterpreted in light of the latter and its true meaning must be discovered.[16]

Clerics, warned Galileo, should realize that what they believe to be absolute truths are not always so, and must therefore tread cautiously when commenting on the conclusions of scientists, not only because their theological conclusions may later prove to be false, but also because scientific knowledge is, by its nature, evolving:

> Indeed, besides saying (as we have) that in many places Scripture is open to interpretations far removed from the literal meaning of the words, we should add that we cannot assert with certainty that all interpreters speak with divine inspiration since if this were so then there would be no disagreement among them about the meaning of the same passages; therefore, I think it would be very prudent not to allow anyone to commit and in a way oblige scriptural passages to have to maintain the truth of any physical conclusions whose contrary could ever be proved to us by the senses and demonstrative and necessary reasons. Indeed, who wants the human mind put to death? Who is going to claim that everything in the world which is observable and knowable has already been seen and discovered?[17]

All of this sounds reassuring to the mind of one concerned by the question of whether science and revelation can coexist. But the method of reconciling the two that Galileo introduced depends on the ability to agree on what constitutes a demonstrated fact of nature, and thus the question of interpretative authority cannot be avoided. While Galileo recognized this challenge, he was careful not to declare who should have the ultimate say. His letter to the Duchess emphasized that only the Pontiff and the Church's Councils have the right to censure scientific opinions as erroneous. But it equally stressed that no one has the right to declare the truth false. Writing about the allegations directed against Copernicus, he stated:

> in regard to these and other similar propositions which do not directly involve faith, no one can doubt that the Supreme Pontiff always has the absolute power of permitting or condemning them; however, no creature has the power of making them be true or false, contrary to what they happen to be by nature and de facto.[18]

Because his letter elevated the observations of scientists above those who lack their qualifications, it was fair to interpret the final sentence as a veiled statement that Galileo and his colleagues in the sciences should have the final word.

It took two more decades for Galileo to be brought to trial, at the end of which he was forced to renounce facts that he knew to be true—without declaring rebelliously *eppur si muove*, "and yet it moves." Two more centuries passed before the Church finally made peace with the heliocentric model. The historical records reveal that a conflation of petty personal and political interests, rather than concern about the implications of Galileo's proposed allegorizing method, led to his perse-cution and prosecution.[19] Had his method been embraced and implemented in practice, the question of interpretive authority would have needed be settled by the Church one way or another, and a clear choice between a theocratic mono-polization of scientific queries and liberation from the shackles of such mono-polization would have had to have been made. A liberal theocracy is an oxymoron, no matter how much one plays with words—whether these words apply to Christian scriptures, Muslim scriptures, or another revelation.

A. The Theory of Evolution in Early Modernist-Apologetic Thought

More than any other scientific theory, the treatment of Darwin's theory of evolu-tion exposes the fragility of the modernist-apologetic promise for a revelation-based social order that guarantees full freedom for scientists who present "proven" facts. A comparative reading of the radical shift in modernist-apologists' treatments of Darwin, from al-Afghani, al-Jisr and 'Abduh to al-Ghazali, al-Qaradawi and 'Imara, demonstrates the great potential of their school to accommodate religiously challenging scientific theories, but also the potentially restrictive implications of their method of accommodation and the risk that this method will result in the imposition of arbitrary theological opinions on scientists. Whereas late nineteenth century and early twentieth century modernist-apologists established and defended the religious legitimacy of the theory of evolution at a time when it tore apart Christian communities in America and was flatly rejected by other eminent Muslim scholars, contemporary modernist-apologists have chosen to characterize and deride Darwinism as a false, disproven theory, a Western exceptionality and a manifestation of atheism that should be shunned by the Muslim community, doing so at a time when Darwinism's status as a foundation of the study of life sciences has been accepted by the majority of scientists worldwide. This shift had little to do with scientific discoveries and much to do with the theological convictions of religious scholars who believed they are qualified to pass ultimate judgments on scientific polemics.

In an apologetic article he published at the conclusion of Darwin's bicentennial in 2009, an occasion marked internationally by numerous books, papers, con-ferences and exhibitions, Muzaffar Iqbal, the founder and president of the Canada-based Center for Islam and Science, argued that the Muslim world's lack of interest in the events proved "yet again that Darwin and what he wrought has little rele-vance to most Muslims."[20] This statement is only partially true. Ever since Charles Darwin's (1809–1882) *On the Origins of Species* was published in 1859, the theory of evolution through natural selection has stirred emotions and religious polemics as no other scientific theory in history has done previously or since. Indeed, the debate over evolutionary theory in Muslim societies has never been as intense as in the West, and Darwin has not become a primary definer of religious attitudes. But the theory of evolution has challenged religious dogmas and stirred an array of conflicting responses also in the Muslim world, where some considered it dangerous blasphemy while others did not. Darwinism has been a cause of distress among some Muslims for the same reasons it has been so for some Christians and Jews. Its implications have the potential to challenge the authority of God over His creation and the unique status He designated for mankind. To make matters worse, unlike other essential scientific models, the core of Darwin's ideas can be easily understood by students of the humanities also.

Analyses of how the early modernist-apologists treated the theory of evolution have not been without misconceptions. Some understood the modernist-apologists to be advocates of the theory. This misconception was popularized to such an extent that a century later Rashid Rida's Wikipedia entry states that "one of his controversial views was his support of Darwin's theory of evolution."[21] The contrary opinion, that "modernist, reforming Islamic thinkers" of al-Afghani's school "found evolution to be unacceptable"[22] is equally misleading. The formative modernist-apologetic texts on Darwin of the late nineteenth and early twentieth century were, in fact, nuanced. With the exception of one text, these works adamantly defended the *potential* compatibility of the Quran and Darwin's ideas, though they did not consider his theory of evolution to have been sufficiently proven scientifically. First and foremost, Darwinism was used by early modernist-apologist thinkers as an example that nothing that science discovers can contradict the final word of Allah as conveyed to humanity by His final Prophet. They considered the ability to make peace, from a religious point of view, with a revolutionary concept that stirred bitter conflicts within Christian societies and among Christian denominations as proof for the validity of the idea that was at the core of their agenda: that the origins of modernity are in Islam, and that Islam, when true to itself, is able to accommodate any useful modern idea.

This early response to Darwinism that considered it to be reconcilable with religious creeds, and even supportive of them, was not unique to Arab-Muslim thinkers, or to Muslim thinkers in general. Across religions and cultures, scholars struggled to accommodate the unsettling theory through familiar religious terminologies and categories. Muslim scholars from India to Turkey introduced hermeneutics reminiscent of those introduced by the early Arab-Muslim modernist-apologists. For example, the Indian-Muslim Sayyid Ahmad Khan (1817–1898), the founding figure of Islamic modernism in South Asia, suggested that Q. 15:26, 23:12, 32:8, which teach that human life began with the fermentation of clay, agree with the idea that human evolution began with lifeless matter.[23] The Turkish scholar Ahmet Hamdi Akseki (1887–1951) explained that Adam's creation from clay does not contradict the theory of evolution because it does not mean that he was created instantly; based on Q. 71:17, Adam may have begun his life as a plant.[24] In other religious traditions, Darwinism was also embraced as commensurate with dogmas and scriptures. As noted in Chapter 1, attempts to reconcile Darwinism with Christian dogmas were, in part, the reason for the emergence of the fundamentalist movement (as well as for its continuing appeal). In the East,

Confucians and Hindus also accommodated their respective teachings to Darwinism. The Chinese scholar and translator Yan Fu (1854–1921) interpreted Darwin's theory in light of Confucian ethical debates, whereas the Bengali scholar and educational leader Satish Mukherjee (1865–1948) considered Samkhya, one of the oldest schools of Hindu philosophy, a precursor to the modern view of evolution (according to Samkhya, the world unfolds as a result of a continuous cycle between creation and dissolution; the cycle, according to the teaching, accounts for the creation of species as well as for the evolution of the universe). Later Indian thinkers followed in Mukherjee's footsteps and considered Samkhya as the theory of evolution applied to the entire cosmos.[25]

Jamal al-Din al-Afghani

The first modernist-apologetic treatment of Darwin left no doubt that his theory of evolution is the enemy of faith. In *The Refutation of the Materialists* (see Chapter 1), al-Afghani's longest and most systematic work, Darwin was ridiculed and disparaged in a way no other scholar was. Al-Afghani's tad too many acerbic insults and general derision of scientific works, which it appears that he had never even read,[26] reveal that he was, contrary to the impression he tried to convey, deeply unsettled by the potential implications of Darwin's theory as he had come to understand them through secondary sources. He considered the theory, as did some in the Christian world before him, a grave threat to the transcendental order centered on the existence of a Creator. It was this order that his treatise sought to protect and uphold.

Al-Afghani portrayed Darwin as the final link in a chain of naïve materialists who spread false ideas. He argued that this chain began in Greece in the fourth and third centuries BC, suggesting that a school of thought developed that denied the existence of anything other than matter, that was in opposition to the school, to which Pythagoras, Socrates, Plato and Aristotle belonged, that believed in one, abstract Creator of all things. According to al-Afghani, the debates between the materialists of his time were a reincarnation of the debates in ancient Greece. After geological findings refuted the notion that the different species on the face of the earth had always existed, a controversy developed between materialists who held that the development of species ended upon the creation of the earth and materialists who held that species continue to develop. Both did an equally poor job presenting credible arguments. The theory that living creatures have existed ever since the earth split from the sun is peculiar, considering the temperature on the planet was so hot that it would have most certainly caused their extinction. The theory that living creatures gradually developed into a perfect form is also baseless, considering that studies in the field of chemistry revealed the similar properties shared between a man's sperm and that of donkeys and bulls; given that the foundations of living creatures are similar, this theory cannot explain why they are so different.[27]

Al-Afghani argued that the theory of evolution—or, as he described it, the idea that living creatures evolve with time from one form to another in response to their needs and external conditions—was born out of the theoretical deadlock that the materialists faced in their endless quest to deny a Creator. Darwin, according to al-Afghani, was a miserable fellow who preached ludicrous ideas. The English scientist argued that due to natural, external conditions, man developed from orangutan into cannibal into negroid and finally into the present form of the caucasian. According to Darwin's logic, argued al-Afghani, it is possible that, with time, a flea could become an elephant and an elephant could become a flea! Based on that logic, Darwin would be unable to answer if asked how it was possible that the old trees in the Indian woods that have been growing in the same soil, exposed to the same wind, and drinking from the same water are nevertheless so dissimilar in their shapes, sizes, tastes and fragrances. Darwin would be equally helpless if asked to explain how it was possible for the fish in the Aral and Caspian seas to differ so greatly in their colors, shapes and behaviors despite their swimming in the same waters and eating the same food. So, too, would he be if asked how it was possible that animals that differ in their shape, size, color, and strength continue living in the same territory without the ability to migrate to another. Faced with such challenging questions that shatter his theorizing, Darwin would have no choice but to curl up and expose his defensive quills like a hedgehog. Another example of the absurdity of Darwin's theory was, according to al-Afghani, his argument that after centuries of cutting the tails off dogs, dogs began to be born without tails, which no longer served any natural function. Al-Afghani wondered whether the miserable Darwin had not heard of the fact that Arabs and Hebrews had been circumcising their boys for thousands of years but, nevertheless, their babies had not been born circumcised.[28]

The Refutation of the Materialists was a protest against the moral impossibility of humanity without a Creator, and al-Afghani's harsh, if unqualified, comments against Darwin were motivated by belief that the theory of evolution is a spearhead of materialism rather than by a rejection of any specific aspect of the theory. Read in this light, it is understandable why al-Afghani's attitude towards Darwinism changed for the better a decade later when he became convinced that Darwin did not deny the existence of God, and that the materialists renounced Darwin's leadership once they concluded he could not contribute to achieving their main objective—establishing that nothing but matter exists.[29] (Al-Afghani could have known about Darwin's theism already when he wrote the *Refutation*: as noted by Moore, in the *Origin of Species*, the word Creation and its cognates were mentioned over one hundred times, and opposite the title is a quotation about studying God's works as well as His Word; and *The Descent of Man* spoke of the "grand sequence of events, which our minds refuse to accept as the result of blind chance."[30] While Darwin revolutionized science as a believer, he ended his life as an agnostic—but that became public knowledge only after the *Refutation* was published.)

Writing on evolutionary theory with the conviction that Darwin believed that life originated with a Creator, al-Afghani changed course and sought to convince his readers that the theory is not entirely an innovation, and that its roots can be found in Muslim thought and practices. For example, he noted that the principle of natural selection is well known in Muslim civilization, where women who possess the best qualities are chosen as wives in order to ensure that the prospective children inherit the best qualities from their fathers as well as from their mothers, and where the Bedouins improve horse species through natural selection.[31]

Husayn al-Jisr

Al-Afghani did not go so far as to argue that the theory of evolution is reconcilable with the Muslim revelation, and, moreover, that its being so is evidence of the truth of that revelation. These notions were first introduced in 1887 by Husayn al-Jisr in his *Hamidiyan Treatise on the Truthfulness of Islam and of the Shari'a*. The book's declared objective was, as noted in Chapter 1, to explain the truth of Islam to Christians; much of it discussed materialism and Darwinism. Al-Jisr argued that materialism must be false, and that the theory of evolution, whether it is credible or not, can only serve to assert the validity of Allah's final revelation and to highlight its superiority to Christianity. His discussion of these issues laid the foundation for the modernist-apologetic treatment of Darwinism in the decades that followed. Moreover, it offered the first systematic and comprehensive theory of modernist-apologetic allegorizing as a means to reconcile the Quran with modern sciences—making it valuable historical work, albeit work that has not been duly recognized as such in academic literature.

There is some irony in the fact that al-Jisr's interest in Darwinism and its theological implications was encouraged, in part, by a bitter polemic between Christian fundamentalists and liberals that took place at the Syrian Protestant College of Beirut (renamed the American University of Beirut in 1920). Surely the day will come when the "Lewis Affair"—an unfortunate conflation of academic power-struggles, religious dogmatism and youthful enthusiasm—will be given the Hollywood or West End adaptation it deserves. Events began to unfold when Dr. Edwin Lewis, a professor of Chemistry and Geology at the College, remarked in his commencement speech to the class of 1882 that Darwin's theory was based on sound research, qualifying his observation by noting that more scientific studies were needed before drawing conclusions as to the validity of the theory. Lewis further noted that even if it was ever established that man had gradually evolved from lower animal forms, such a fact would be irrelevant to the origin of the first man or the responsibility imposed on him by God.[32] While the speech unequivocally committed to the existence of God as the Creator of humankind and to the limitations of science in understanding His deeds, it enraged the President of the College and members of its Board of Managers and Board of Trustees. They believed Darwinism to be an unfounded theory that denies Biblical truths and, thus, a theory that should not be taught at one of the Arab world's main missionary institutions.[33]

Following Lewis' speech and amid the growing anger of the Syrian Protestant College's administration, a series of events ensued that greatly impacted intellectual life in the Arab-speaking world. Lewis was forced to resign, a student rebellion against the administration ended in the administration's favor, and professors at the

College were required to pledge to a Declaration of Principles that forbade instruction against the revealed truth.[34] Several of the College's teachers and students, who left Beirut for Cairo, transformed Egypt's capital into the hub of Arabic rationalist, scientific-minded journalism at the turn of the century. Faris Nimr (1856–1951) and Ya'qub Sarruf (1852–1927) were junior professors at the College. Sarruf taught Arabic and Physics, Nimer taught Latin and served as research assistant in the observatory. In 1876 they established al-Muqtataf, a monthly scientific journal that published and promoted even-handed accounts of Darwin's views.[35] The two added much to the fury of the College's management over Lewis' speech by publishing it in full in the August 1882 edition of their journal,[36] and giving generous space to conflicting views about the speech in subsequent issues.[37] This action ultimately frustrated their hopes for academic promotion, and as a result they migrated to Egypt.[38] The ardent materialist Shibli Shumayyil (1853–1917) completed his medical studies at the College in 1875 and moved to Paris before settling in 1885 in Cairo.[39] Shumayyil was impacted by the teachings of Lewis and the 1882 scandal.[40] His subsequent writings greatly contributed to the association of evolutionism with atheism in the minds of some of his Arab contemporaries, including al-Afghani.[41] Jurji Zaydan (1861–1914), a medical student and leader of the failed rebellion, moved to Cairo and founded in 1892 al-Hilal, perhaps the most popular of Egypt's highbrow magazines. He popularized modern science and philosophy, and vastly contributed to the development of an Arab national-ethnic identity.[42]

Another important impact of the Lewis Affair was on the evolution of modernist-apologetic thought. According to Ebert, in the summer of 1882, al-Jisr, the newly appointed headmaster of al-Madrasa al-Wataniyya in Beirut, took advantage of his relocation and frequently visited the library of the Syrian Protestant College, where he read translated works in the natural sciences.[43] Elshakry observes that he closely followed the Lewis Affair. When composing his apologetic treatise about the truth of Islam, the inability of Christian professors to accommodate the theory of evolution was in the back of al-Jisr's mind, emboldening him to highlight the potential of Islamic hermeneutics to succeed in doing so.[44] Still, al-Jisr was motivated by more than a longing to cast aspersions on Christianity. Reading his treatise, one is left with the impression that al-Jisr was deeply distressed by the possibility that the theory of evolution would be proven to be true, and, unlike al-Afghani when he initially engaged the subject, was fearful that this may eventually be the case. Thus, he was eager to demonstrate, first and foremost to himself, that there is nothing in the theory that can undermine the three fundamental truths on which his religious thought rested—there is a Creator, Muhammad was His final Prophet, and the Quran is His final, perfect revelation.

As in al-Afghani's discussion, al-Jisr's treatment of Darwin was part of his broader rejection of materialism. He attacked the notion that only things that can be experienced through one of the five senses should be acknowledged: given that certain things in this world can only be observed using a microscope, i.e. that there are limitations to our senses even with regard to things that belong to this world, is it not possible that there are things in the beyond that our senses cannot expose?[45] Al-Jisr invoked the watchmaker analogy (without explicitly alluding to William Paley and his Natural Theology) to argue that the materialist contention that matter gradually evolved from itself and without a cause from a simple form into its many sophisticated, splendid variations is just as incredibly foolish as the argument that a watch, which can only be produced through the meticulous application of mechanical and engineering laws, came into existence through the work of a blind amputee.[46] The metaphor clearly impressed him. He used it later in the book to ridicule materialists who, while denying the existence of Allah, do not deny that they do not know a great deal about a great many things. Thus, the materialists should recognize the existence of Allah just as a person who looks at a watch recognizes the existence of a watchmaker, even if he cannot explain all of its different components.[47]

Al-Jisr introduced two conflicting arguments according to which both the order in our world, and lack thereof, are proof of Allah's existence. When one notices the perfect order and harmony in the world, the functionalist utility of what is in it—for example, how winds allow ships to sail and plants to grow—clearly one must acknowledge that all of this cannot be a coincidence and a Creator exists.[48] But, conversely, according to al-Jisr, when one notices the great variations in the shapes and appearances of animals, one realizes that their Creator is not subject to any rules and can do whatever He pleases; there can be no greater logical proof than this for the existence of the Creator.[49]

Satisfied that he had refuted the possibility of a world in which nothing but matter exists, al-Jisr turned to explaining why the theory of evolution cannot damage the truths of Islam and why materialists would be wrong to believe that evolution teaches that there is no such thing as a soul and that human beings are a form of animal. His discussion included three main parts:

a   Introducing the concept of allegorizing revealed verses that guarantees, in a way unique to Islam, the reconciliation of the revelation with scientific findings;
b   Explaining why the theory of evolution, if ever proven true, is reconcilable with the Quran;
c   Analyzing why the theory of evolution was not validated in a satisfying manner at that point in time.

The first part was already discussed in chapter 1; al-Jisr argued that whenever—and only whenever—a conclusive logical proof appears to contradict the literal meaning of the revelation, that meaning should be allegorized in a way that accommodates the proof. He explained that it was not the purpose of the Quran to give a detailed account of the laws of nature, including of how life came into being; the purpose of the Quran is to teach about Allah, and the ways to worship Him. Human beings should learn about the laws of nature using their minds. The natural issues that are mentioned in the revelation are addressed in general terms, and only for the purpose of providing logical proof for the existence of Allah.[50]

Turning to the theory of evolution (without explicitly mentioning Darwin's name even once), al-Jisr stated that Allah created everything that is in nature from nothing. The rules according to which variations exist are His rules. Whether or not the minerals, the plants and the animals were created by Him directly or through gradual evolution is not an important question, because He is capable of doing both. Evolution is commensurate with the Muslim faith just as direct creation is, provided that the theory is grounded in recognition of Allah as the Creator.[51]

Al-Jisr alluded (without citing precisely) to several verses in the Quran that deal with creation, including Q. 21:30 (that every living thing was made from water), 24:45 (that states the same) and 42:29 (on Allah's dispersing of animals in the heavens and the earth). These are commensurate with the theory of evolution. Other verses, e.g. 39:6 (on the creation of male and female) and 51:49 (that creatures were created in pairs), contradict the theory because they suggest that the creatures on the face of the earth were created by Allah directly and independently.[52] Q. 4:1, according to which Allah "created you from one soul, and created from it its mate, and dispersed from both of them many men and women," means, literally, that Allah created man directly, and thus also contradicts the theory of evolution (as we shall see below, the meaning of this verse became a focal point in the debate over the legitimacy of the theory, and 'Abduh's—and Rida's—understanding of it was different than al-Jisr's).[53]

According to al-Jisr, the theory of evolution was still no more than an unsubstantiated hypothesis and mere speculation. Given the guideline that verses should be understood literally unless an unequivocal rationalist proof contrary to such an interpretation exists, he believed that the theory should be rejected and Muslims should, at that time, believe that Allah created all the species on the face of the earth directly. If proof of the theory should be established in the future, then providing a reconciling interpretation for verses that literally read as contradicting the theory would become obligatory. This being the case, he believed that embracing Islam is a win-win situation for materialists who hold evolution to be true. If ever the theory would be solidly proven, nothing should hinder them from allegorizing verses to accommodate the scientific truth. However, he cautioned the materialists to not confuse a definite truth and a hypothesis, which is what the theory of evolution is; only the former allows for allegorizing.[54]

Al-Jisr wrote, confidently, that it would require an entire book to explain why the theory of evolution is merely a hypothesis, but that it was not the subject of his study. He nevertheless treated the issue in some detail, suggesting that he had not only read on the subject but had also given it considerable thought. The impression is that while he stated that the theory of evolution bears no theological implications for Muslims, he was not at ease with it and very much wished for it to be false. His main argument against the validity of the theory was that adherents of evolution are wrong to hold that the fact that certain animals have vestiges of certain extraneous organs is proof against direct creation. According to al-Jisr, this condition is true only for a minority of animals, which underwent a process of evolution, a process directed by Allah; it is possible, for example, that the agama had to hide itself for a time because its existence was threatened by another animal, and during that time Allah changed its nature and its legs disappeared, though leaving their remains visible. However, the fact that in a majority of animals the remains of superfluous organs cannot be found suggests that they were directly created. The implication is that the theory of evolution had not been proven, because its adherents hold it to be universally true for all creatures. Al-Jisr was equally unimpressed by claims that fossils that show evolution from simple to more complex life forms constitute proof that the theory of evolution is true. There was nothing preventing Allah, he wrote, from first creating the more simple creatures and then, independently of them, creating the more complex creatures; with time, the simple creatures perished, either because they could not endure certain climates, or because more complex creatures, created after them, overcame them, or for any other reason. Thus, fossil findings do not validate the theory of evolution.[55]

Another proof discussed by al-Jisr was that the similarity between men and monkeys suggested common ancestry. Affirming his concept of allegorizing he argued that the possibility of something does not imply, from the standpoint of followers of Muhammad, that it contradicts the revelation. Moreover, there is evidence against the hypothesized common ancestry: when a monkey is born, it is stronger than a human baby, who is unable to walk or sit by himself. However, with time, humans become stronger than monkeys. This, according to al-Jisr, is one of Allah's marvelous deeds, and proof of His immense abilities—as well as proof that man did not evolve from monkeys.[56]

It is unlikely that any of the above reasonings will impress students of biology, but al-Jisr was not a scientist. His treatise was not scientific, rather it was theological. It introduced a conceptual framework that made it theoretically possible for Muslims to accept, based on a method of interpretation strongly rooted in Islamic tradition, a scientific theory with which many Christians across the world, including in his own country, could not make peace. In this sense, his discussion was a masterful demonstration of the potential of the modernist-apologetic school to integrate revolutionary scientific theories into Muslim societies. But one crucial question remained unanswered. His hermeneutics rested on the assumption that it is possible to unmistakably distinguish between proven, yet-to-be-proven and unproven scientific theories, between hypotheses and theses. But it did not commit to how precisely that should be done. His refutation of Darwinism, a theory that, at the time, had already gained wide acceptance among life scientists (albeit not an absolute consensus), which was based on his own unqualified doubts, implied that he did not believe it was for scientists to determine when the time for allegorizing had ripened. But it did not explain what made his verdict the credible one.

Muhammad 'Abduh and Muhammad Rashid Rida

In its almost four decades of existence, Rashid Rida's al-Manar served as the primary venue propagating the idea that the theory of evolution is reconcilable with the Quran. The pages of the mouthpiece of modernist-apologetic thought testify that Rida was consistent and adamant in his defense of Darwinism's *potential* religious legitimacy, but also that this defense met with strong resistance among other Islamic scholars, who were convinced that the theory of evolution amounted to blasphemy. In his analysis of Darwinism, Rida (whether in publishing his own thoughts, those of his teacher 'Abduh or those of others), did not make any contribution that was radically different than that of al-Jisr. Like al-Jisr, Rida was reluctant to consider the theory of evolution as more than a flawed hypothesis. As al-Jisr, he cited and interpreted verses in the Quran as being supportive of Darwin's theory, provided the theory was to be found true (he was less ready to concede that certain verses contradicted it). Also, as was the case with al-Jisr, Rida's apologetics left a crucial question unanswered: how, and by whose ultimate judgment, should one determine whether controversial scientific theories, including Darwin's, have matured to the point that allows, in fact requires, allegorizing that would legitimize their full embrace?

The first thorough defense of Darwinism's compatibility with Islam's revelation was published in the pages of *al-Manar* in 1905, in the fourth and final part of a series written by the physician Muhammad Tawfiq Sidqi (1881–1920) titled "Religion in Light of the Sound Mind." Sidqi described the theory of evolution as the best explanation for a variety of scientific problems (including the similarities between animals) that human beings have made to date. He emphasized that the theory should not be considered a final, decisive truth, but contended that the Quran is compatible with evolution, explaining that the revelation does not depict Adam as the first man to ever exist, and neither does it mention that Adam was directly created from clay.[57] Following the publication, several readers protested and demanded that *al-Manar* issue a retraction and refutation of the claims that had been made. Rida declined the request based on two arguments:

a   an editor is not required to pass judgment on everything he publishes;
b   Sidqi's opinion, that the Quran can be interpreted in a way that does not contradict Darwin's ideas should the theory of evolution be verified, is sound.[58]

In 1909, four years after 'Abduh's death, Rida published 'Abduh's exegesis of Q. 4:1. The text demonstrates that 'Abduh was aware of the need to accommodate scientific findings that undermined belief in Adam as the father of mankind, and understood the debate surrounding the religious legitimacy of such findings as an opportunity to emphasize the truth of Islamic revelation. There is some evidence that 'Abduh had been cognizant of the theory of evolution, and concerned with its implications, since the 1880s, though his sporadic observations did not accumulate into a coherent concept of the theory's potential legitimization or de-legitimization. In 1882, in an essay addressing the shortcomings of parliamentary decisions, he noted that it is Allah's law that things reach perfection only gradually.[59] Fifteen years later, in *Risalat al-Tawhid*, he argued that it is Allah's way to proceed in stages as man is nurtured from his birth to adulthood, and so is His way with the nurture of nations.[60] As noted in the previous chapter, in that book, 'Abduh rejected the theory of natural selection without specifically mentioning it.[61]

According to 'Abduh's 1909 exegesis, the statement in Q. 4:1 that Allah created human beings from one soul does not necessarily relate to Adam; this is one of several possible interpretations. In support of his position, 'Abduh argued that "one soul" is not in the definite article, and that the verse tells of dispersing from that one soul *many* males and females, rather than all the males and the females. This being the case, the notion that all of humanity directly descended from Adam should not be regarded as a conclusive text. The implication of this position is that holding that humanity descended from several sources does not contradict the revelation. 'Abduh saw the ambiguity of the Quran with regard to the origin of man as proof that it is an authentic revelation. Had the Prophet Muhammad composed the Quran himself, he would have presented a conclusive narrative commensurate with the beliefs of the monotheists of his time, i.e., a text whose literal meaning suggests that Adam was the father of all mankind. Instead, the Quran relates to the origin of man in a way that can be neither rejected by Jews nor by contemporary scientists who had presented proofs against the belief in common descent.[62]

A month after 'Abduh's exegesis appeared in *al-Manar*, Rida published—and wrote his own response to—an angry attack against Shibli Shumayyil penned by a Lebanese educator and journalist whom he greatly respected, 'Abd al-Qadir Qabbani. Rida's response amounted to another defense of the legitimacy of Darwin's ideas in *al-Manar*. According to Qabbani, Shumayyil's advocacy of the theory of evolution was a denial of creation and amounted to waging war against all monotheistic religions that should disqualify Shumayyil from serving as an elected representative in Istanbul. Qabbani wondered how it was possible that medical doctors, who of all people know the complexity of the human body, could deny creation. He further called for a distinction to be made between useful European sciences, which should be taught in Muslim lands and which Muslims can greatly contribute to their advancement, and the blasphemous, imaginative hypothesis called Darwinism, which should be rejected.

Rida did not find Qabbani's words unsettling at all, and used the controversy to highlight the idea that was at the core of his life-project: Islam is not the problem of Muslim societies, but rather misinterpretations and wrongful implementations of it are. He assured Qabbani that if Darwin's theory would be validated at some point, it would not contradict any principle of Islam and any verse in the Quran. Rida agreed that there are indeed, and regrettably so, medical doctors and other educated individuals who deny creation, but emphasized that there are also medical doctors who accept Darwin's theory while remaining faithful and devout Muslims. He suggested that the reason for disbelief among some educated individuals is due to having not been introduced to the one and only religion that is commensurate with science in the course of their studies. That "one and only religion" is Islam, but not Islam in its popular, distorted forms that allow room for superstitions such as grave-worshiping; those distortions damage Islam more than Darwin's theory does. An Islam true to itself, purified, will be embraced by medical doctors and chemists, by biologists and astronomers, and by jurists and politicians.[63]

A period of silence on Darwin followed. Then, in 1930, in response to a series of questions from members of an Islamic youth group, Rida published his most thorough treatment of Darwinism's legitimacy. By that time, particularly in the United States following the rise of the American fundamentalist movement and the 1925 Scopes Monkey Trial in Tennessee, the theory of evolution became the common point of division between loyalty to scientific truth and religious dogmatism. *Al-Manar* frequently reported and commented on events of import around the world, particularly those affecting the state of Muslims, including those addressing either their plight, or their inevitable ascendance. Nevertheless, the Scopes Monkey Trial, an event that could have potentially served to epitomize the modernist-apologetic claim for Islam's ability to better accommodate scientific discoveries than Christianity does, was not mentioned in Rida's discussion. It is not clear whether news about the trial reached Rida at all, and to what extent he was exposed to new literature that cast doubts on Darwin. It is evident, however, that by the 1930s he had become less impressed with the theory of evolution than he had been two decades earlier. Nevertheless, he remained convinced that theory posed no threat to the Muslim creed, but rather presented an opportunity to demonstrate its inherent truth.

Rida stated that his objective in discussing Darwinism was to examine whether the theory of evolution supports the principle, which he had repeatedly stressed elsewhere, that one of Islam's miracles is that not a single conclusive scientific truth contradicts the fundamentals of faith or conclusive verses from the revelation, which was transmitted in the seventh century by a Prophet who was illiterate upon receiving it. His inquiry suggested that the miracle remains intact; while the theory of evolution contradicts the Bible, it does not contradict the Quran.[64]

The editor of *al-Manar* wrote that some scholars in the West endorse Darwin's theory as the most logical explanation to date for the diversity of species and their origins, but even they do not consider it a final truth that could never be refuted, as the laws of math are; others reject the theory. While in the past the supporters of evolution had the upper hand, discoveries in psychology have increased the number of scholars who believe that human beings have independent souls that greatly affect their existence.[65] Many scholars have found flaws in the theory of evolution; some had been correct in their arguments against it, and some wrong.[66] Yet even if validated, Darwin's ideas do not contradict the revelation. Gradual evolution is supported by Q. 21:30 and 41:9–12 (describing Allah's gradualist creation of the heavens, earth and living creatures), as well as by 71:14 (according to which the creation of man was gradualist) and 15:26 (according to which man was created from clay). While several verses reveal that Allah created the heavens and the earth in six days, a day in Arabic does not necessarily imply 24 hours and thus this time span should be interpreted as describing ages in which different stages of evolution occurred, an interpretation that the Biblical account of Creation does not allow.[67]

Rida noted that the likeness between certain fossils, the likeness between certain fossils and certain living creatures, and the likeness between certain living creatures that have no matching fossils had not been sufficiently explained by Darwin's theory (Indeed, in the early twentieth century, the dominant view among paleontologists, particularly in Germany and the United States, was anti-Darwinist; they held that discovered fossil records do not support the theory).[68] Nevertheless, Rida maintained that much of Darwin's explanation with regard to such likenesses asserts Allah's control over His Creation and, if the explanation would be proven true, it would not contradict any verse in the Quran.[69] Islamic religious scholars, long before Darwin, had noted the likenesses and differences between species, as well as the hierarchy between them. However, this does not suggest that species have the same common origin, but rather that they originate from one Creator.[70] Furthermore, the claim that some organs have no function in the body (and thus prove that evolution occurred), even if proven true, neither contradicts any verse or fundamental of the faith nor does it demonstrate that one species evolved from another. Indeed, the fact that we do not know today what functions those organs play does not mean that we will not know what those functions are in the future.[71]

The final time Rida addressed the theory of evolution, two years before his death, was an addendum to his broader, bitter quarrel with Yusuf al-Dajawi, a member of al-Azhar's Council of Senior Scholars. Their sardonic exchanges reveal just how controversial the religious legitimacy of evolution was in Egypt in the mid-1930s; they also show that Rida, as he neared death, was more disposed than ever before to the position that Darwin was wrong, but this did not affect his steadfast conviction that the Quran is reconcilable with Darwin's theory. In September 1932, al-Dajawi, apparently convinced that Rida's views on the origin of man were a soft spot, attacked *al-Manar*'s interpretation of Q. 4:1, and Rida's contention that Darwin's theory is reconcilable with the Quran, noting that the theory of evolution contradicts 3:59 (on the creation of Adam from dust) and other information given in the Quran and in the traditions. Adding that many Europeans despise the theory of evolution, he implied that Rida's opinion amounts to blasphemy.[72] It took Rida half a year to respond. He referenced his previous writings on the matter, including 'Abduh's exegesis, his response to Qabbani from 1909, and his detailed essay from 1930 (he also referenced al-Jisr's treatise), and asserted that even if Darwin's theory were proven, it would not affect the foundations of Islam. However, Rida also emphasized that he never believed that the theory of evolution had been proven true.[73]

A Contested Legacy

The Cairo Trilogy by Naguib Mahfouz offers a masterful depiction of Egypt's struggle for independence and ill-timed transformation from a revelation-based to a doubt-based society. The novels, written in the 1950s, describe the disintegration of a patriarchal family in Cairo between the two World Wars. The youngest son, Kamal, loses his faith and becomes an ascetic teacher and confirmed bachelor. His heart is wholly given over to Western philosophy and science; he even publishes an article about Darwin in a literary journal. To his horror, his father, the daunting and unwaveringly religious—yet hypocritical and morally corrupt—Ahmad 'Abd al-Jawad, gets his hand on the piece. The father summons his son and orders him to recant his heresy. Darwin, says the father, is "certainly an atheist trapped by Satan's snares." He continues:

> If man's origin was an ape or any other animal, Adam was not the father of mankind. This is nothing but blatant atheism. It's an outrageous attack on the exalted status of God. I know Coptic Christians and Jews in the Goldsmiths Bazaar. They believe in Adam. All religions believe in Adam. What sect does this Darwin belong to? [...] You can rely on a fact that's beyond doubt: God created Adam from dust, and Adam's the father of mankind. This fact is mentioned in the Quran. Just explain the erroneous aspects of the theory. That'll be easy for you. If it isn't, what's the use of your education?[74]

It follows from the survey of early Muslim views on Darwin and the responses those views provoked that 'Abd al-Jawad's fictional words echoed ideas articulated by Egyptian religious scholars. These religious figures considered Darwinism to be a blasphemous attack against Islam and monotheism at large that cannot be reconciled with the Quran in any way, and regarded its teaching in schools, universities and media to be a conscious attack on the foundations of society. The unease these Muslims felt with Darwin was similar to that which consumed American fundamentalists.

Contrary to some common misconceptions, the formative works of the modernist-apologetic approach itself were ambiguous with regard to the theory of evolution. Al-Afghani's first treatment utterly rejected the validity of the theory and Rida's final treatment, five decades later, stated that the theory had not been proven. No modernist-apologetic text written in the meantime accepted Darwinism as a confirmed scientific theory. For al-Jisr and Rida, however, the theory of evolution became an essential demonstration of the marvel of Islamic revelation and its potential to be reconciled with any discovery or innovation. In presenting it as such they supported an argument that was at the core of the modernist-apologetic view. They also, inadvertently, exposed a lacuna in their theorization on the relation between Islam and science—the absence of a systematic, clear method as to how and who should decide when a scientific theory has been proven beyond doubt and reached the stage that calls for allegorizing of verses whose literal meanings seem contradictory. The judgments they passed so confidently on scientific issues on which they were not experts suggest they considered religious scholars to be qualified to serve as ultimate arbitrators. But no method was offered as to how differences *between* religious scholars should be resolved.

During the 1940s and the 1950s, apologetics on Darwinism such as those introduced by al-Jisr and Rida diminished and views describing the theory of evolution as blasphemous found ardent supporters among influential intellectuals in the

Muslim world. One of them, the Indian Abu al-A'la Mawdudi (1903–1979), the founder of Islamism in South Asia, argued in an article published in 1944 that the theory of evolution is unsubstantiated and logically unsound. He considered it a materialist philosophy that contradicts Islam because it denies that life began by God's order, and considered its moral effects on humanity devastating because by teaching humans that they are just one kind of animal it turned them into animals.[75] Mawdudi's anti-evolution position was adopted by several of his disciples. His most renowned student in the Arab world, Abu al-Hasan al-Nadwi (1914–1999), argued in *What the World Lost with the Downfall of the Muslims*, a book that had a profound impact in Egyptian Islamist circles in the early 1950s, that the theory of evolution greatly enhanced the rise of materialism in the West, that it contradicted both religion and logic, and constituted a new religion that undermined the foundations of Old Europe. He suggested that the theory attracted Westerners despite its falsity because it challenged religion and the Church establishment.[76] Sayyid Qutb (who was greatly impressed with al-Nadwi's work,[77] and possibly influenced by it on this point), rejected Darwin's theory in his exegesis of the Quran, specifically the idea that humankind can be the result of "blind coincidence."[78]

The two conflicting legacies of late nineteenth and early and mid-twentieth century Islamic scholarship on the theory of evolution—that it is potentially true and reconcilable with the Quran and that it is invalid and a heresy—echoed decades later in the scholarship of Muhammad al-Ghazali, Yusuf al-Qaradawi and Muhammad 'Imara. Unlike the luminaries of the modernist-apologetic school, they came to be convinced that Darwinism was a fraudulent lie and an anti-Islamic theory. This radical shift was encouraged by events that took place thousands of miles away from Egypt.

B. The Evolution of Darwin to a Christian Peculiarity in Contemporary Modernist-Apologetic Thought

In a book he published in 1980, the turn of a new Muslim century, Muhammad al-Ghazali suggested that Darwinism should not be regarded as part of the modern scientific revolution, but rather as one of its unfortunate by-products. Al-Ghazali listed, with great admiration, several achievements of modern science, including the discoveries of epidemic bacteria, electricity and the position of earth in the solar system, as well as the utilization of nuclear energy and the conquest of space. Yet, he lamented that this scientific renaissance had come at a price. Many Westerners began to believe in science alone, worshiping and sanctifying it. They preached that the age of religion had come to an end and was never again to return. The process of religious decline, argued al-Ghazali, was encouraged in the West by two theories. The first was Freud's, which claimed that human beings, just as animals, are subordinate to beastly whims and passions. The other was Darwin's, which argued that man belongs to the *fasila* (species or family) of the apes, and, in doing so, contradicted the narrative of all monotheistic religions on the creation of Adam by God as His successor (*khalifa*) on earth.[79]

Writing in 1985, al-Ghazali further delegitimized the theory of evolution. He accused Darwin of introducing the notion that man, having originated from apes, is nothing more than a developed animal, and, moreover, should take pride in his lineage because apes are morally better than humans, who kill one another for no reason. According to al-Ghazali, this notion clearly contradicts the religious belief that Allah distinguished between human beings, His successors on earth, and other animals.[80]

If any doubts were left as to Darwinism's standing in al-Ghazali's thought, his aforementioned column from 1992 on the implications of Islamizing the sciences dispelled them. In that article, he promised that this process would only reform, rather than terminate, the treatment of modern, empirical sciences. Yet, this reform would not allow space for erroneous theories. Life sciences, he wrote, would still be studied, but they would be studied in line with Allah's verses on the universe which He created, and Darwin's fairytales about the origin of species, natural selection and evolution would be recognized, from a scientific point of view, for what they really were—baseless notions that people will finally be protected from.[81] Writing a year later, al-Ghazali argued that in studying the natural world Darwin had fulfilled an Islamic duty; however, Darwin's great shame was that he was not aware of the final revelation when he came to his conclusions.[82]

Al-Ghazali's comments marked a break from the modernist-apologetic legacy on Darwin. Whereas al-Jisr and Rida did not accept the theory of evolution as more than a hypothesis—but nevertheless defended its potential religious legitimacy should it ever be satisfactorily proven—al-Ghazali believed that the theory inherently conflicted with Islam and undermined its foundations. His words also marked a shift – albeit a less pronounced one – from his own sympathetic position towards Darwin's legitimacy in the 1960s, which was consistent with al-Jisr's and Rida's theorizing. At that time, he emphasized, while describing how blood circulates through the body and suggesting that no reasonable person could argue that this system developed without a designated purpose, that Darwin himself was not an atheist; that the theory of evolution did not suggest that the world was not formed by a Creator; and that even if the theory were proved right, it would not have any effect on faith.[83]

The view of Darwin's theory as wrong, blasphemous, corruptive, dangerous, and the epitome of a declining, Godless culture has been articulated also by al-Qaradawi and 'Imara since the 1980s. In 2003, a woman asked whether it was permissible to play the popular Japanese video-game Pokémon. Al-Qaradawi ruled that it was not, and listed a number of reasons. The first suggested he believed the theory of evolution to be a great danger:

> The cartoon contains items that run counter to the Muslim's creed, as it indirectly tries to give support to the controversial Darwin's theory of evolution, which indicates that every living species undergoes a gradual development, in the sense that the existing species produce new ones through adaptation to new surroundings. According to this theory, man, before

reaching his present form, has undergone a series of evolutionary changes, from simpler forms up to the stages of being in the form of an ape, deemed to be closely related to man. This cartoon tries to enhance this theory, by instilling in children's minds Darwin's idea on the gradual development of characteristics of insects.[84]

The issuance of *fatwa*s that are detached from the reality of popular culture and are easy prey for ridicule, such as the one above, is not common for al-Qaradawi. His unease with Darwinism is demonstrated by the fact that the other reasons for the impermissibility of Pokémon only appear further down on his list, including that the game encourages violence and gambling, and that it "contains some signs that have their meanings and [are] known to their proponents, like 'The Hexa Star', which has something to do with the Zionists and Masons."[85]

Other discussions by al-Qaradawi further revealed unfavorable views of Darwinism and the delegitimizing of its teaching in Muslim societies. In a book exploring, ironically, Islam's concept of democracy, al-Qaradawi assured his readers that the Islamization of the natural sciences would have only one impact—an affinity would be established between the way these sciences are studied and the philosophical view that man was created by Allah, that the laws governing man are the laws of Allah, and that nothing in the world happens by chance. This statement practically closes the door to the teaching of Darwinism in Muslim schools.[86]

Another example is al-Qaradawi's book *The Culture of Proselytizing*, in which he explained why it is imperative that proselytizers acquire scientific knowledge. Proselytizers should gain knowledge in humanistic fields and social studies to better understand people, *zeitgeist*s and discourses, and in the life and the exact sciences, because these fields have become a vital aspect of modern life and, furthermore, can be utilized to support religious truths. However, caution must be exercised in the process of study, so as to not allow the penetration of ideas which are contrary to the foundations of Islam. In social studies al-Qaradawi warned against Freud's, Durkheim's and Marx's theories,[87] while in the life sciences he warned against Darwin's theory, as means that undermine the truth of Islam.[88]

Speaking on the occasion of Darwin's bicentennial, al-Qaradawi argued that the direct, intended creation of man is a foundation of all monotheistic religions and that Allah created man to be His successor on earth. While belief in evolution does not necessarily lead to denial of the Creator, it runs the risk of persuading people that everything is transitional and there are no constants in life, whereas in Islam the foundations of faith and its moral values do not change. Applying the cyclical logic of the modernist-apologetic school, he stated that Islam encourages free thinking and investigation of Creation, but only if drawn from the premise that a Creator exists.[89]

'Imara further developed the rejection of Darwinism arguing that the theory was no more than an aberration that reveals the uniqueness of Western societies and their troubled history. Writing in the late 1980s in a book on the reality of a Western "cultural attack" on the Muslim world, he began by noting that evolution is an inseparable part of existence. He cited several verses to support this statement (Q. 23:12–16; 40:67; 32:8–9; 75:36–40; 30:54; 22:5; 2:260, all but the last of which deal with Allah's Creation of humankind). All human civilizations, argued 'Imara, including Muslim civilization, acknowledge evolution to be true, but Western society is the only civilization that used evolution as the foundation of an ideology that holds everything, rather than some things, to be subject to constant change. 'Imara considered Darwin to both represent and shape the Western mindset that rejects constants. He suggested that the flawed theory according to which all living species have one common origin and that man originated from an ape should be regarded as a "Western addition" of materialist-atheist essence to the universal rule of evolution. This "Western addition" and its concept of the "survival of the fittest" had served as justification and legitimization for the colonialist enterprises that wrought destruction in other civilizations.[90]

According to 'Imara, Darwin's theory is not the only Western theory that claims to be universally true but in fact constitutes an expression of Western uniqueness; so is Hegel's interpretation of history. Hegel's dialectical philosophy correctly acknowledges that ideas evolve as societies progress, but mistakenly holds that all ideas are subject to change, as if change is the only constant thing in life, failing to recognize the existence of fundamentals that are not subject to change. Karl Marx, too, represents the Western mindset that rejects constants; Marxism is the social variation of Darwin's belief in constant biological evolution and Hegel's belief in constant ideological evolution. The theory on a totalistic class struggle should be considered another demonstration of "Western uniqueness" that falsely portrays itself as a universal truth.[91]

Why has Western civilization so eagerly embraced mistaken concepts of constant evolution? 'Imara suggested as an explanation a core narrative of the modernist-apologetic approach, according to which relations between Christianity and sciences are a tragic historical exception: in the days when the Church dominated Christian societies, it froze any advancement and progress, whether material, ideological or scientific; the Church regarded as constants even those things which are universally recognized as subject to change. When Western societies experienced their Renaissance, they reacted by exaggerating the importance of change at the expense of constants.[92]

In essence, Western obsession with evolution is, in 'Imara's view, a product of the heritage of a despotic Church that was an enemy of scientific thought; given that Islam's approach to science is different, as is the historical experience of Muslims, there is no reason for Muslims to accept the Western canard that is the theory of evolution as a universal truth. Whereas Rida considered Darwin's theory an example of the advantage of Islam over Christianity because, unlike the Bible, it demonstrates the harmony of the Quran with empirical science, 'Imara considered Darwin's theory an example of that advantage because its acceptance in the West despite its falsity tells of the scientific freedom that Islam allows and Christianity does not.

In his book *The Islamic State between Secularism and a Religious Regime*, 'Imara elaborated on the crucial difference between Islam's heritage of scientific freedom and the heritage of Christianity. Christian clerics, he argued, held that their religion has a say in all scientific fields, and that they have the right to declare certain theories and ideas as blasphemous. In Islam, however, a division was established between *shar'i* sciences, that relate to the foundations of religion and whose primary reference is the revelation, and worldly sciences, such as chemistry, astronomy and medicine, which are universal, and whose primary reference are facts derived through rationalist investigations.[93] According to 'Imara, the reason there is no animosity between Islam and the worldly sciences is that, unlike in Christianity, in Islam religion is not relevant (*la madkhal*) to those sciences.[94] 'Imara's treatment of Darwin contradicts his historical-philosophical observations: his rejection of the theory of evolution as a Western ideological peculiarity was not based on relevant expertise and constitutes theological intervention in the field of the life sciences.

The notion of Darwinism as an ideology, rather than a scientific theory, resonated in other Arab-Islamic apologias. A number of Islamists argued, based on the fabricated "Protocols of the Elders of Zion," that the Jews propagated Darwin's theory in order to destroy what remained of faith in Western societies and subordinate those societies to Jewish interests (Western imperialism, in turn, sought to destroy faith in Muslim societies through the diffusion of Darwinism and other infidel ideologies).[95] Darwinism's unique position in Arab scholarship is revealed by the fact that no other leading figure from the fields of the exact or life sciences is the subject of similar conspiracy theories (Einstein received similar treatment in the Palestinian newspaper *Filastin* in 1923, but Arab reactions to his personality and work generally showed great respect,[96] and his theory of relativity is not challenged today by Islamic scholars). There is no trace of anti-Semitic comments in 'Imara's writing on evolution. However, he does consider Muslims' embrace of Darwinism as submission to the grand Western conspiracy that utilizes an array of cultural and ideological means to undermine faith and subordinate Muslim societies without resorting to arms. To accept the ideology of Darwinism is, in 'Imara's view, an act of Westernizing and, thus, a betrayal of Islam.[97]

The Rise of Scientific Creationism

Why have contemporary modernist-apologists so confidently shifted from the opinion of their school's founders, according to which Darwinism is potentially compatible with Islam, to the opinion that it is a dangerous, anti-Islamic theory, a Western aberration and exception? The answer is revealed in passing in a number of their texts.

Whereas al-Jisr and Rida considered Darwinism a hypothesis that had not yet been proven or disproven, the scholars who built upon their legacy became convinced that Darwin's theory had been, over the course of time, proven false. 'Imara suggested that Western scientists acknowledged that the theory of evolution was based on deficient induction.[98] Al-Ghazali was convinced that there are "missing links" in the theory that invalidate it; discussing the "disease of atheism," he wrote that Darwin's "closest students" refuted the majority of his hypotheses and, as a result, the theory declined in importance.[99] In yet another article he recalled that in high school he had learned that man originated from an ape; that theory, he wrote, negates religion, yet it had been undermined over the years.[100] Relying on al-Jisr, al-Qaradawi stated that should the theory of evolution ever be validated, it would be possible to reconcile it with the Quran through allegorizing; however, in the same breath, he added that the theory had been refuted "even" by "the biologists." The biologists came to hold that Darwin fabricated some of his proofs, and, moreover, that Darwin based his conclusions on artifacts that were later found to have been forged by others.[101]

As stated before, the modernist-apologetic theory recognizes three possible situations with regard to scientific theories and their reconciliation with the reve-lation: they either have been proven true, in which case possible contradictions with the literal meaning of the revelation require the reinterpretation of verses; have neither been proven true or false, in which case caution and further inquiry are required; or have been disproven scientifically, in which case allegorizing becomes illegitimate, and the theories must be vociferously rejected if they expli-citly undermine the foundations of faith. Based on this equation, the shift of the contemporary modernist-apologists to unmitigated rejection of the theory of evo-lution makes perfect sense. Having been convinced that a theory that had never been popular in Islamic religious circles, and which had challenged their intuition, their core religious beliefs and their literal interpretations of the revelation had been sufficiently disproved by science, contemporary modernist-apologists were content that attacking Darwinism did not risk undermining their core concept of absolute reconcilability between science and revelation, and were thus ready, even eager, to present it as fraudulent and unacceptable.

A more complicated question is why and how the contemporary luminaries of the modernist-apologetic school came to be convinced that the theory of evolution is a fallacy. To answer it, we must turn our attention to the development of the anti-evolutionist discourse in the United States and the incorporation of this dis-course into Arab, and other Muslim, discourses on Darwin. Exploring these develop-ments conveys much about the potential implications of the modernist-apologetic method of allegorizing for scientific freedom.

On January 15, 1927, a bare majority of Tennessee's Supreme Court upheld the constitutionality of the law prohibiting the teaching of Darwinism, while also reversing John Scopes' verdict on a technicality.[102] Following the Scopes affair, efforts to criminalize the teaching of evolution declined across Southern states in America. Only one—Mississippi—followed Tennessee by enacting a similar law to that effect. In Tennessee, while attempts to repeal the law were rebuffed by the Tennessee State Legislature in 1927 and 1929, and two high school principals were charged with violating it, a more tolerant spirit nevertheless manifested itself and, in some parts of the state, educators did not hesitate to teach the theory.[103] But the trial also yielded consequences that equally damaged the cause of science. For the next three decades, responding to market pressure, and in the case of several Southern states, to official requirements, virtually all publishers removed Darwin's ideas about evolution as the unifying theme of life from their biology textbooks, or treated them with great caution.[104] By 1942, less than 50 percent of American high school biology teachers included the theory of evolution in their curriculum.[105]

Then, a dramatic change occurred. Following the Soviet Union's successful launch of the artificial satellite Sputnik in October 1957, a wave of panic swept across an American public who had seen its technological superiority challenged, and President Eisenhower led an initiative to massively reform and fund science education. Amid the intensity of the Cold War, subordinating science to religious dogmas was a luxury the United States could not afford. A primary consequence of the new reforms was the introduction of new and improved biology textbooks including sections on evolution, which were integrated in classrooms across the country despite some protest from Christian fundamentalists.[106]

In 1968, the U.S. Supreme Court overturned an Arkansas law forbidding the teaching of evolution, deeming it unconstitutional. The ruling established that a state was not permitted to prohibit the teaching of a scientific doctrine merely because it conflicted with the doctrines of a particular religious denomination.[107] The fundamentalists realized that the battle to forestall the teaching of evolution in classrooms was lost. This realization, coupled with concern that a new, more skeptical generation would not accept the Biblical account of creation based exclusively on theological argumentations, encouraged a major shift in tactics. Instead of trying to ban evolution, anti-evolutionists began fighting to give the Creation narrative equal time in classrooms, and instead of appealing to the authority of the Bible, they consciously downplayed the Genesis story in favor of developing and propagating pseudoscientific argumentations.[108]

At the heart of the position promoted by Creationist scientists is the idea that there are two, and only two, possible answers to the question of the origin of the universe and all life: the theistic model of creation, and the "atheistic" model of evolution.[109] Scientific Creationists focused on exposing discrepancies and gaps in the theory of evolution and arguing that the idea that the earth and all living organisms originate from the Almighty's deliberate actions provides a more satisfactory explanation of the scientific evidence.[110] In its various forms—some reluctant to accept any scientific theory or finding that appears to contradict a literal reading of Genesis, and others that are more accommodating—Scientific Creationism characterized the theory of evolution as something that fell between a flawed scientific theory and a religious creed which is not scientific at all. A favored argument they promoted, drawn from Popper, is that since Darwinism could not be falsified, it is by definition not science.[111] Since the 1970s, Creationists intensively circulated their ideas through conferences, public lectures and debates, articles, newsletters, books and movies with scientific pretense. Some of their activities acquired an institutionalized academic form with the establishment of research centers—such as the Institute for Creation Research, founded by the Texas engineer and preeminent Creationist author Henry Morris (1918–2006).[112]

The core of Scientific Creationism as it developed in the United States—the assumption that a supernatural Creator functions outside the constraints of natural law—cannot be accepted as scientifically meaningful by mainstream scientists.[113] The lack of Creationists possessing academic credentials also undermined their authority in the eyes of qualified biologists; save few exceptions—most notably, the passionate debater Duane T. Gish (1921–2013), who held a doctorate in biochemistry from the University of California—most were not trained in the life sciences.[114] Nevertheless, they remained undeterred despite being dismissed by confirmed life and exact scientists as religious crusaders masking themselves as scientists. One of their more appealing arguments has been, drawing on Kuhn's study on *The Structure of Scientific Revolutions*, that scientists should not be denied space within the scientific curriculum just because they are an embattled minority, and that denying them such space amounts to censorship and the prevention of a legitimate and essential competition between scientific models.[115]

Throughout their struggle, American Creation scientists continuously failed to make their case not only on the academic front, but also on the legal one. Bills passed during the 1980s in at least 26 state legislatures, which required teachers to dedicate equal time to the instruction of the Creationist narrative and evolution, were declared unconstitutional.[116] But while Scientific Creationism lost the battle for institutional and constitutional legitimacy in the United States, it has not entirely lost the battle for the hearts and minds of the American public. One reason for this is that the literature Creationists produce can, to quote Barker, "appear highly impressive not just to the already committed fundamentalist but also to the intelligent lay person who is prepared to listen."[117] Among substantial segments of American society, the theory of evolution has remained doggedly illegitimate. A 2005 poll conducted by the Pew Forum on Religious and Public Life reported that 38 percent of Americans would prefer that creationism was taught instead of evolution theory.[118] A national survey conducted in 2007 among American high school biology teachers found that 17 percent do not cover human evolution in the classrooms, and no less than 25 percent taught Creationism, of which half agreed or strongly agreed that is a valid scientific alternative to Darwinism.[119] In a Gallup poll conducted in 1982, 45 percent of the American public agreed with the statement that "God created human beings pretty much in their present form at one time within the last 10,000 years or so"; the results were similar in a poll conducted in 2004.[120]

Scientific Creationism in the Arab World

Another achievement of American Scientific Creationism was the spread of its literature and the diffusion of its agenda across the globe,[121] even among non-Christian societies. In the Arab world, beginning in the 1980s, a wave of publications that celebrated Darwin's "final" defeat appeared. These included Muhammad 'Ali Yusuf's *The Downfall of Darwinism* (1983), 'Abd al-Razzaq Nawfal's *Man and Monkey and the Downfall of Darwin* (1984), Mahir Khalil's *The Downfall of Darwin's Theory in Light of New Scientific Discoveries* (1986), Ziyad Abu Ghanima's *Science Disavows from Darwin's Theory, The Greatest Case of Scientific Fabrication in the History of Science: Documented Investigations* (1989), and Talib Janabi's *Darwin's Evolutionism: Superstitions Disguised as Science* (1989). As observed by Danner, there developed no Arab equivalent to the American phenomenon of "Creationist scientists."[122] However, partly due to the impact of Christian fundamentalist scholars, theological treatises bearing the appearance of scientific literature came to dominate the Arab religious discourse on Darwin. Authors, none of whom were life scientists by training, eagerly embraced pseudoscientific refutations of a theory which contradicted some revealed passages and which had drawn strong denunciations from Islamic scholars from its beginning. They argued that Darwin's ideas have been discredited by all Western scientists who are not agenda-driven, and suggested that one cannot be a believer and accept the theory of evolution.

Yusuf opened his book by declaring that while Darwin was not the first to theorize on evolution, he was, nevertheless, interested only in Darwin because of his unparalleled impact on atheist thought that fights against faith.[123] Yusuf's book suggested that Darwinism had been refuted in the West, or had become, at the very least, highly controversial. He relied on a number of American anti-Darwinist sources, including Norman Macbeth, author of *Darwin Retried* (1971) and the aforementioned Duane Gish. He quoted Gish's words that to many "well-informed" scientists creation seems to be far superior to evolution.[124] While Yusuf remained loyal to the early modernist-apologetic opinion that Darwin's theory, if validated, would be reconcilable with the Quran, he argued that it is "impossible" that Darwinism would ever be validated.[125]

Nawfal (d. 1984), an Egyptian agronomist by training and author of treatises on Islam's compatibility with science, argued that scientists in the West acknowledge that they hold firm to the unsubstantiated theory of evolution only because the alternative is believing in direct creation by Allah.[126] Khalil, an Egyptian and geologist by training (who was encouraged to investigate the topic by Anwar al-Jundi (d. 2002), a prolific author of Islamic apologias) presented a plethora of findings to contradict Darwin's theory, in part based on American Creationist literature. He argued that faced with these findings, contemporary scientists in the West had divided into two camps: irrational atheists, who still accept Darwin's theory even though it had been invalidated, and scientists who, having realized that the theory is a fabrication, reject it.[127] He divided Muslim scholars, historically, into three camps: those who utterly rejected Darwinism outright (he praised al-Afghani for his early insightfulness); those who utterly embraced Darwinism as part of their secularizing agenda; and those, like Rashid Rida, who erroneously toiled to reconcile the theory of evolution with Islam, despite the fact that there is nothing in the Quran or the Prophetic traditions to suggest that man evolved from animals.[128]

Abu Ghanima (b. 1937), a Jordanian historian and Muslim Brothers activist who, in the 1980s and early 1990s, served as head of the movement's Jordanian communication bureau, based most of his refutation of Darwinism on Western sources. He presented the polemic on the theory of evolution as a clear-cut struggle between the faithful, who cannot accept any truth other than that Allah created man, and the atheists, who deny this truth and claim that man developed independently.[129] Abu Ghanima's refutation rested on two foundations. One, a personal attack on the character of Charles Darwin in which Abu Ghanima, drawing on a selective reading of biographical data, presented Darwin as a troubled individual who could not be trusted because he suffered from family issues, ill health and mental problems, and was judged by those who knew him to lack the diligence and the methodicalness that are essential for a scientist.[130] To his personal defamation of Darwin, Abu Ghanima added a lengthy deliberation in support of his argument that there is no single piece of evidence that proves Darwin's theory true, while there is plenty of evidence that invalidates it. Notable on the list of American and English anti-Darwinists discussed by Abu Ghanima is Duane Gish.[131] As did Khalil, Abu Ghanima did not consider the criticism of anti-Darwinist scholarship in the West and ignored the fact that Darwin's theory is broadly accepted by qualified scientists in contemporary times. Thus, it was reasonable for him to conclude that a faithful Muslim cannot interpret the Quran in a way that is reconcilable with Darwin's theory, as a number of verses (Q. 32:7, 10:34, 41:21, 18:48, 6:94) indicate that man was created in his full and perfected form by Allah.[132]

Science-laden criticisms of Darwin were introduced into the Arab world also by non-Arab propagators. In Turkey during the 1970s, some religious scholars began to more vocally express their opposition to the theory of evolution. Their concerns, which were inspired in part by the works of American Creation scientists, won, in 1983, official endorsement in a national cultural policy plan that attacked Darwin as an apostle of materialism. This endorsement was part of the Turkish military government's attempts to reach out to religious conservatives and, later, constituted part of the conservative government's policies.[133] In the 1990s, Scientific Creationism began to flourish in Turkish popular and academic discourses.[134] Pseudoscientific refutations of Darwin have arguably gained their broadest reach through the initiatives of the prolific Turkish author Harun Yahya ('Adnan Oktar, b. 1956 in Ankara), who heavily borrowed his negative observations on the theory of evolution from the aforementioned Institute for Creation Research.[135] Yahya's intense efforts (over 200 books have been released in his name)[136] have achieved global notoriety,[137] and some of his literature has been translated into Arabic.[138] His preaching that Darwinism is a "satanic plot" that nurtures terrorism around the world is diffused through a massive media operation whose financers have never been disclosed.[139]

Across Muslim communities, including in the West, rejection of the theory of evolution has come to be promoted as a hallmark of religious devotion.[140] Islamic Creationist literature makes it clear, as does its American predecessor, that one can either believe in the theory of evolution or in God, and that the former belief is both blasphemous and absurd. In the words of the leaflet "Dialogue with an Atheist," added to this author's collection during a visit to Reykjavik's al-Rahman mosque:

> Evolution theory or "Darwinism" is a desperate try to explain the existence of
> life on earth. This theory serves as the scientific foundation of the philosophy

of "materialism" that rejects the existence of God the Creator [...] the evolution theory depended mostly on a person's powers of imagination due to the lack of high technology at the time. After the discovery of inheritance laws by Gregor Mendel in 1865 and the discovery of the DNA in 1950s, the evolution theory collapsed. This is because DNA molecule and cell construction are so complex that is it impossible to believe that such complexity could happen by chance through the evolutionary mechanisms proposed by Darwinism. Thousands of scientists around the world refuted the evolution theory and many books have been written to clarify its invalidity. Nowadays evolution theory is nothing but history.[141]

Efforts to delegitimize the theory of evolution have failed to banish it from public education in much of the Muslim world. Saudi Arabia, where the biology textbook produced by the Ministry of Education disparagingly characterizes Darwin as an atheist who denied Creation and laments the acceptance of his theory by some Muslims, is the exception not the norm.[142] Nevertheless, where it is taught, caution is exercised. A survey of high school textbooks from 2014 established that in Egypt, Malaysia, Pakistan, Syria and Turkey Darwin's theory of natural selection is discussed with examples, and paleontological evidence supporting evolution is provided—but human evolution is not mentioned.[143] The theory is highly unpopular among the general publics in most Muslim countries surveyed, indicating that the campaigns against it are effective. A survey of religious patterns conducted in 2007 suggests that only eight percent of Egyptians agree that it is probably or most certainly true, compared to 16 percent of Indonesians, 14 percent of Pakistanis, 11 percent of Malaysians, and 22 percent of Turks who agree with this statement.[144]

How much from the plethora of anti-Darwinist pseudoscientific literature, in Arabic and other languages, reached al-Ghazali, al-Qaradawi and 'Imara and aided in shaping their firm delegitimization of the theory of evolution? As is often the case in their writings on areas of knowledge that is not theological, their conclusion that the theory of evolution had been proven wrong was not supported by references. One cannot avoid the impression that they have not read any relevant primary texts. It is, however, evident that what they have learned about Darwin was, in their minds, trustworthy enough to dispel any doubts as to the falsity of theory of evolution in scientific terms.

In the context of our discussion on the modernist-apologetic concept of scientific freedom, identifying the precise texts that swayed the three away from considering Darwinism religiously tolerable is of lesser importance. Of greater importance is recognizing that this shift occurred at a time when the theory of evolution had already been firmly established by biologists as the foundation for the study of the life sciences, and its religiously motivated scientific refutation had already been rejected by mainstream scientists as groundless. In declaring Darwinism a baseless, illegitimate theory, the luminaries of contemporary modernist-apologetic thought acted as the ultimate arbiters of scientific truth and fallacy—and of the permissible and prohibited—and in this role they chose a non-scientific refutation of science over actual science only because it better conformed to their preexisting beliefs and agenda.

C. Modernist-Apologetic Scientific Freedom in Liberal Thought

It follows from this discussion that the modernist-apologetic school has not introduced a coherent concept of scientific freedom, one that lives up to its core promise of closing the door to arbitrary theocratic interventions in the conclusions reached by scientists based on empirical observations and logical analyses. On the one hand, the modernist-apologists have consistently presented, since the late nineteenth century, a revivalist approach to Islam that elevates the advancement of science and technology to a principle religious duty, and reestablishes a centuries-long method of allegorizing that makes possible the reconciliation of any scientific theory, model or fact with the Quran. These achievements should not be understated, or discounted. They create, drawing on a claim of fundamentalist authenticity, potential space for revelation-based acceptance of scientific discoveries that contradict the literal meaning of revealed passages, which Christianity, in its fundamentalist forms, has denied.

But the restrictive aspects of the modernist-apologetic approach to science are far greater than it its propagators have ever been ready to admit. First, while the modernist-apologists suggested that everything, first and foremost faith in Allah, His Prophet and His revelation, is subject to independent rational inquiry, their argumentations have made any choice other than absolute faith in the fundamentals of Islam unacceptable, and practically excluded matters of theological creed from the domain of legitimate academic investigations. Second, while they praised the importance of the exact, life and social sciences, they left no room for scientific explorations that are independent of religious motivations or contexts. Third, while they emphasized that their methodology can always accommodate revelation to proven science they did not debate the problem of certainty and never introduced a clear concept of interpretive authority. The problem of certainty was avoided for a reason. To recognize that the implementation of their concept of scientific freedom requires the formation of a mechanism to determine scientific certainty and legitimacy would have required the modernist-apologists to consider whether that arbitrating-mechanism should be dominated by theologians. A society in which religious scholars hold the ultimate authority to legitimize scientific inquiries has a name, according to the terminologies applied by the modernist-apologetics themselves: a theocracy. The establishment of such a society would undermine the entire modernist-apologetic project, which rests on the promise that an Islamized, revelation-based society will not be theocratic.

Darwin's theory of evolution is the most significant example, but only one of several, of the potential implications of subjecting the legitimacy of scientific theories to the approval of theologians, whether they are literalist or modernist. Decades-long treatments of Darwinism by modernist-apologists concluded in opposition to the theory of evolution in a way that is not dissimilar to the criticisms leveled by literalist elements in both Christian fundamentalist and Muslim *wahhabi* orientations. In theory, the modernist-apologetic concept of science and religion allows for the reconciliation of any scientific theory with the revelation. In practice, some of the most basic and essential modern scientific theories have been rejected by contemporary modernist-apologists as being unqualified to justify reconciliations.

This raises questions regarding the ultimate fate of scientific inquiries in a Muslim society that embraces the modernist-apologetic concept of science in an institutionalized form. For what is to become of scientific studies and scientific education in a society where, in the name of complying with religious injunctions, and despite the promise for an everlasting peace between science and religion, the theory of evolution—as well as the Big Bang Theory, psychoanalysis and other essential concepts—will be banned?

In Egypt, as elsewhere in the Arab world, it is hardly permitted, today, to apply critical scientific methods in the study of religion (even less than was permitted a hundred years ago). But studies of the natural world have, at least officially, been protected from direct theological interventions. One can only speculate whether a regime inspired by and committed to modernist-apologetic teachings will, de facto, introduce limitations along the lines suggested by al-Ghazali, al-Qaradawi and 'Imara. The brief spell of the Muslim Brothers' rule in Egypt did not see the imposing of any measures that limited scientific freedom, but it was too brief and fragile to provide a true indication. The constitution they passed in December 2012 maintained a sense of ambivalence: while it safeguarded and emphasized the importance of scientific freedom and the independence of universities (part 2, article 59), it also stressed that universities are obliged to educate students on the moral values that pertain to different disciplines (part 2, article 60).[145] The experience of Muslim governments of other orientations that are committed to a revelation-based order is quite diverse, and, thus, also fails to provide an indication: as Burton pointed out, while Saudi Arabian scientific education is captive to restrictive and castrating theological notions, Iran's tradition of rationalist scientific education was not much affected by the Islamic Revolution of 1979, and contemporary biology textbooks in its state schools discuss Darwinism in greater depth than that allowed in state schools in Israel, where warnings against the "Iranization" of public life are often articulated in public debates on the role of religion in society.[146]

Still, the restrictive implications of the modernist-apologetic approach to scientific studies and education should not be deliberated just as a matter of potential future legal institutionalization. In Egypt and other Arab societies, the broad diffusion of this approach has contributed to shaping social expectations as to how scientists should conduct their studies and how science teachers should conduct their classes. It has played a vital role in the preservation of academic and scholastic cultures where scientific inquiries are not thought by some scientists to be an open-ended adventure in which everything believed to be a fact is to be doubted, questioned and challenged, but as a process of asserting fundamental truths and revealed passages; in which even scientists in fields where religious scholars have no formal legal say are under pressure to accommodate the unqualified opinions of theologians; and, most astonishingly, in which these limitations are broadly believed to not inherently impede the ability of scientists and future scientists to break new ground.

Since the late 1960s, several Arab-Muslim thinkers have recognized the caveats of a revelation-based contextualization of scientific studies, and called for a complete separation between science and Islam. These calls, which brought to mind aspects of the secular-Islamic debates of the late nineteenth century and early twentieth century (although the former was then led by Christian Arabs), were part of broader reflections on the relation between conceptual and terminological trends, social norms, and the scientific and technological stagnation of Arab societies. The issue was, and remains, extremely sensitive. Denial of the divinity and inerrancy of the revelation amounts to refuting a fundamental foundation of faith. But even its contextualization as an inerrant, divine text that is irrelevant to the understanding of the natural world challenges ideas that have become almost conventional wisdom in Arab societies: i.e., that the Quran is relevant to modern scientific inquiries and is miraculously compatible with modern discoveries.

The most formidable challenge to modernist-apologetic ideas on science and religion was introduced in 1969, when Sadiq Jalal al-'Azm released his *Critique of Religious Thought*. Arguably no book written by a respected contemporary Arab-Muslim scholar and published by a mainstream press came so close to denying the Quran's inerrancy. Al-'Azm, a Syrian professor of philosophy (1934–2016) who earned his doctorate from Yale University and specialized in Kantian thought, mercilessly attacked each and every modernist-apologetic notion of compatibility between revelation and the modern study of the natural world (without recognizing their modernist-apologetic roots). Applying a Marxist-materialist approach, his book did not beat around the bush. It described religions as reactionary forces that, in Muslim societies just as in Christian societies, had always stood in support of the existing oppressive hegemonic orders.[147]

Al-'Azm's most radical statement was that the conflict between religions—including Islam—and science is inherent, and that attempts to deny this conflict constitute no more than an effort to defend the authority of religious creeds.[148] He argued that:

a   It took over 250 years for science to triumph over the Church in Europe, whereas in developing countries, including in the Arab world, the battle continues.

b   Islam contains ideas and beliefs about the evolution of the universe, its structure and nature, and the history of humanity, which clearly contradict the rationally obtained knowledge on these issues[149]—no sensible twentieth-century Muslim can believe in the fairytales of the Quran about how man was created, or about angels, demons and devils.[150]

c   There is a basic disparity between the methods through which scientific knowledge and religious knowledge are obtained: whereas in Islam and other religions the source for knowledge on the natural world is a revelation believed to be inerrant, or works of religious scholars on a revelation believed to be inerrant, scientists reach their conclusions exclusively through observations that lead to analytic conclusions based on the commensurability of the results with previous results and with the reality.[151]

d   Because of their conviction that the basic truths about human life had already been revealed, Muslims always look to the past, and believe that the task of scientists is not to bring forward new truths but to more correctly understand revealed passages through allegorizations and allegorizations of allegorizations. The true spirit of science is the converse of this attitude, as it does not deem anything to be beyond the pale of objective criticism and thorough investigations; should that spirit of discovery weaken, science would die.[152]

Al-'Azm articulated his views in Lebanon at a time when the country was politically dominated by a Christian majority, and home to the most liberal and vibrant Arabic press. Still, they led to his dismissal from the American University of Beirut even before the book was published, and to his arrest and indictment (together with his publisher) following the book's release. He was charged with aiming to provoke sectarian feuds and released several weeks later. The book was banned in Lebanon as well as in other Arab countries.

In hindsight, Al-'Azm said that despite the harsh criticisms his work encountered, it was debated by religious scholars in a serious way, and not for a moment did he feel that his life was under threat. He also mentioned that despite it being banned, the book was always available in the markets. He found these to be positive signs for the future of the Arab world.[153] Empathetic observers described his experience differently. Fouad Ajami (1945–2014), another Arab intellectual who never shied from speaking his mind, wrote that there was a novel theme to al-'Azm's life—"novel in the Arab context of this period: It is the story of an affluent young man who could have chosen acquiescence and security but instead chose to oppose, to dissent and to lose out."[154] This depiction should be revisited. Al-'Azm indeed paid a price, first and foremost living under the constant shadow of threats, but his is hardly a story of defiance and downfall; he has remained to this day a prolific author and a professor in both his native Syria and Western universities.

Bassam Tibi, yet another audacious Arab intellectual, wrote in the early 1990s that the Arab secularists' protests against al-'Azm's oppression in the early 1970s had become, only a few years later, "no longer conceivable." The reason for this is that "the imprint of Islamic fundamentalism has become the salient feature of public life in the Middle East" as it transformed to "a widespread intellectual approach to all major issues, including the question of the appropriation of modern science and technology. The prevailing argument is that Islam is not only compatible with modern science and technology; rather, it is ultimate source of modern science and technology."[155] The first part of this analysis was possibly exaggerated also for its time, and is certainly not applicable to the Arab discourse of the 2000s, in part due to the diverse array of opportunities provided by advanced media technologies to access and propagate various viewpoints. Moreover, aspects of what Tibi described as "fundamentalist thought" have been openly and blatantly challenged by contemporary Arab liberals other than al-'Azm—including the notion of the compatibility between revelation and science.

One determined voice against the foundations of modernist-apologetic thought on science was Shakir al-Nabulsi's (1940–2014), a Jordanian-American professor of literature and an adamant advocate for the separation between politics, science and religion in Arab societies. Al-Nabulsi ridiculed the argument that in Islam, as opposed to Christianity, religion and science are not at odds. If this is so, he asked, why do so many schools across the Arab world still avoid teaching scientific theories that contradict the Quran's version of creation, first and foremost, Darwin's theory of evolution and Freudianism? Equally, why is teaching Marxism prohibited in Arab religious academic institutions, particularly in those in Arab Gulf countries, despite its importance for understanding modern economic, social and political history? Al-Nabulsi concluded that a reign of religious scholars over science has been established in the Arab world through the publication of personal decisions on scientific theories that, with time, were popularized as revealed words that are undebatable.[156]

The Egyptian medical doctor, television sex-adviser and columnist Khalid Muntasir (b. 1960) has acted as another champion for the separation of science and religion. Unlike al-Nabulsi, who dispatched his challenges from the West, Muntasir's base is Egypt. His ability to present his ideas on mainstream media platforms suggests his is not an esoteric voice. Muntasir has railed against what he sees as the excessive indulgence of Arab societies in religious affairs. He holds the neglect of rationalist thinking and technological innovation to be the main problem of the Arab world. In his book *The Phobia of Science*, he cautioned against the sanctification of the past and argued that the root of Western Renaissance was the West's rejection of culture that relied on existing books and over-indulged in their interpretation in favor of pursuing new methods that encouraged observing nature afresh.[157]

In his writings on the Arab-Israeli conflict, Muntasir argued that the Arab world should turn its focus from religion to science if it wished to overcome its enemy. In an article he published in March 2009 titled "Israel Leads the Way in Physics While We Lead the Way in Religious Jurists," he recalled two headlines that alarmed him: "Russia Purchases Drones from Israel" and "India Buys a Spy Satellite from Israel." As he understood it, Israel has become a major player in the market of high technology because of its investment in scientific education:

> We will not overcome them in the realms of science, military or the economy by preaching in mosques, portraying them as monkeys and pigs and creating a preacher for every citizen and a religious jurist for every household. We will overcome them only through science.[158]

The Technion, Israel's highest institute of technology, is for Muntasir the model for the revolutionary path Arabs should take, because (so he claims) its slogan, "science is the solution," is a reversal of the Muslim Brothers' slogan, "Islam is the solution."[159] In an article he wrote after the 2011 Noble Prize in chemistry was awarded to Professor Dan Shechtman from the Technion, he defined it as the "*qibla*" (the direction of prayer in Islam) for scientists, that attracts chemists, physicists, engineers and computer scientists from around the world.[160]

Muntasir holds that the revelation should not serve in any way as a reference for scientific issues. In a book dedicated entirely to refuting the notion of the Quran's reconcilability with science, he warned that the mixing of science and religion injures the advance of the former and is the reason for the great disparity between the West's scientific achievements and those of the Arab world. While he accepted the divinity of the Quran, he suggested that the revelation applied concepts and language that the people of the time could understand, and the erroneous scientific notions it contains should be understood in the context of the necessity to reach out to those people.[161]

There is an inherent caveat to denying the revelation a place in science drawing on the recognition (or, at least, silent acknowledgment) of its divinity and inerrancy as undeniable, almost axiomatic, facts. It implies that scientific matters should be independent of religious considerations based on an interpretation of the revelation itself rather than based on a philosophy that is external to the revelation. As such, it indirectly allows for the authority of religion in science to be decided based on a competition between ideas as to the true meaning of the revelation. As we will see in the next chapter, this weakness is particularly characteristic of Arab-Muslim liberal works on the relation between the revelation and democracy.

A curious aspect of Arab-Muslim liberals' efforts to disassociate science and religion is that the founding fathers of the modernist-apologetic approach are not critically discussed. While those who seek the liberation of science from religion have identified the restrictive implications of the modernist-apologetic view of scientific freedom—specifically the risks of allegorization-based reconciliations between scientific discoveries and the revelation—they have not associated these views with the modernist-apologetic legacy itself. It is remarkable, for example, that al-'Azm's *Critique*, the most systematic attack on al-Afghani's, 'Abduh's, al-Jisr's and Rida's ideas and their lingering impact on Arab-Muslim scientific thought, does not recognize their importance in this context, and, in fact, does not address them at all. It is just as remarkable that Muntasir's attack on the culture of searching for verses in the Quran that are commensurate with empirical findings ignores the group that contributed more than any other to the contemporary prevalence of this method in religious circles. It is understandable why 'Abdallah b. Baz (1910–1999), the Grand Mufti of Saudi Arabia, is a focus of Muntasir's attention in a book aimed at charging against theological interventions in science[162]—but is b. Baz's infamous belief that the earth does not orbit the sun any more alarming than some of the views presented by the religious scholars who championed the reconcilability of science and revelation, starting with al-Afghani and his denigration of Darwin?

Rather than identify the modernist-apologetic approach to science as a primary rival to theirs, contemporary Arab liberal thinkers have tended to identify it as an ally. There was much to encourage this perception. Contemporary liberals realized that their worldview is countered by numerous and formidable rivals—*wahhabi* literalists, who care little about scientific research or about the ridicule that their opinions on science and technology encounter, the offspring of Qutbist *jihadi* thought, who hasten to excommunicate and kill those who think differently, stagnated religious establishments, and progressive and conservative regimes alike that meddle in academic studies. Then there are the wider publics and their general suspicion of secularism to consider. Whereas at the turn of the century the call to separate science and religion was introduced as a silver bullet for societies overwhelmed by Western strength, contemporary liberals have offered the same solutions to societies where liberalism has been tried and broadly judged to be a failure. Azzam S. Tamimi, in his dual role as an academic specialist in modernist-apologetic ideas and a propagator of these ideas, argued that secular Arab writers of the early twentieth century failed to:

> recognize that Islam is a religion that continues to shape and influence the lives of its adherents, who believe its values and principles are aimed at liberating mankind, establishing justice and equality, encouraging research and innovation, and guaranteeing freedom of thought, expression and worship.[163]

This statement is factually wrong with regard to the Muslim authors that Tamimi's essay addressed, none of whom doubted the revelation or called for the secularization of their societies. However, it reflects a perception shared also by contemporary liberals—that agendas perceived as anti-religious, whether they actually are or not, stand no chance of swaying the Arab masses in their favor.

Unlike other revelation-based Islamic approaches to modernity, the modernist-apologetic approach, at the very least, creates the potential for accommodating discoveries that challenge literal readings of the Quran, and emphasizes the importance of science and technology in language reminiscent of that used by liberals. It states that scientific progress is an important foundation of Islam and is inseparable from it, and declares that Islam guarantees scientific freedom. Its teachings can easily be confused, or conveniently interpreted, as ushering in a liberal agenda that releases science from any theological shackles.

Faced with a number of antagonistic views, and appreciating the need to place their ideas in a religious context, the temptation for some liberals to see the modernist-apologetic approach as an inspiration and a partner has been strong. One illuminating example is al-Nabulsi's historical chain of Arab liberals. It begins with al-Afghani and concludes with the efforts of a third, contemporary generation of liberals with which he associated.[164] This chain is reminiscent of Hourani's definition of early modernist-apologetic works as central part of a "liberal age," which, as noted in chapter 1, he later rethought. Al-Nabulsi ignores the crucial difference between a view intent on reestablishing the authority of the revelation and his agenda, which was to establish total separation between religion, politics and science.

Another instructive example of the liberal enchantment with the modernist apologists is the Egyptian Nasr Abu Zayd (1943–2010), a professor of literature and Islamic studies. Abu Zayd's life project was the liberation of Arab thought and politics from submission to interpretations of the Quran. He was careful not to cross the line of explicitly doubting the revealed essence of the Quran, but he was, nevertheless, unequivocal and reasoned in presenting his understanding of the implications of having the revelation serve as a basis for the social order (The misfortunes this position brought him are discussed in the next chapter). Historically analyzing 'Abduh's place in Islamic reformation movements, Abu Zayd described him as an intellectual whose discourse was "liberal," whose ideas excluded "any attempt of comparison between the Quran and science," and who "prepared the ground for Muslim intellectuals throughout the twentieth century to open up the meaning of the Quran and hence the meaning of Islam."[165] The impression taken from Abu Zayd's text is that 'Abduh's ideas are a precursor to his own, and that he continues his legacy. What Abu Zayd failed to note is that 'Abduh's theory of hermeneutics not only allowed for a comparison between the Quran and science, it required such a comparison as part of a process of distinguishing between legitimate and illegitimate science. As seen in this chapter, it encouraged theological intervention in the study and teaching of science. All of these run counter to Abu Zayd's core objectives.

Perhaps the most revealing demonstration of the liberals' inclination to embrace the early modernist-apologists as the pioneers of their own ideas on science and religion is none other than al-'Azm's reflections on the relation between Islam and empirical, rationalist studies, written almost four decades after the publication of his *Critique*. Al-'Azm asked whether Islam "can ever reconcile itself" with the "new and reigning" model on which the pursuit of knowledge has been based ever since the Western-originated scientific revolution began. The answer, according to al-'Azm, points to a division between two camps: the "yes" camp, comprised of those who confidently take their cues from the "classic movement of liberal reform and latitudinarian religious interpretation" initiated by al-Afghani and 'Abduh, and the "no" camp, comprised of adherents of the twentieth-century counter-reform, antimodern, and anti-rationalist fundamentalism of the Muslim Brothers and its excommunicating *jihadi* offspring. As an example of the mindset of the latter camp he quoted the words of the Shukri Mustafa (1942–1978), leader of *al-Takfir wal-Hijra* (Excommunication and Migration), who said that it was impossible for Western scientists and builders of civilization to be also obedient servants of Allah, and who emphasized that the Prophet and his Companions had no interest in the exact sciences, and therefore those who argue that Islam cannot be reestablished unless it becomes a pupil of Western sciences are imposters.[166]

In the dichotomous world of Islamic revivalist thought created by al-'Azm, the founders of the modernist-apologetic approach provide a historical legacy that has the potential to facilitate a desired rationalist-empiricist transformation. By associating their project with his, he adorned his views with plumes of widely respected Islamic scholarship. This explains why his discussion of 'Abduh suggests that the Grand Mufti of Egypt was, in fact, a secularist,[167] a summation of 'Abduh's biography that is no more loyal to the facts than al-'Azm's depiction of Hasan al-Banna and the Muslim Brothers, who have been, in general, loyal standard-bearers of modernist-apologetic ideas on science (and of modernity at large) as a counter-reformist faction.

The motivations for these analogies are clear. But a gaping chasm separates al-'Azm's work from that of al-Afghani, 'Abduh and those who followed in their footsteps. His has aimed to free scientific inquiries from theological notions and from the intervention of religious scholars. Theirs aimed to reassert the revelation as an all-encompassing, binding authority, and has created a space for theocratic monopolization of scientific studies. In his essay from 2007, al-'Azm described his troubles as history repeated: more than eight decades after Edwin Lewis, a Christian, was forced to resign from what later became the American University of Beirut for praising Darwin, he, al-'Azm, a Muslim, was dismissed from the same institution for critically discussing the conflict between science and religion.[168] A closer reading of verdicts passed on the theory of evolution and other scientific theories could have convinced al-'Azm that loyalists of the modernist-apologetic approach are far from trusted allies if one wishes to protect the freedom of scientists to speak their mind.

Notes

1   Muhammad al-Ghazali, "Hadha Dinuna," *al-Sha'b*, no. 540, April 3, 1990, 12.
2   Muhammad al-Ghazali, *'Ilal wa-Adwiya* (Doha: 1984), 203.
3   For a debate between two Americans, a theologian and a professor of philosophy, on whether the Big Bang theory supports the belief that the universe was created by God, or an atheistic view: William Lane Craig, *Theism, Atheism and Big Bang Cosmology* (Oxford: Clarendon Press, 1993).
4   Muhammad Asad, *The Message of Quran* (Gibraltar: Dar al-Andalus, 1980), 698, accessed July 20, 2015: www.usc.edu/schools/college/crcc/private/cmje/religious_text/The_Message_of_The_Quran__by_Muhammad_Asad.pdf.
5   Zakir Naik, *The Quran and Modern Science: Compatible or Incompatible?* (Riyadh: Darussalam, 2007), 10–11.
6   Muhammad al-Ghazali, "Hadha Dinuna," *al-Sha'b*, no. 645, April 21, 1992, 12.
7   Thomas S. Kuhn, *The Structure of Scientific Revolutions* (Chicago, IL: University of Chicago Press, 1970).
8   Norman Cohn, *Noah's Flood: The Genesis Story in Western Thought* (New Haven, CT and London: Yale University Press, 1996), 47.
9   Don Cameron Allen, *The Legend of Noah* (Urbana: University of Illinois Press, 1963), 92–112.
10 Muhammad 'Abduh, "Tufan No'ah … Hal 'Amma al-Ard Kulha?" in Muhammad 'Imara (ed.), *al-A'mal al-Kamila lil-Imam Muhmmad 'Abduh*, vol. 3 (Beirut: al-Mu'assasa al-'Arabiyya lil-Dirasat wal-Nashr, 1972), 511–13.
11 Muhammad al-Ghazali, *Zalam min al-Gharb* (Cairo: Dar al-Kitab, n.d.), 252–53.
12 John L. Heilbron, *Galileo* (Oxford and New York: Oxford University Press, 2010), 201.
13 John Hedley Brooke, *Science and Religion: Some Historical Perspectives* (Cambridge: Cambridge University Press, 1991), 44–45, 84.

14 Ludovico Geymonat, *Galileo Galilei: A Biography and Inquiry into His Philosophy of Science* (New York: McGraw-Hill Book Company, 1965), 45.

15 Ibid., 59, 67.

16 For the text of the letter: Maurice A. Finocchiaro (ed. and translator) *The Galileo Affair: A Documentary History* (Berkeley, Los Angeles and London: University of California Press, 1989), 87–118.

17 Ibid., 96–97.

18 Ibid., 114.

19 Heilbron, *Galileo*, 303–17; Pietro Redondi, *Galileo Heretic*, translated by Raymond Rosenthal (Princeton, NJ: Princeton University Press, 1987), 227–71.

20 Muzaffar Iqbal, "Darwin's Shadow: Evolution in an Islamic Mirror," *Islam & Science*, 8:1 (Summer 2010), 13.

21 "Rashid Rida," Wikipedia entry, accessed July 12, 2015: https://en.wikipedia.org/wiki/Rashid_Rida.

22 Taner Edis, "Modern Science and Conservative Islam: An Uneasy Relationship," *Science & Education*, 18:6–7 (2009), 889.

23 Martin Riexinger, "Responses of South Asian Muslims to the Theory of Evolution," *Die Welt des Islams*, 49:2 (2009), 217–19.

24 Veysel Kaya, "Can the Quran Support Darwin? An Evolutionist Approach by Two Turkish Scholars after the Foundation of the Turkish Republic," *The Muslim World*, 102:2 (April 2012), 358–64.

25 Marwa Elshakry, "Global Darwin: Eastern Enchantment," *Nature*, 461:7268 (October 2009), 1200.

26 Adel A. Ziyadat, *Western Science in the Arab World: The Impact of Darwinism, 1860–1930* (London: Palgrave Macmillan, 1986), 86; Damian Howard, *Being Human in Islam: The Impact of the Evolutionary Worldview* (London and New York: Routledge, 2011), 37–38.

27 Jamal al-Din al-Afghani, *al-Radd 'ala al-Dahriyyin* (Cairo: Dar al-Karnak, n.d.), 38–42.

28 Ibid., 42–45.

29 Jamal al-Din al-Afghani, "al-Nushu' wal-Irtiqa'," in Muhammad 'Imara (ed.), *al-A'mal al-Kamila li-Jamal al-Din al-Afghani* (n.d.), 249–51.

30 James Moore, "That Evolution Destroyed Darwin's Faith in Christianity—Until He Reconverted on His Deathbed," in Ronald N. Numbers (ed.), *Galileo Goes to Jail And Other Myths about Science and Religion* (Cambridge, MA: Harvard University Press, 2009), 147–48.

31 Al-Afghani, "al-Nushu' wal-Irtiqa'," 252–53.

32 Donald M. Leavitt, "Darwinism in the Arab World: The Lewis Affair at the Syrian Protestant College," *The Muslim World*, 71:2 (April 1981), 85–86; Nadia Faraj, "The Lewis Affair and the Fortunes of al-Muqtataf," *Middle Eastern Studies*, 8:1 (January 1972), 76–77.

33 Leavitt, "Darwinism in the Arab World: The Lewis Affair at the Syrian Protestant College," 87, Faraj, "The Lewis Affair and the Fortunes of al-Muqtataf," 78.

34 Leavitt, "Darwinism in the Arab World: The Lewis Affair at the Syrian Protestant College," 89–97.

35 For examples of articles which dealt in depth with the theory, as well as with the responses it stirred in the Christian world, "Charles Darwin," *al-Muqtataf*, 7:1 (June 1882), 1–6; "al-Madhhab al-Darwini," *al-Muqtataf*, 7:2, 7:3 (July and August 1882), 65–72, 121–27.

36 Edwin Lewis, "al-Ma'arfa wal-'Ilm wal-Hikma," *al-Muqtataf*, 7:3 (August 1882), 158–67.

37 "Al-Munazara wal-Murasala," *al-Muqtataf*, 7:4 (September 2, 1882), 233–36, "Al-Munazara wal-Murasala," *al-Muqtataf* , 7:5 (October 1882), 287–92.

38 Faraj, "The Lewis Affair and the Fortunes of al-Muqtataf," 80–82.

39 Johannes Ebert, *Religion und Reform in der Arabischen Provinz* (Frankfurt am Main: Peter Lang, 1991), 132–33.

40 Howard, *Being Human in Islam: The Impact of the Evolutionary Worldview*, 42–43.

41 Al-Afghani, "al-Nushu' wal-Irtiqa'," 252.

42 Leavitt, "Darwinism in the Arab World: The Lewis Affair at the Syrian Protestant College," 97–98.

43 Ebert, *Religion und Reform in der Arabischen Provinz*, 84.

44 Marwa Elshakry, "Muslim Hermeneutics and Arabic Views of Evolution," *Zygon*, 46:2 (June 2011), 332.

45 Husayn al-Jisr, *al-Risala al-Hamidiyya fi Haqiqat al-Diyana al-Islamiyya wa-Haqqiyyat al-Shari'a al-Muhammadiyya* (Cairo and Beirut: Dar al-Kitab al-Misri, Dar al-Kitab al-Lubnani, 2012, originally published 1888), 147.

46 Ibid., 172–74.

47 Ibid., 263–64.

48 Ibid., 206–09.

49 Ibid., 232, 236.

50 Ibid., 279–82.

51 Ibid., 289–90.

52 Ibid., 290–91.

53 Ibid., 295–96.

54 Ibid., 292, 296.

55 Ibid., 301–07.

56 Ibid., 315–16.

57 Muhammad Sidqi, "al-Din fi Nazr al-'Aql al-Sahih" (fourth section), *al-Manar*, 8:19 (November 28, 1905), 737–44.

58 *Al-Manar*, "Abuna Adam wa-Madhhab Darwin, min Bab Intiqad al-Manar," 8:23 (January 26, 1906), 920.

59 Muhammad 'Abduh, "al-Shura wal-Qanun," in Muhammad 'Imara (ed.), *al-A'mal al-Kamila lil-Imam Muhmmad 'Abduh*, Vol. 1 (Beirut: al-Mu'assasa al-'Arabiyya lil-Dirasat wal-Nashr, 1972), 365.

60 Muhammad 'Abduh, *The Theology of Unity*, translated by Ishaq Musa'ad and Kenneth Cragg (London: George Allen & Unwin, 1966), 130–31.

61 Ibid., 48–49.

62 *Al-Manar*, "Bab Tafsir al-Quran al-Karim – Surat al-Nisa'," 12:7 (August 16, 1909), 483–91.

63 *Al-Manar*, "Dar al-Munazara wal-Murasala: al-Duktur Shibli Afandi Shumayyil," 12(1):8 (September 14, 1909), 632–37.

64 *Al-Manar*, "Nazariyyat Darwin wal-Islam," 30:8 (March 1, 1930), 596.

65 Ibid., 594.

66 Ibid., 597.

67 Ibid., 596–97.

68 David Sepkoski, "Evolutionary Paleontology," in Michael Ruse (ed.), *The Cambridge Encyclopedia of Darwin and Evolutionary Thought* (Cambridge: Cambridge University Press, 2013), 356.

69 *Al-Manar*, "Nazariyyat Darwin wal-Islam," 598.

70 Ibid., 598–99.

71 Ibid., 599–600.

72 Yusuf al-Dajawi, "Sahib al-Manar: wal-Salat wal-Salam 'ala al-Rasul Sala Allah 'Alayhi wa-Salam: Ba'd al-Adhan," *Nur al-Islam*, 3:5 (September 1932), 335–40.

73 *Al-Manar*, "Al-Maqal al-Thalith 'Ashar: al-Buhayta al-Sabi'a Ma Samaha Tatbiq al-Qur'an 'ala Madhhab Darwin," 33(1):1 (March 3, 1933), 58–64.

74 Naguib Mahfouz, *The Cairo Trilogy, vol. 2: Palace of Desire*, translated by William Maynard (New York: Knopf, 2001, first published in Arabic 1957), 891, 893.

75 Riexinger, "Responses of South Asian Muslims to the Theory of Evolution," 227–30.

76 Abu al-Hasan al-Nadwi, *Madha Khasara al-'Alam bi-Inkhitat al-Muslimin* (Cairo: Maktabat al-'iman, 1994), 170–72.

77 Sayyid Qutb, "Madha Khasara al-'Alam bi-Inkhitat al-Muslimin" (a review), *al-Risala*, 19:947 (August 7, 1951), 965–7.

78   Sayyid Qutb, *Fi Zilal al-Quran, Surah 23 (al-Mu'minun),* English translation, 154–56. accessed March 30, 2014: http://tafsirzilal.files.wordpress.com/2012/06/al-mukminun-eng.pdf.

79   Muhammad al-Ghazali, *al-Da'wa al-Islamiyya fi al-Qarn al-Hali* (Cairo: Dar al-Shuruq, 2000), 128–29.

80   Muhammad al-Ghazali, *Sirr Ta'akhkhur al-'Arab wal-Muslimin* (Al-Jiza: Nahdat Misr, March 2005, originally written 1985), 85.

81   Muhammad al-Ghazali, "Hadha Dinuna," *al-Sha'b,* no. 645, April 21, 1992, 12.

82   Muhammad al-Ghazali, "Hadha Dinuna," *al-Sha'b,* no. 771, August 31, 1993, 12.

83   Muhammad al-Ghazali, *Raka'iz al-'Iman bayna al-'Aql wal-Qalb* (Kuwait: Maktabat al-Amal, 1967), 64–71.

84   Yusuf al-Qaradawi, "Pokemon Games," posted December 30, 2003, accessed December 10, 2013: http://www.onislam.net/english/ask-the-scholar/arts-and-entertainment/cinema-theatre-and-tv/174701.html?TV=.

85   Ibid.

86   Yusuf al-Qaradawi, *Min Fiqh al-Dawla fi al-Islam* (Cairo: Dar al-Shuruq, 2001, first published 1997), 75.

87   Yusuf al-Qaradawi, *Thaqafat al-Da'iya* (Cairo: Maktabat Wahaba, 1996, 10th printing), 104–05.

88   Ibid., 113–15.

89   Yusuf al-Qaradawi, *Bidayat al-Khalq wa-Nazariyyat al-Tatawwur,* transcript of a discussion in the television program "al-Shari'a wal-Hayat," February 25, 2009, accessed December 20, 2013: http://www.aljazeera.net/programs/pages/af1ea016-4280-4a0d-838f-8ca05f31c8df.

90   Muhammad 'Imara, *al-Ghazw al-Fikri Wahm am Haqiqa?* (Beirut and Cairo: Dar al-Shuruq, 1997, first published 1989), 110–18.

91   Ibid., 119–25.

92   Ibid., 122.

93   Muhammad 'Imara, *al-Dawla al-Islamiyya bayna al-'Almaniyya wal-Sulta al-Diniyya* (Cairo: Dar al-Shuruq, 1988), 62.

94   Ibid., 63.

95   Muhammad Qutb, *Waqi'una al-Mu'asir* (Cairo: Dar al-Shuruq, 2006, written in 1986), 220–23; Abdallah 'Azzam, "*al-Saratan al-Ahmar,*" n.d., accessed January 1, 2014: http://www.moslim.se/maktaba/kotob/melal-saradan-azzam.htm; Ziyad Abu Ghanima, *al-'Ilm Yatabarra'u min Nazariyyat Darwin: Akbar Jarimat Tazwir 'Ilmi fi al-Ta'rikh: Dirasat Watha'iqiyya* (Amman: Dar 'Ammar, 1989), 157–59.

96   Adel A. Ziadat, "Early Reception of Einstein's Relativity in the Arab Periodical Press," *Annals of Science,* 51:1 (1994), 32.

97   'Imara, *al-Ghazw al-Fikri Wahm am Haqiqa?* 118.

98   Ibid., 114.

99   Al-Ghazali, *Sirr Ta'akhkhur al-'Arab wal-Muslimin,* 87.

100 Muhammad al-Ghazali, "Hadha Dinuna," *al-Sha'b,* no. 944, May 9, 1995, 12.

101 Al-Qaradawi, "*Bidayat al-Khalq wa-Nazariyyat al-Tatawwur*".

102 Randy Moore, "Creationism in the United States" (part 2), *The American Biology Teacher,* 60:8 (October 1998), 572.

103 Norman F. Furniss, *The Fundamentalist Controversy, 1918–1931* (Hamdan, CT: Archon Books, 1963), 92.

104 Randy Moore, "Creationism in the United States" (part 2), 576; Judith A. Villarreal, "God and Darwin in the Classroom: The Creation/Evolution Controversy," *Chicago-Kent Law Review,* 64:1 (January 1988), 343.

105 Ibid., 344.

106 Ibid.; Moore, "Creationism in the United States" (part 2), 576; Eugenie C. Scott, "Antievolution and Creationism in the United States," *Annual Review of Anthropology,* 26 (1997), 272.

107 Villarreal, "God and Darwin in the Classroom: The Creation/Evolution Controversy," 346.

108 Robert L. Numbers, "Creationism in 20th-Century America," *Science*, 218:5 (November 1982), 543.

109 Villarreal, "God and Darwin in the Classroom: The Creation/Evolution Controversy," 351.

110 Eileen Barker, "Let There Be Light: Scientific Creationism in the Twentieth Century," in John Durant (ed.). *Darwinism and Divinity: Essays on Evolution and Religious Belief* (Oxford and New York: Basil Blackwell, 1985), 184–92; Ronald L. Numbers, *The Creationists* (Berkeley, Los Angeles and London: University of California Press, 1993), 243–49.

111 Numbers, "Creationism in 20th-Century America," 543.

112 Scott, "Antievolution and Creationism in the United States," 268; Numbers, "Creationism in 20th-Century America," 541–42.

113 Villarreal, "God and Darwin in the Classroom: The Creation/Evolution Controversy," 356.

114 Ibid., 363–64.

115 Numbers, *The Creationists*, 247; "Creationism in 20th-Century America," 543.

116 Scott, "Antievolution and Creationism in the United States," 273–74; Villarreal, "God and Darwin in the Classroom: The Creation/Evolution Controversy," 348.

117 Barker, "Let There Be Light: Scientific Creationism in the Twentieth Century," 193.

118 Michael B. Berkman, Julianna Sandell Pacheco and Eric Plutzer, "Evolution and Creationism in America's Classrooms: A National Portrait," *PLoS Biology*, 6:5 (May 2008), 920.

119 Ibid., 922.

120 Randy Moore, "Creationism in the Biology Classroom: What Do Teachers Teach and How Do They Teach It?" *The American Biology Teacher*, 70:2 (February 2008), 79.

121 Numbers, "Creationism in 20th-Century America," 544.

122 Victor Danner, "Western Evolutionism in the Arab World," *The American Journal of Islamic Social Science*, 8:1 (1991), 79–80.

123 Muhammad ʿAli Yusuf, *Masraʿ al-Darwiniyya* (Jedda: Dar al-Shuruq, 1983), 14.

124 Ibid., 188.

125 Ibid., 202.

126 ʿAbd al-Razzaq Nawfal, *al-Insan wal-Qird wa-Suqut Darwin* (Cairo: Matbuʿat al-Shaʿb, 1984), 119.

127 Mahir Khalil, *Suqut Nazariyyat Darwin: Fi Dawʾ al-Iktishafat al-ʿIlmiyya al-Haditha* (Alexandria: al-Markaz al-ʿArabi, 1986), 157–65.

128 Ibid., 165–68.

129 Abu Ghanima, *al-ʿIlm Yatabarraʾu min Nazariyyat Darwin*, 5–6, 124–52.

130 Ibid., 8–20.

131 Ibid., 50–64.

132 Ibid., 126–27.

133 Edis, "Modern Science and Conservative Islam: An Uneasy Relationship," 890.

134 Ibid., 891.

135 Salman Hameed, "Science and Religion: Bracing for Islamic Creationism," *Science*, 332 (December 12, 2008), 1637.

136 Salman Hameed, "Evolution and Creationism in the Islamic World," in Thomas Dixon, Geoffrey Cantor and Stephen Pumfrey (eds), *Science and Religion: New Historical Perspectives* (Cambridge: Cambridge University Press, 2010), 139.

137 Anne Ross Solberg, *The Mahdi Wears Armani: An Analysis of the Harun Yahya Enterprise* (Stockholm: Södertörns högskola, 2013), 6–10.

138 For example, "Destruction of Evolution Theory in Twenty Questions" is a lengthy attack on both the scientific credibility of natural selection as well as the possibility of reconciling faith with Darwin's theory. Yahya claims that there exists not a single

scientific discovery or experiment to support the theory (7). See: *Hadm Nazariyyat al-Tatawwur fi 'Ishrin Su'alan* on ar.Harunyahya.com (accessed December 10, 2014).

139 Steve Paulson, *Atoms and Eden: Conversations on Religion & Science* (Oxford and New York: Oxford University Press, 2010), 304–07; Solberg, *The Mahdi Wears Armani*, 13–14; Edis, "Modern Science and Conservative Islam: An Uneasy Relationship," 891.

140 Salman Hameed, "Making Sense of Islamic Creationism in Europe," *Public Understanding of Science*, 24:4 (2015), 388–99.

141 Manea H. Al-Hazmi, *Dialogue with an Atheist* (Alexandria: Conveying Islamic Message Society, n.d.), 7–8. See also the words of the leaflet "A Design Indicates a Designer," Published by Islamreligion.com, and added to this author's collection in the same mosque: "If you examine your eyelashes, you will notice that the upper ones turn upwards and the lower ones extend downwards. If the matter was the opposite, it would have impaired one's vision. Who is it that directs every eyelash of every human being and animal other than God? [...] the whole of existence bears witness that everything is the work of the one and only true God [...] those who believe that nature created them contradict the intellect and reject the truth."

142 Elise K. Burton, "Evolution and Creationism in Middle Eastern Education: A New Perspective," *Evolution*, 65:1 (2010), 303.

143 Anila Asghar, Salman Hameed and Najme Kishani Farahani, "Evolution in Biology textbooks: A Comparative Analysis of 5 Muslim Countries," *Religion and Education*, 41:1 (2014), 8.

144 Hameed, "Science and Religion: Bracing for Islamic Creationism," 1637; for a survey of studies on the predominantly negative approaches to the theory of evolution among Muslim students and teachers in high schools: Zoubeida R. Dagher, Saouma Bou-Jaoude, "Science Education in Arab States: Bright Future or Status Quo?" *Studies in Science Education*, 47:1 (2011), 83–84.

145 Constitution of Egypt, December 2012, accessed August 18, 2015: www.sis.gov.eg/newvr/theconistitution.pdf.

146 Burton, "Evolution and Creationism in Middle Eastern Education: A New Perspective," 301–4.

147 Sadiq Jalal al-'Azm, *Naqd al-Fikr al-Dini* (Beirut: Dar al-Tali'a lil-Tiba'a wal-Nashr, November 1969), 23.

148 Ibid., 24.

149 Ibid., 22.

150 Ibid., 36–37.

151 Ibid., 22.

152 Ibid., 22–23.

153 Sadek Jalal al-Azm and Abu Fakhr, "Trends in Arab Thought: An Interview with Sadeq Jalal al-Azm," *Journal of Palestine Studies*, 27:2 (Winter 1998), 73.

154 Fouad Ajami, *The Arab Predicament: Arab Political Thought and Practice since 1967* (Cambridge: Cambridge University Press, 1989), xii.

155 Bassam Tibi, "The Worldview of Sunni Arab Fundamentalists," in Martin E. Marty and R. Scott Appleby (eds), *Fundamentalisms and Society: Reclaiming the Sciences, the Family and Education—The Fundamentalist Project*, vol. 2 (Chicago, IL and London: The University of Chicago press, 1993), 78.

156 Shakir al-Nabulsi, "Limadha Yu'adi Rijal al-Din al-'Almaniyya?" *al-Hiwar al-Mutamadin*, no. 1508, April 2, 2006, accessed August 1, 2015: www.ahewar.org/debat/show.art.asp?aid=61203.

157 Khalid Muntasir, *Fubya al-'Ilm* (Cairo: Dar Akhbar al-Yawm, December 2008), 22.

158 Khalid Muntasir, "Isra'il Tataqaddamu bil-Fiziya' wa-Nahnu bil-Fuqaha'," March 26, 2009, accessed July 6, 2013: www.ahl-alquran.com/site/arabic/show_article.php?main_id=5053.

159 Khalid Muntasir, "Hal bil-Adabi wa-Alfiyyat Ibn Malik sa-Yatafawwaq al-'Arab 'ala Isra'il?!," June 27, 2008, accessed April 10, 2014: www.elaph.com/Web/ElaphWriter/2008/6/343355.htm.

160 Khalid Muntasir, "Hum Ikhtaru al-Kimiya wa-Ihna Ikhtarna al-Fustan al-Bumbay,"
     October 10, 2011, accessed April 16, 2014: www.almasryalyoum.com/node/503303.
161 Khalid Muntasir, *Wahm al-I'jaz al-'Ilmi* (Egypt: Dar al-'ayn lil-Nashr, 2005), 5–21,
     219–22.
162 Ibid., 52–54.
163 Azzam S. Tamimi, "The Renaissance of Islam," *Doedalus*, 132:3 (July 2003), 57.
164 Shakir al-Nabulsi, *al-Libaraliyyun al-Judud: Jadal Fikri* (Cologne: Manshurat al-Jamal,
     2005), 19–20, 43–55.
165 Nasr Abu Zayd, *Reformation of Islamic Thought: A Critical Historical Analysis* (Amsterdam:
     Amsterdam University Press, 2006), 32–34.
166 Sadik Jalal Al-Azm, "Islam and the Science-Religion Debates in Modern Times,"
     European Review, 15:3 (2007), 291–93.
167 Ibid., 289.
168 Ibid., 286.

3

ISLAM AND DEMOCRACY

The establishment of a revelation-based society that maintains scientific freedom is one promise the modernist-apologetic school made. Another promise, which has been repeatedly articulated in modernist-apologist texts since the late nineteenth century, is the foundation of a revelation-based regime in which politics are neither despotic nor theocratic. An obscure endorsement of some form of participatory politics, first articulated by al-Afghani, 'Abduh and their early twentieth century disciples, was further developed during the second half of the twentieth century by al-Ghazali, al-Qaradawi and 'Imara into a far more detailed commitment to the establishment of a regime in which the public elects and dismisses its leadership, an elected parliament legislates, and basic freedoms, including the freedom to criticize and oppose government officials, are safeguarded—however, all within the confines of the permissible and the prohibited as delineated by the *shari'a*.

The modernist-apologists' argument about the similarities between the Islamic concept of government and liberal principles and conceptions of democracy primarily centered on the term *shura* and the command to consult, as instructed in the following two verses: "consult them in the matter" (Q. 3:159) and "[those] whose affair is [determined by] consultation among themselves" (Q. 42:38). They also interpreted numerous traditions to be endorsements of political participation, pluralism, majority rule, political opposition and individual freedoms. They suggested that certain democratic and liberal values that are so cherished in the West are not only compatible with Islam but had, in fact, been introduced by Islam in the Muslim world before they were introduced in the West. Moreover, they have argued that it is desirable, indeed even a requirement, for Muslims to learn from Western achievements in governance and develop the application of *shura* based on critical imitations of Western examples. As they did in the field of science, their theorizing implied that one need not and should not choose between a liberal, doubt-based political reference and an Islamic, revelation-based reference because all that is desired in the former can be safeguarded and promoted by the latter, and the latter is devoid of the weaknesses and moral corruption of the former.

These synthesizing theories were not intended to remain, and have not remained, in the realm of theological inqueries only. Political ideas articulated by the modernist-apologists in the late nineteenth century served as the foundation for Hasan al-Banna's response to the reality of a quasi-democratic Egypt in the 1920s and 1930s. Later they served as the primary inspiration for more elaborate and detailed theorizing offered by contemporary modernist-apologists. The writings of contemporary modernist-apologists, in turn, have served as the basis for the numerous political agendas championed by Islamist movements across the Arab world.

As a political program, the modernist-apologetic theory of government has failed to materialize. Throughout the Arab world, movements and individuals who represent it have been ousted from democratically won power, forced to concede power, or denied outright the opportunity to contest for power. It is just as remarkable that, almost without exception, in the few instances during the past four decades when those calling for a revelation-based *shura* democratic system stood for elections they won, almost without exception, in impressive landslides (when the elections were entirely competitive), or emerged as the strongest and most credible political force (when the elections were not entirely competitive). It goes without saying that the reason for those achievements was never solely due to the promise of a democratic, revelation-based society. Other factors, primarily social and organizational, also played a significant role. However, to disregard the importance of ideological motivations when assessing the continuous appeal of ideological movements is as simplistic as overstating them. The modernist-apologist theory of Islam and democracy has been, and remains, the most vibrant, popular alternative to the existing political structures in the Arab world, rendering it all the more a worthy topic for study.

The Quest for "Sincerity": Contextualizing the Academic Discourse

Academic literature has extensively addressed the implications of Islamic revelation on the politics of Muslim societies. Two approaches have dominated this discourse. One, almost a-historical, asked what "Islam" says about democracy. Another inquired what Muslims say that Islam says. The former applied reasoning similar to that of the modernist-apologists, according to which a coherent view on politics can be deduced from the revelation; the latter evaluated political interpretations of the revelation made by Muslim scholars and activists. Both approaches introduced considerable analytic difficulties.

Essentialist explanations for the absence of political freedoms in Muslim societies are almost as old as modern democracy. Already in the mid-nineteenth century, Alexis de Tocqueville, a firm believer in the positive contribution of religion and religious dogmas to human life, as well as an advocate of their separation from politics, argued in his study on democracy in America that Islam would decline in influence in an enlightened, democratic era because of the political and legalistic nature of its revelation.[1] At the turn of the same century, French historian and politician Gabriel Hanotaux wrote (as discussed in chapter 1) that separation between state and religion is crucial if Muslim societies wished to advance. Half a century later, English historian Arnold Toynbee described the rejection of demo-cratic institutions as a characteristic of "zealot" Muslim leaders who, due to their stubbornness, face extinction.[2]

During the second half of the twentieth century, with the collapse of democracy across an ethnically and culturally diverse spectrum of societies, modernization-theory and socio-economic factors dominated the study of the reasons for the failure of liberal regimes in the Arab world.[3] Then, in the early 1990s, when a global wave of democratic revolutions passed over the vast majority of the Muslim world, the religious-cultural argument found renewed favor. For some scholars, "Islamic political culture" shone brightly as the key factor that explained why Muslim countries were an exception to the global democratic trend.

This essentialist argument is problematic in a number of ways. The assumption that a "democratic culture" is a precondition for the emergence of a democratic society is illogical: if a democratic "present" could only result from a democratic "past," no country in the world would be democratic. From an empirical point of view, developments since the late 1990s have rendered obsolete the argument that a society with an "Islamic tradition" can never be democratic. With Indonesia, the world's most populated Muslim country, embarking on a stable process of demo-cratization, and an impressive list of other Muslim countries joining it, an essenti-alist understanding of Islam can no longer be seriously singled out as the one reason why *some* Muslim societies have not been democratized.

Exploring what "Islam" has to say about democracy is a historical anachronism: from a historical, rather than theological, perspective, Islamic revelation and tradi-tions say nothing about democracy. They say no more about democracy than they do about space shuttles for the simple reason that democracy, as practiced in modern times, was not a concept that early Muslims were familiar with or concerned about.

Even if we insist on the credibility of analyzing "Islam's" attitude to democracy we will find that in a corpus so rich and open to interpretation there is an ample amount of evidence to support conflicting approaches. Thus, findings pointing in one direction can always be contradicted with contesting findings. Two examples from post-Cold War academic works on Islam and democracy clarify this point. In an historical overview, Bernard Lewis argued that "we can discern elements in Islamic law and tradition that could assist the development of one or another form of democracy," among which he listed the disapproval of arbitrary rule, the call not to obey a command that violates divine law, and the legitimization of the plurality of opinions.[4] Another formidable scholar of Islamic history, Elie Kedourie, offered an argument to the contrary: there is nothing "in the political traditions of Islam" which might "make familiar, or indeed intelligible, the organizing ideas of con-stitutional and representative government." Kedourie invoked the religious duty of obeying the leader, and the culture of political passivity it engendered, as a characteristic of the despotic heritage of Muslim societies.[5] Neither Lewis nor Kedourie were wrong; there are certain elements in Islamic revelation and history (as there are in Judaism and Christianity) that can be interpreted as supporting democratic tendencies, and there are other elements that can be interpreted as supporting autocratic tendencies. A discussion of what "Islam" commands with regard to democracy is therefore certain to enlighten us more about what the analyst wishes to highlight than about Islam.

Scientific analyses should thus focus, as suggested by Gudrun Krämer, on what "Muslims living and theorizing under specific historical circumstances" have said and not on what "Islam" says about democracy.[6] Indeed, numerous studies written since the 1990s have adopted this approach. And, due to both the popular appeal of Muslim Brothers movements and to the elusive and controversial nature of their texts on democracy, particular attention has been given to modernist-apologist theorizing in this field. However, as was regrettably the case with other contentious issues, and perhaps more than has been the case with any other contentious issue, the debate over the role of Orientalism in scholarship overshadowed many of those studies as cyclical arguments and elusive definitions were invoked at the expense of systematic analyses. Studies set criteria for what democracy is, or should be, and then examined the trustworthiness of what Islamists say about democracy (or of what other scholars, from the "other camp," say about what Islamists say). The eagerness to demonstrate that "positive" views of Islamists' relation to democracy are indicators of Western liberal self-defeatist syndrome or the contrary urge to expose "negative" views as indicators of Western imperialist-Orientalist mindsets sometimes resulted in analyses that left their readers with little substantive knowledge of what Islamists themselves actually say and believe.

David Bukay, for example, declared that the "Islamic world is not ready to absorb the basic values of modernism and democracy,"[7] and added that "the popularity of post-colonialism and post-modernism within the academy" impels intellectuals to find a compatibility between Islamism and democracy that doesn't exist.[8] His rather shallow survey of what Islamists have written about democracy, which stressed that democracy cannot be judged by its electoral component only, stated (based on secondary sources) that al-Qaradawi considers elections as heresy and legislators as unnecessary, and noted that Hasan al-Banna considered democracy as infidelity.[9] Both statements are misleading, but nevertheless bolstered the argument that the academic establishment twists facts for fear of being labeled "Islamophobic." In the same vein, Bassam Tibi, a fierce critic of Islamism, claimed in an essay on why Islamists "can't be democratic" that what Islamists really aim to do is reshape the world based on an "invented tradition" of an Islamic state and the rule of *shari'a*. [10] In doing so, Tibi ignored the fact that all interpretations of what "Islam" really is (or is not), including his own that contradicts that of Islamists, are, at least to a certain extent, invented and reflexive.

Scholars calling for a positive approach to the Islamist discourse on democracy also failed to make a convincing case often times. Arguing against a dismissive attitude to this Islamist discourse, John Esposito and John Voll, in what became one of the better-known studies on the subject, emphasized that there is no universal definition or model for democracy. Thus, according to Esposito and Voll, democracy can be established not only through the adoption of Western democracy but equally through "the adaptation of Western democratic forms or the formulation of indigenously rooted forms of political participation and empowerment."[11] The cyclical essence of this argument, in a discussion that was far from systematic, cannot be overstated: if "democracy" is anything that one makes it, as they suggest, it becomes a term bereft of meaning, rendering any examination of whether a certain approach is compatible with it or not meaningless. Ahmad Moussalli's study, an apologetic defense of Islamist apologists that emphasized it was not apologetic, introduced a cyclical argument of another sort. His discussion of *shura*, which embraced the elasticity of the term as an opportunity to develop a method of democratic politics grounded in Islam,[12] undermined his core normative distinction between "moderate Islamists" who adopt liberal democracy in an "Islamic fashion" and "radical Islamists" who adopt an authoritarian approach.[13] If Islam is anything that people make it, then who is to say that one interpretation of *shura* is more Islamic than another? The bottom line of Raghid El-Solh's essay (which largely focused on the works of Muhammad al-Ghazali and Muhammad 'Imara) was that misjudging the works of Islamists who are "responsive to the idea of parliamentary democracy" may "eventually contribute to the weakening of democratic tendencies in the Arab region."[14] This observation was borne out of El-Solh's analysis that focused on his positive evaluations of al-Ghazali's and 'Imara's positive evaluations of Western democracy. Yet, his analysis dismissed the more critical aspects of their "responsive" approach and the potential implications their belief that *shura* must be limited by the boundaries of the *shari'a* may have.

This chapter applies a different approach than those introduced in previous studies on Islamic discourses on democracy. Rather than invoke contested empirical definitions of the essence of democracy, the essence of Islam, or both, with the intention to demonstrate that certain interpretations of Islam are incompatible, compatible or potentially compatible with those definitions, the chapter examines whether the ideal and the structure of the Islamic regime put forward by the modernist-apologists (and adopted by the Muslim Brothers) are consistent and coherent. In this way, the caveat of considering one's normative preference as universal and objective is avoided. Specifically, instead of asking whether the modernist-apologists are "really" democratic or "sincerely" support human rights, the chapter aims to discern whether they have managed to put forward a political theory that reconciles their promise for a non-despotic, non-theocratic regime in which the religious establishment does not possess power over political decisions with their insistence that the regime will be *shari'a*-based and will never breach Islam's unequivocal regulations on the permissible and prohibited.

This premise is indeed conceptually minimalist; it narrows the democracy debate to the issue of whether the power to peacefully depose a government resides with the people or not. It should be noted, however, that this kind of reductionism is not unknown in liberal scholarship and is especially prevalent among those who emphasize freedom of thought as the most important aspect of liberal, open societies. To resort once more to Karl Popper, his definition of democracy is nothing more than a regime in which it is possible to remove the government without bloodshed, and of tyranny as a regime in which it is possible to do so only through revolution.[15] Popper did not argue that a regime qualifies as "democratic" only in cases where certain freedoms and values exist. His democracy was not judged by the freedoms it grants women, gays, religious minorities, or gamblers, but by one single criterion—whether it allows a substantial enough measure of freedom to render a peaceful electoral transition of power possible.

Political agendas often introduce contradictions and lacunas; they must have a certain measure of ambivalence and fluidity if they wish to attract the broadest possible support and provide flexibility for the leadership. However, if those presenting agendas wish them to be judged as serious and applicable, certain contradictions are impossible to avoid. A government, for example, cannot at the same time universally raise and reduce the value added tax on all commodities, and if politicians running for power would make the illogical argument that they intend to do so, they would be rightly suspected of either outright deception or intellectual ineptitude. Similarly, a regime cannot be non-theocratic and theocratic at the same time: either the people are the ultimate source of legitimacy for political decisions, or unelected religious scholars are. Herein lies the importance of examining the modernist-apologist school on its own terms and ascertaining whether its theory of government is consistent and coherent. To be judged as such, it must involve a workable, coherent model for a regime in which the *shari'a* is the exclusive reference while the people are the source of all legislative and governmental powers.

Shari'a *and Theocracy*

A crucial distinction has to be drawn already at this point. Grounding a system of government in a revelation, and constraining legislation to the confines of that revelation, does not, in itself, create the political rule of a religious establishment. A theocratic regime is one that vests religious scholars with the ultimate and unchecked authority on political decisions. It rests on three foundations, not one: a revealed text is its exclusive reference; it is not legitimate to challenge the status of the text; and religious scholars who are not elected are the ultimate authority entrusted with the interpretation and implementation of the text.

The line between a theocratic and a non-theocratic regime can easily be blurred and it is important to recognize this line if we wish to judge the coherence of the modernist-apologetic promise of a government that is freely elected by the people yet is also *shari'a*-based. In a comparative investigation of the American constitution and the Quran as constitutional foundations, Azizah al-Hibri suggested that the contradiction between the people's will and the Quran is superficial. Al-Hibri listed the following similarities as potential foundations for a revelation-based Islamic democracy: Americans have adopted a formative political document, which in essence does not change (the constitution), and so have Muslims (the Quran, their constitution); the annulment of laws enacted by representative bodies based on their incompatibility with the Quran should not be regarded as different from their annulment based on constitutional grounds by the U.S. Supreme Court; and, the argument that the Quran cannot be amended and the American constitution can is semantic because the constitution has hardly ever been changed, and the Quran is open to flexible interpretations just as the constitution is.[16]

None of these arguments is incorrect in itself, but al-Hibri's comparison is not exhaustive. It ignores two principles that are inseparable from the American constitutional order and establish the people's sovereignty. First, while American society is governed by a document written in the eighteenth century, the electorate holds the power to amend *any* of its clauses. While the process of doing so is complex, it implies that the constitution is a living document rather than a static, revealed text immune from challenge, and a number of important amendments have in fact been introduced over the years. Second, the justices authorized with passing their verdict on the constitutionality of legislation are indirectly nominated by the people (who elect the electors who elect the president who nominates the justices), and the laws governing their operation (for example, the number of justices) are subject for legislative change. Thus, a comparison between the *shari'a* and the American constitution cannot stop at the potential of both to be interpreted in flexible, creative ways. It must address additional questions: Who is the ultimate reference for constitutional authority in a society that has the Quran as its constitution? And, what are the means of electing the panel authorized to disqualify legislation on constitutional grounds?

The answers to those questions, which structurally determine whether a *shari'a*-based regime is theocratic or not, are not as simple as they may seem. *Shari'a* can be established as the constitutional reference for legislation and political action in different ways:

a   The people choose to have Islam as their constitutional reference, for example, through a referendum. That choice bears certain implications, including that politics should abide by the principle of *shura*, and that political action and legislation are restricted by the prohibited and permissible. However, it is valid only to the extent that a majority continues to wish it.

b   Islam is the a priori exclusive and only legitimate reference for politics. Because *shura* is ordained by Allah, it is a *shar'i* duty to apply it, i.e., to practice democratic politics and to respect certain individual rights. But this duty does not differ from other religious duties; therefore it is illogical that in exercising it other duties should be denied.

While (b) can easily be confused as identical to (a), and while the two can potentially lead to the same practical results, they are different. In (b), democratic practices are legitimized because of their Islamic reference, whereas in (a) Islamic practices are legitimized because of their democratic reference. Under (a), the notion that Allah wanted Islam to be the exclusive constitutional and legislative framework has to be continuously legitimized by a majority vote, suggesting that individuals who believe that Islam is the only legitimate reference need to hypothetically acknowledge the right of a majority to replace it with another reference. Under (b), the right of individuals to reject the notion that Islam should serve as the exclusive reference and strive to establish alternate references can only be legitimized or denied based on justifications drawn from that reference, creating a paradoxical result in which pluralism is sanctioned only to the extent that it ensures the triumph of one specific view.

Option (b) is inherently anti-liberal as it grants supremacy to one revelation and to one specific interpretation of the relationship between politics and that revelation. However, if we understand theocracy as the rule of an unelected religious establishment monopolizing the interpretation of the revelation, rather than as merely the rule in accordance with a revelation, then (b) is not *essentially* theocratic. The *shari'a*, as any textual corpus, is what people make of it, and people can make of it almost anything. Even its most clear-cut, self-evident prohibitions are susceptible to suspension based on mechanisms that are understood and applied differently by different jurists. Thus, to determine whether (b) is theocratic the crucial question is: who is the ultimate interpreter? Is it the majority, exercising their interpretive authority directly or indirectly, or is it a body that is external to the electoral process? There are at least four options:

b1) The decisions of the people's representatives constitute a confirmed and legitimate interpretation of the revelation. The representatives abide by the spirit of the *shari'a* and its limits as they understand them.

b2) A panel of experts in Islamic law, serving as a form of constitutional supreme court, has the final say on whether political actions and legislation are compatible with the *shari'a*. The panel's structure and the identity of its members are determined by the people's representatives, who have the right to change both by democratic vote.

b3) A panel of experts in Islamic law has the final say on whether political actions and legislations are compatible with the *shari'a*. The panel's structure and the identity of its members are determined by the people's representatives, but once established, the panel, as the ultimate arbitrator with regard to Allah's laws, enjoys the ultimate authority to rule whether decisions pertaining to its functioning are lawful or not.

b4) A panel of experts in Islamic law, selected and governed by a larger body of experts in Islamic law, has the final say on whether political actions and legislation are compatible with the *shari'a*. The existence of the panel as an organ independent of the political system and the pressure of public opinion, and its overriding authority over them, cannot be challenged.

The difference between (b1) and the other three options is obvious. In (b1) the electorate (or its elected representatives) and the application of the *shari'a* are one. Structurally, options (b2), (b3) and (b4) appear identical: in all three a panel of

expert religious jurists has the ultimate authority over all political decisions. However, whereas in (b2) the panel is indirectly governed by the people's will, and thus
the regime is not theocratic, in (b3), and far more drastically in (b4), the panel is
not subject to the will of electorate; once established, its authority is based not on
the public's consent, but on the expert status of its members as confirmed by other
experts. Thus, whereas (b2) can be considered (even if very narrowly) as a form of
a non-theocratic regime, (b3) and (b4) constitute a theocracy.

Reading one hundred and fifty years of modernist-apologetic political theorizing
in Arabic exposes a lacuna: early texts did not broach the topic of who holds the
ultimate authority for interpreting the divine. Yet, almost without exception, even
contemporary, more comprehensive texts, written by scholars quite aware of the
need to structurally ensure the harmony of electoral democracy with the *shari'a*,
did not provide a definitive answer to this question. Modernist-apologetic scholars
adopted option (b) rather than (a), either by taking it for granted or by stipulating
that the Islamic reference is not negotiable, but almost without exception did not
provide a full, systematic, unequivocal description of the structure of (b).

This long-enduring ambiguity, in works so nuanced and informative in other
respects, cannot be a coincidence. It reflects an onerous dilemma that modernist-
apologists have found hard to resolve. To fully equate the interpretation and the
application of the *shari'a* with the will of the people would amount to recognizing
the legitimacy of any decision taken by the masses, or their representatives, who
have been corrupted by decades of Western cultural attacks and living in a post-
shar'i world. On the other hand, establishing independent religious scholars as the
ultimate constitutional authorities would amount to creating the kind of regime
Islam detests according to modernist-apologists. Neither embracing one option nor
the other is the one position that allowed the promise for a *shari'a*-based, yet
non-theocratic, regime to remain intact.

The result of this ambiguity is that despite pledging that an Islamic regime would
not privilege religious scholars with a monopolizing voice, modernist-apologists
have left the door wide open to the establishment of a revelation-based theocratic
regime in which unelected *'ulama'* speak in the name of Allah and impose their
individual, possibly controversial, interpretations of His words. As examined in the
following discussion, while the modernist-apologists promised the very best of
two worlds—the world of revelation and the world of pluralistic doubt—they
managed to no more reconcile them in the political sphere than they did in the
scientific one.

A. *Shura*, Democracy and the Early Modernist-Apologists

Early modernist-apologetic literature introduced a set of ideas on despotism and
political participation that became the basis for the political theorizing of their
contemporary disciples. Al-Afghani, expressing sympathy for republicanism, argued
that despotism is morally wrong and socially destructive. 'Abduh gave this argument an apologetic context, suggesting that Islam was not to blame for the

despotism in the Muslim world, and this notion was then further developed by his students. The prevalence of despotism in Muslim societies, late nineteenth-century modernist-apologists argued, is not sanctioned by Islam, but is the tragic result of its misinterpretation and neglect. To abide once again by the teachings of Allah and His Prophet, Muslim societies should apply *shura*, which is a foundational Islamic principle. Applying *shura* involves accountable leaderships, freedom of speech, and the public's participation in the decision-making process. In creating the mechanisms to secure these aspects of *shura*, there is no harm in imitating Western democracies. The reasons imitation is not harmful are that *shura* may develop and be applied in different times through different means, and has been developed and applied more successfully in the West than in Muslim countries.

The underlying ambition of these arguments was similar to the ambition that encouraged early modernist-apologist theorizing on the compatibility of modern sciences and the Quran. The modernist-apologists wanted to demonstrate that a central, desired aspect of Western strength can be incorporated into Muslim societies without those societies having to relinquish Islam as their exclusive reference and framework of identity. However, their hermeneutics on politics were less coherent than on science. In identifying certain Quranic verses as retrospective forerunners of scientific discoveries, the early modernist-apologists equated specific revealed words with specific empirical facts. One could doubt, or ridicule, their writing on the heliocentric model or photography. But there could be no confusion as to what they intended to recognize as credible in Islamic terms. In contrast, in equating revealed words with modern political norms, ambiguities were not dispelled. The early modernist-apologetic writers were clear as to what Islam stands against—despotism; their sympathy for constitutionalism, electoral politics and legislative parliaments was also evident. But their texts did not put forward a specific political structure, and some left the reader uncertain as to whether or not they demand an open, consultative form of monarchism or authoritarianism, or would settle for nothing less than pluralistic electoral politics with the people as the source of all political powers. The potential clash between Islam as a reference for both political freedom and political action was almost completely ignored. They did not care to explain whether the freedom sanctioned by the Islamic reference allows undermining or doing away with Islam as the reference. Neither did they address the possibility that disagreements would arise over how specific aspects of divine directives should be applied, let alone provide a mechanism for settling such disagreements. From their point of view, once the Islamic ideal of government is reinstated, then core doctrinal or religio-legal disputes become impossible. But this belief contradicts some of the historical evidence they provide in support of their arguments.

By the time the first modernist-apologists began theorizing on despotism and political freedom, participatory institutions of governance had already been introduced in the Ottoman Empire. As mentioned by Lewis, already in the mid-eighteenth century Ottoman writers noted the existence of democratic institutions and republican principles in European countries. However, Western political structures received little attention and, following the French Revolution, were described pejoratively.[17] It was only in the mid-nineteenth century, with the rise of the Young Ottoman movement, that constitutionalism and parliamentarism began to be championed as prerequisites for imperial revival, and their reconciliation with Islamic norms, including the concept of *shura*, was considered. The Young Ottomans did not envision a secular regime; they conceptualized *shari'a* as the foundation for reform and freedom.[18] The pinnacle of that movement's achievements, the Ottoman constitution of 1876, which was modeled on the Belgian constitution of 1831, established an appointed upper house of parliament and an elected lower house with legislative authorities. This development signified a shift toward a civic Ottoman identity, but did not challenge the traditional structure of the state. The Sultan was not accountable to the elected assembly, and was authorized to dissolve it and to suspend the constitution whenever he wanted,[19] which is indeed what 'Abd al-Hamid II did in February 1878 when he was convinced that the democratic experiment weakened his position.[20]

Egypt's more prolonged and turbulent experiments with representative assemblies served as the main theatre for modernist-apologist conceptualizations of politics and, as such, merit particular attention. None of the advisory institutions established in Cairo during the nineteenth century involved rulers conceding their monopoly on decision-making. But they did signify the emergence of a link between political freedoms and social progression, and their creation was explained through terminological parallelisms between Islamic traditions and modern Western forms of government.

In September 1829, Muhammad 'Ali (reigned 1805–1848) convened, for the first time, an appointed consultative council (*Majlis al-Mushawara*). The Council, consisting of 156 members, was presided over by 'Ali's son Ibrahim and gathered once a year to carry out its advisory role on matters of administration, education and public works.[21] Its assembly indicated that Egypt's modernizer had reached the conclusion that some institutionalized form of public participation in the affairs of the state would enhance his political standing. 'Ali's official bulletin, *al-Waqa'i' al-Misriyya*, compared the Council to the British Parliament and the French National Assembly, and Rifa'a al-Tahtawi, head of Egypt's language school and the state's translation department, invoked the term *shura* to describe the American Congress.[22] It is not clear whether the terminological confusion between elected councils with legislative and supervisory authorities and an appointed council without any actual power was deliberate. Sa'id, 'Ali's third successor (reigned 1854–1863), created an appointed State Council that also remained purely advisory. In November 1866, his successor, Isma'il, established an assembly of 75 delegates (*Majlis Shura al-Nuwwab*) elected by Egypt's male population. Prior to the publication of the decree announcing the establishment of the assembly, French, Belgian and English journalists got wind of the project, and some were convinced that the prospective assembly was the equivalent of the French legislative bodies. As its predecessors, the assembly possessed only advisory authority. Isma'il was under no obligation to accept its advice, and he alone had the authority to convene, adjourn or dissolve it. However, to impress his European creditors with his constitutional aims, he consulted with the assembly on various matters, particularly those related to finance and infrastructure.

Jamal al-Din al-Afghani

By early 1879, members of Egypt's elected assembly, partly inspired by the teachings of Jamal al-Din al-Afghani, became more confident and were not wary of criticizing the Khedive. They pressed for greater authority, including the demand that the Assembly should be consulted before any decision affecting the Egyptian populace was taken.[23] Isma'il, on his part, struggled to assert his authority, and al-Afghani became his rival.[24]

On February 15, 1879, al-Afghani published his most elaborate commentary on despotism in *Misr*, a weekly edited by Syrian émigrés who were his disciples, and, though it did not explicitly address the situation in Egypt, it could not have been read outside of the context of the intensifying political battle for meaningful representative politics. Hourani argued that al-Afghani was, by temperament, autocratic and impatient, and that his ideal of government was not constitutionalist in principle, but "rather that of the Islamic theorists—the just King recognizing the sovereignty of a fundamental law."[25] Yet, al-Afghani's article suggests the contrary. In it, he expressed his heartfelt preference for a republican form of government, and was willing to endorse enlightened autocracy only based on pragmatic considerations. In *Misr*, he lamented the lack of discussion on republicanism in the East and that the true nature of republicanism, as well as the happiness it brings to those enjoying it, are not acknowledged because of the arbitrary reign of unrestrained despots who rob their subjects of their rights, reduce them to the level of beasts, and hinder the teaching of the true sciences. He then distinguished between different categories and sub-categories of despotic regimes, some cruel, some crueler, and some blatantly incompetent and naïve. The "compassionate-informed-enlightened government" was the only one described positively; such a government acts like a provident father toward his children. It applies a just system of law, develops the economy, the education system and the sciences, provides for the welfare of the population, and prevents corruption. While this was evidently not al-Afghani's desired system of government, he promoted it as the most feasible transformation Eastern societies could hope for in the foreseeable future.[26]

The abovementioned was not the only instance in which al-Afghani expressed his position against despotism, his praise of republicanism, and his support of enlightened autocracy as compromise between the first two extremes. In May 1879, four months before he was expelled from Egypt, he argued that the weakness of Eastern countries was due to their fanaticism and despotism, which he described as shackling a nation with the chain of one will and acting only to please that one will.[27] In another text he characterized one-man rule as the commonplace form of government in Muslim societies, the result of the nations' ignorance, and, in contrast, the people's rule as the commonplace form of government in Europe, associated with wisdom, knowledge and advancement. He argued that it is one of Allah's laws that nations that become knowledgeable do away with despotism, and that gradually, with time, the people are to rule themselves in all the nations of the world.[28] In yet another text, he argued that, in order to be meaningful rather than artificial, legislative assemblies must be elected by the people rather than appointed by the leader.[29] Despots, he suggested elsewhere, never concede their powers voluntarily. Moreover, he continued, true freedom and true independence are never delivered to people on a golden plate; they must be fought for and the fight is bloody. Being that neither Egypt nor the East are ready to transition to a republican regime, and since their renewal requires an end to despotism, they should hope that Allah will provide them with the rule of strong, just leaders who would not rule as despots and whose powers would be limited. Indeed, a transition from despotism to a *shura* regime is more achievable than to a republican regime because rulers may find that a *shura* regime enables them to consolidate their power and garner public support without compromising their authority.[30]

Islamic jargon and justifications were strikingly negligible in al-Afghani's work. His were the comments of a perceptive political scientist who has learned much about human nature and the shortcomings of various governing systems. He did not suggest that republicanism is sanctioned by Allah or is rooted in the Quran or in Muslim history. *Shura*, for him, was the equivalent of the participatory, consultative authoritarianism he was ready to settle for rather than the foundation of Islamic political philosophy as it was later considered by his disciples. Even his pragmatism was not couched in Islamic terms. There is nothing in al-Afghani's texts that indicates he was concerned with the historical linkage between Western republicanism, constitutionalism and secularization.

Muhammad 'Abduh

The apologist argument against despotism and in favor of electoral politics was introduced by 'Abduh. In 1881, as the nationalist officers movement led by Ahmad 'Urabi grew in influence, a petition signed by 1,600 individuals demanded that Tawfiq, the successor of the disposed Isma'il, grant the assembly authorities similar to those enjoyed by European parliaments. However, the assembly that he convened on December 26, 1881, had no such authorities. Shortly before the delegates convened, 'Abduh published three essays on the meaning of *shura*. The essays constituted an effort to support demands for reforms without challenging the authority of the Khedive or expressly siding with one of the factions competing for influence in the country. In the process, 'Abduh laid the foundations for a theory on the relation between *shura* and freedoms. Whereas al-Afghani's broaching of the subject three years earlier was devoid of an overtly Islamic context, 'Abduh's views, as expressed in those three essays, reveal a determination to show that Islam is the remedy for—rather than the cause of—oppression and injustice. His essays presented Islam as a reference that allows for a strong ruler, an elected legislative council, and the wise, binding advice of religious scholars to coexist in harmony in a society that is free from tyranny *because* it is loyal to the divine decrees on governance.

In his first essay, "On *Shura* and Despotism," 'Abduh distinguished between two types of despots. One type, the totalitarian, rules as he sees fit and his will is the only thing that matters. The other type applies the *shari'a* and acts in accordance with Allah's laws. According to 'Abduh, the former type contravenes *shari'a* itself, which commands leaders to abide by the laws of Allah and apply them. In contrast, the latter type is not really a despot for two reasons. The *shari'a* speaks of the need for an *imam* who applies Allah's laws and protects religion. And common sense holds that an individual who applies the *shari'a* is not a despot because he is constrained by Allah's laws and is not able to contravene them.[31]

Had 'Abduh stopped there, his essay would have constituted an endorsement of the classic model, according to which a Muslim ruler's ability to govern effectively and apply Allah's decrees are the only criteria for legitimacy. But he went further. He argued that while the *shari'a* limits rulers, and thus prohibits despotism, it does not suffice in itself as a guarantee against wrongdoing. Allah ordained that religious scholars, who are required to command the good and forbid the evil, alert the ruler when he contravenes Allah's laws. In this context, 'Abduh cited a tradition according to which Allah wanted three things: that He alone would be worshipped, that He would not be associated with others, and that the leader would practice *shura*.[32] Thus, contrary to the implication of 'Abduh's previous statement, a one-man-regime is never acceptable, even if that one man is committed to the *shari'a*, as the *shari'a* itself requires that a leader must be advised and a leader is certain to commit errors without sound advice from knowledgeable individuals.

While 'Abduh did not say so explicitly, he appeared to distinguish between two types of advice: the advice of religious scholars that serves as a check and balance against breaking the *shari'a*, and the advice of the body politic as a means of reaching decisions on issues on which the *shari'a* leaves room for human discretion. The latter is, according to 'Abduh, ordained by the command in Q. 3:159, and supported by Abu Hurayra, who testified that he had never seen anyone willing to consult others more than the Prophet. 'Abduh emphasized that the words of 3:159, "And when you have decided, then rely upon Allah," should be interpreted as applying to decisions reached after consultation.[33]

How should *shura* function precisely? What exactly are its prerogatives? In his first essay on the subject, 'Abduh did not go into details, but his words clearly indicated his hope that something akin to the elected parliaments of the West would be established in Egypt—and in other Muslim societies. There should be no objection, he wrote, to us accommodating the way we exercise *shura* to that of nations that learned *shura* from us and apply it using certain methods, so long as doing so would benefit the *umma* and Islam. Indeed, if learning from the experience of others serves the interests of Muslims then it is their duty to do so. The point that adopting external political models is actually a return to authenticity could not have been stressed more: 'Abduh concluded the essay by conveying his hope that he had managed to convince his readers that the quest for *shura* and the rejection of despotism are not the result of imitating foreigners but of a desire to implement the *shari'a*.[34]

'Abduh's second essay on *shura* directly addressed Egypt's newly elected assembly and reads as an encouragement for the Khedive to broaden its authorities. He wrote that Egyptians are ready for *shura*, as they had come to learn the difference between the beneficiary and the harmful, and that the Khedive desires *shura* because he rejects despotism, seeks the good of his country and abides by the *shari'a*. Given the existence of a sufficient number of Egyptians who know what *shura* is and how it will benefit the country, and, given that many of those elected to the Egyptian assembly belong to this group, it is indeed right for *shura* in Egypt to be facilitated through its elected assembly.[35]

The third and final segment of 'Abduh's series on *shura* constituted another, albeit indirect call to entrust the newly elected assembly with meaningful legislative powers. 'Abduh alluded to Rousseau as he passionately advocated for political pluralism and for the necessity of an elected, representative and legislative council. While he did not explicitly mention Egypt, his previous essay suggests that he wrote with his homeland in mind when stipulating the social conditions that allow the existence of electoral politics and legislative assemblies. He wrote that the best and most useful laws are those that result from the "general will" (*al-ra'i al-'amm*). As such, they are based on the principles of *shura*, which are beneficial only in societies where a general will has been established. The general will is an enlightened stage of development, in which people are united in purpose and prefer the communal benefit to their individual benefit. When members of a nation reach this stage they will not be satisfied with anything less than just laws that fit their situation and their interests. Such laws cannot be enacted by one single individual because one person does not possess the ability to correctly identify the interests of the entire nation. At the same time, it is also impossible for everyone to participate in the legislative process. Thus, the one and only alternative is to elect an appropriate number of legislators, and empower the press to present to the public the delegates' debates and proposed pieces of legislation.[36] 'Abduh addressed the potential shortcomings of parliamentary politics in a way that actually affirmed his deep belief in its advantages. It is possible, he wrote, that legislators would not reach the best decisions. But even in such cases, they should not be reprimanded because Allah has decreed that things reach their desired stage only gradually.[37]

As a political commentary, there was little audacity in 'Abduh's three essays. When he directly addressed the political situation in Egypt he expressed his trust in the Khedive, and when he advocated for a legislature with actual powers he refrained from directly mentioning Egypt or criticizing the regime. He desired a parliament with legislative authorities but was careful not to argue that a regime that negates this desire is, in Islamic terms, illegitimate. The importance of the essays as an intellectual legacy, on the other hand, cannot be exaggerated, as they introduced a set of interwoven ideas that became the foundation of the political thought of the modernist-apologetic school: Western systems of government are rooted in Islam; their adoption, to the extent that it is beneficial, is not an act of imitation but of restoration; *shari'a* is the best guarantee against despotism; the system of government ordained by the *shari'a* places limits on the leader's power, requires him to consult the people, and, when a general will is reached, implies that a legislative council, popularly elected, be established.

Shari'a in 'Abduh's political writing is a three-fold framework: the primary and comprehensive source for all authorities; a constitution determining the pluralistic nature of the regime; and, a legal codex. The possibility of an alternative to Islam as the exclusive reference was so fanciful that he did not engage with the notion in any way. Neither did he discuss the theoretical potential for clashes between an elected legislator and the revelation. As noted in the introduction, in his apologetic works written two decades later, responding to the argument that Muslim societies are despotic *because* of Islam, 'Abduh presented *shari'a* as a protector against one-man rule and the rule of religious scholars, as all must equally abide by it and apply it. Yet absent from his theorizing in both the early 1880s and later was any idea as to how a participatory system with the *shari'a* as its reference would actually function. Specifically, he did not address the mechanism that would resolve disagreements over interpretations of the *shari'a*, should they arise between the different actors in the system envisioned. Which religious scholars should have a say in politics and how will they be elected or selected? What if the ruler or the assembly do not heed the advice of religious scholars that a certain measure contravenes the laws of Allah? What if the ruler vetoes legislation enacted by a council elected by an enlightened public that represents the general will and that, according to all interpretations, does not negate the Quran? The essays on *shura*, in particular, reveal an understanding that politics involve, by their very nature, struggles for power, but they nevertheless failed to address the possibility that a society that abides by true Islam could face conflicts between different factions, all of which speak in the name of Islam.

'Abd al-Rahman al-Kawakibi

The failure of the 'Urabi revolt in September 1882 and the British occupation that followed did not end Egypt's parliamentary experiment. But both did cripple what had been a growing movement promoting the transfer of governmental authorities to elected representatives. An elected Legislative Council (*Majlis Shura al-Qawanin*) was established in 1883, but its de facto role was merely an advisory one and it proved to be submissive to the demands of the government.[38] The powerlessness of parliamentary life in English-occupied Egypt and the rigid authoritarianism that developed in the fragile, disintegrating Ottoman Empire served as the backdrop for 'Abd al-Rahman al-Kawakibi's treatise against despotism. Al-Kawakibi, a politician, journalist and victim of 'Abd al-Hamid's political oppression, found shelter in Egypt in 1898 and joined Rida's al-Manar project. By that time, the foundations of the modernist-apologist's interpretive synthesis of Western advancements and Islamic revelation had already been solidly laid. His book demonstrated his mastery of that synthesis, and further developed 'Abduh's apologetics on the anti-despotic nature of Islam, but also introduced a number of additional ambiguities.

Al-Kawakibi's definition of a despot was essentially akin to those of al-Afghani and 'Abduh: a leader who is satisfied with his own opinion when deciding on matters that require consultation. He defined despotism as a trait of an absolutist government that rules as it sees fit, without regard for the law or the people's will.[39] Such governments, he made clear, are not unique to the lands of the East. Constitutions and electoral procedures are not guarantees against despotism, as the authority of the majority of elected governments in the world is limited only in theory. In practice, he argued, these elected governments are not beholden to the legislative body, and are not subjected to critical oversight or held accountable; thus, they are despotic. In the history of humankind, non-despotic regimes had proven fragile, with England's being the only exception, having never been destroyed by the depression of defeat or the arrogance of victory.[40]

Having established the universality of despotism and its enduring nature, al-Kawakibi could safely turn to the apologetic argument that was the heart of his discussion. European political commentators are entirely wrong, he wrote, in suggesting that political despotism in Muslim lands is the result of religious despotism, or that the two are fraternal-despotic systems that cooperate with each other. The Quran does not endorse despotism; on the contrary, the Quran rejects it, as seen in Q. 3:159 and 42:38, as well as in revealed narrations. One example is the Queen of Sheba, to whom King Solomon sent a letter requiring her to submit to Allah. Upon receiving it she conferred with her advisers: "She said, 'O eminent ones, advise me in my affair. I would not decide a matter until you witness [for] me.'" The dignitaries humbly told their Queen: "'the command is yours, so see what you will command.'" (Q. 27:32–33). This story, according to al-Kawakibi, instructs that it is the duty of rulers to seek the advice of the nation's dignitaries and reach a decision based on these consultations alone. It also teaches that power should be preserved in the hands of the people. Another example is Q. 7:109–112 and 20:62, which tell of Pharaoh's consultations with his advisors.[41] Indeed, Allah cursed despotism.[42] Loyalty to Allah requires educating the people against despotism, to prepare an alternative, and then to oppose despotism gently and gradually.[43]

Al-Kawakibi's bottom line is far-reaching: Islam is based on the foundations of "democratic administration, or republicanism ('umumiyya), or aristocratic shura or the shura of dignitaries."[44] He used these terms interchangeably, as if they were identical, possessing the same meaning. The suggested parallel between the Islamic model and the Westminster model fit with the general admiration for England and the defense of its democratic character that resonated in his work.[45]

The opposite of despotism is freedom, and as much as Islam forbids the former, it protects the latter. In a subsequent book, Umm al-Qura, a precursor of Arab nationalism, al-Kawakibi described the foundations of freedom as equal rights, the subjection of leaders to criticism, the lack of fear to advise them, and the protection of various liberties, including the right to teach, preach and publish. In his mind, there was an inseparable link between adherence to true Islam, the establishment of freedom and the resurrection of the people; freedom is the spirit of religion, the most cherished of human possessions except life itself, and a prerequisite for hope and action.[46]

But what *precisely* is the non–despotic regime ordained by Islam? And what precisely are the freedoms ordained by Islam? Al-Kawakibi's discussion left these questions unanswered, and was not without its contradictions. It is not clear whether he envisioned an electoral democracy in which the people, represented by their delegates, are the ultimate reference for political decisions, or if he would settle for an enlightened, devout monarch who consults others. The story of Queen Sheba exemplifies the ambiguity of his text. Contrary to what al-Kawakibi wrote, even the most generous interpretation of the verses on the Queen's deliberations with her dignitaries cannot suggest a requirement to entrust the powers of government with "the people," or even a requirement to abide by the results of a consultative process. The story tells of an absolute monarch who consults with a select group, and is not obligated, even by the standards of the noblemen who give her counsel, to accept their advice. This is a far cry from al-Kawakibi's praise of governments that are answerable to parliaments, and, together with other examples and definitions he provided, the result is confusion as to what exactly he had in mind.

Another contradiction is history as a guide. Al-Kawakibi narrated the chronicles of Muslim political history as a process of decline, in which the neglect of true Islam and the embrace of ideas alien to Islam allowed despotism to prosper. He was satisfied that in the days of the four righteous successors the Islamic foundations of government were maintained in the most perfected and comprehensive way.[47] He compared the opposition to 'Uthman b. 'Affan with the Dreyfus affair in France, suggesting it demonstrates that government at the time of the four righteous successors was subject to the kind of scrutiny and criticism that prevents despotism.[48] But rather than support his argument that the solution to all problems lies in the return to a golden past, the experience of 'Uthman's days implies that even the most righteous and closest companions of the Prophet failed to implement Allah's ideal of government. If al-Kawakibi's sympathies lay with the opposition to the third Khalifa (and indeed, that is also 'Imara's understanding of his text),[49] then he would have to concede that the *salaf* failed to practice *shura* properly at times. Considering that even the righteous forefathers failed, why hold with such certainty that those who can merely hope to follow their example would succeed?

This question leads to another inconsistency in al-Kawakibi's argument. He presented Islam as a reference for political freedom within the broader context of his defense of Islam as the all-encompassing reference for all aspects of life, but, like his intellectual mentors, did not address the potential challenges resulting from this formulation. For example, do political freedoms, including the freedom of speech that he clearly cherished, involve the right to undermine the legitimacy of Islam itself as the all-encompassing reference? What if a people, living in a free society in which their freedom of expression was secured, were to decide that they wished to speak against religion, or even eliminate it from their lives?

For al-Kawakibi this prospect was unthinkable and, thus, undeserving of attention in the same way it was for 'Abduh. He was less dismissive of the potential contradiction between his desire to have religious law as the all-encompassing reference and his wish to have elected assemblies that democratically enact legislation. His brief comment that the Prophet and his righteous successors were able to maintain democratic foundations because in Islam religion is paramount only on matters that are pertinent to its fundamentals,[50] suggests he was satisfied that Islam allows broad enough discretion on most matters so as to allow English or French-styled elected assemblies to function with *shari'a* as their reference. But al-Kawakibi did not address this issue in a detailed manner. What if different actors debated the interpretation of specific religious "fundamentals," or debated whether certain issues should be considered "fundamentals" at all? Who then should have the final say as to what accords with Islam and what does not? The analytic acumen al-Kawakibi demonstrated on other issues, specifically showing Muslim societies were not spared such controversies even in their golden days, emphasizes the absence of these questions from his discussion.

Muhammad Rashid Rida

Muhammad Rashid Rida expressed his views on despotism in a number of essays, but given the copious amount of his intellectual output over the course of thirty-seven years, the lack of a systematic concept of the ideal Islamic regime, or of the relationship between Western political systems and the Islamic ideal, is surprising. In one of his first commentaries on despotism, published in 1906, six years after he reprinted al-Afghani's analysis of despotism in al-Manar, Rida distinguished between two types of societies in which *shura* is not applied and the will of one person is the law. According to Rida, when a despot is righteous, just, vigorous, knowledgeable, and promotes the sciences, nations can be happy, rich and competent. When the despot is corrupt and weak, nations become corrupt, poor and desperate, and the strong injure the rights of the weak. Such nations are easy prey for occupation. Rida accepted al-Afghani's notion that not all despots are the same and that a certain type of tyranny can do good, but unlike al-Afghani, he did not argue that a republican regime is the desired alternative.[51]

Rida's most detailed framework for Islamic government appears in his treatise *al-Khilafa*, which he published in 1922. In the treatise, Rida discredited the failing political ambitions of the Sharif Husayn of Mecca, who had, by then, become his archrival. The despotic, unconstitutional conduct of the Sharif, "who does whatever he wants and rules however he deems fit" was specified as one of several reasons for why the title of *Khalifa* was unsuitable for him.[52] According to Rida, in the Islamic state the *Khalifa* will be chosen by *ahl al-hall wal-'aqd* of the nation, which he defined, in line with the classic definition of the phrase, as a group of religious scholars, leaders and dignitaries. The nation has the right to depose the *Khalifa* after weighing whether the continuation of his reign may cause greater harm than the *fitna* (civil strife, in this context) that may result from a rebellion.[53] Relying on Q. 3:159, 42:38 and a number of traditions according to which the Prophet practiced *shura*, and even changed his mind following consultations, Rida argued that it is mandatory for the Muslim leader to seek counsel before deciding on issues the Quran and Prophetic traditions do not address, or on issues incon-clusively addressed.[54] As his predecessors had done, he too ignored the reality that the decisive status and meaning of revelations is subject to debate, and did not offer a way or mechanism to resolve them.

While Rida did not explicitly state that he considered the outcomes of con-sultations to be binding, not optional, his use of the example of the Prophet, who preferred the opinions of others to his own, imply that in his opinion *shura* was indeed binding. This view renders his conception of *shura* to be similar to a par-liamentary regime in which the executive must abide by the decisions of the leg-islature. But this is not an argument Rida himself made. The historical examples he provided for the exercising of *shura* pointed not only to consultations with the public, but also to consultations with a small group of senior confidents, thus allowing for an interpretation of *shura* as a form of both republican and mon-archical regimes. His comments that the Prophet did not offer specific regulations on the practice of *shura* and that *shura* should accommodate current circumstances and conditions also allowed diverse interpretations.[55] Al-Kawakibi's writings were similarly vague as to whether *shura* is the equivalent of a republic or of an enligh-tened monarchy, but Rida's ambiguity on this point is more striking: he presented his ideal for an Islamic regime at a time when Western liberal democracies were at a historic pinnacle of strength, and Egypt had gained official independence and was in the process of adopting a constitution that was not revelation-based. *Al-Khilafa* sought to reverse a reality of Western domination by providing a framework for a viable, authentic, unified Islamic regime. As such, Rida perhaps thought it counter-productive to engage with parallelisms between liberal political concepts and Isla-mic ones. But this does not explain why Rida published his most detailed political treatise without specifying precisely how *shura* should be implemented in his day and time. The book ended a period of four decades of modernist-apologetic poli-tical theorizing that presented the Islamic ideal of government as similar to Western democracies, but always fell short of expressing exactly how the ideal should be implemented in practical terms.

Hasan al-Banna

Hasan al-Banna was in a more challenging position than the forefathers of the modernist-apologetic school. A leader of a mass movement that sought to revolu-tionize Egypt through political activism, he operated at a time when democratic elections became the conventional wisdom for legitimizing governments. In 1923, Egypt adopted a constitution that did not recognize Islam as the exclusive or even primary reference, declared the nation the source of all powers and established an elected parliament, though it vested ultimate executive and legislative authorities with the King. The parliament was dominated during the 1920s and 1930s by liberal parties that differed in their opinions of Britain and the Palace. In devising a political strategy, al-Banna had to decide whether he accepted representative par-liamentary monarchism as being a legitimately Islamic political system. He offered his most detailed answer in 1939 during the fifth conference of his movement while being faced with intense pressure from activists calling on him to consider launching a violent revolution immediately.[56] His answer relied on the legacy of early modernist-apologists, and did not avoid a crucial question they had ignored: what is the verdict on democratic legislation that contradicts Allah's law?

Al-Banna put forward a simple equation that limitedly recognized the legitimacy of Egypt's constitution based on its accordance with Islam, while delegitimizing particular pieces of legislation approved by the parliament elected in accordance with that constitution. He declared that constitutional government is closer to Islam than all other existing forms of government because certain norms it promotes are Islamic norms, including protecting personal freedoms, exercising *shura*, establishing the people as the source of the regime's authority, holding the leadership accountable, and clearly defining the powers of different government authorities.[57]

From this followed that the constitution, and electoral parliamentary politics, are legitimate not because of the liberal values they manifest and maintain, but because these liberal values are in fact Islamic; in other words, that they are legitimate not because the people decided so, but because they represent certain Islamic principles. The difference is not a matter of splitting hairs, as indicated by the subsequent argument al-Banna presented. Islam, he wrote, enacted laws on numerous issues, from finances to crimes, from commerce to international relations. It is thus incomprehensible and illogical that any law enacted in a Muslim nation should contradict the laws of its religion, its Quran and the example of its Prophet. Drawing on Q. 5:49–50, which commands Muslims to abide by Allah's laws, al-Banna warned of the likely conflicts between man-made and divine laws, for example those prohibiting and permitting prostitution, interest-based loans, alcohol and gambling, and stated that the Muslim Brothers would never abide by laws that contradict those of Allah and would use "all means" to replace them with Islamic laws.[58]

Al-Banna presented his case as a defense of the liberal constitution itself: since the constitution declared Islam as the religion of the state, laws that contradict *shari'a* should be regarded unconstitutional.[59] This argument makes sense, if one accepts his view of the meaning of designating Islam the religion of state. But the implications of this argument were not raised by al-Banna. If one accepts that majority rule must be servile to Islamic law, one must clarify who should possess the authority to determine whether certain legislation contradicts Allah's laws. Is it the king, the parliament, a council of religious scholars, al-Banna himself? Given that the politicians who enraged al-Banna considered themselves loyal to Islam no less than he, the indispensability of a mechanism that would resolve such controversies could not have escaped him. His silence on the matter is revealing. That of the fathers of modernist-apologetic thought could possibly be explained by the theoretical nature of their discussion but this was not the case with al-Banna. Confronted by an actual conflict between Islamic law and the people's law, he still avoided addressing any issues that would have forced him to recognize the fine line between the sovereignty of the people and theocracy.

B. *Shura*, Democracy and Contemporary Modernist-Apologists

The writings by Muhammad al-Ghazali, Yusuf al-Qaradawi and Muhammad 'Imara on the relation between Islam and democracy drew from foundational modernist-apologetic texts, and asserted several core arguments that had already been introduced in the late nineteenth century, often invoking similar revealed texts and apologetic statements. Specifically, these included the views that Islam forbids despotism and negates a theocratic regime; that Islam commands leaders to engage in *shura*; that the methods of practicing *shura* can change in order to accommodate changing times and needs; and, that it is not prohibited to learn how to practice *shura* from non-Muslim societies, to the extent that these practices are beneficial. However, while inspired by formative modernist-apologetic scholarship, al-Ghazali's, al-Qaradawi's and 'Imara's political theorizing was not merely a replication of the existing intellectual project they so admired; rather, it was a bid to expand and accommodate that project to new realities. On the one hand, they introduced, particularly since the 1980s, a broader and more detailed commitment to pluralistic, competitive electoral politics overseen by an elected, representative legislature; on the other hand, they emphasized that Islam is the reference for their democratic agenda, and stressed that in their envisioned Islamic state, democratic decisions could not breach the limits of the *shari'a*.

Both distinctions corresponded to international, regional and local developments. The three matured as thinkers in an Egypt where liberalism was viewed as a failed experiment with a foreign political theory, unfaithful to its own promises, but where democratic elections and the existence of certain liberal freedoms—or, more correctly, the appearance of democratic elections and the existence of certain liberal freedoms—had nevertheless been established as the only means to legitimize governments. Furthermore, casting votes at the ballot box seemed to be the most feasible way to peacefully transform the country to a *shari'a*-based society. In the 1980s, the collapse of communism, the failure of Pan-Arabism and the "third wave of democratization" encouraged the reemergence of liberal democracy as a viable universal system in the eyes of some Egyptian—and Arab—intellectuals and activists.[60] In response to these developments, al-Ghazali, al-Qaradawi and 'Imara began to place the democratization of Muslim societies at the core of their agenda. They emphasized the democratic essence of Islam and further developed apologetic arguments on the similarities between *shura* and liberal democracy.

Fitting with their emphasis on the democratic essence of *shura* and, thus, of Islam, al-Ghazali, al-Qaradawi and 'Imara also stressed something the early modernist-apologists hardly found the need to address at all: that revelation must serve as an exclusive reference and that the institutions of *shura* must never breach the limits of the divine law. While this may seem significant, the difference between them and their intellectual forefathers on this matter does not indicate a theoretical transformation of any kind. For late nineteenth-century and early twentieth-century modernist-apologists, the possibility of a government and legislature not committed to the revelation was unthinkable and, thus, they saw no reason to underscore the point that a participatory regime should abide by the *shari'a*. In contrast, for al-Ghazali, al-Qaradawi and 'Imara, the status of the *shari'a* as an exclusive, all-encompassing, standard that every piece of legislation and every executive measure must accommodate was something that needed to be explained and defended. Throughout the course of their own lives they witnessed Egyptian regimes allow the supremacy of Islamic law to be challenged to a certain extent. Beginning in 1923, when the constitution failed to even mention Islamic law as a source of legislation, subsequent Egyptian regimes made similar challenges, including Nasser entirely ignoring the *shari'a* in his temporary constitutions and Sadat describing the *shari'a* as only *a* main source of legislation in the 1971 constitution. Intended as a positive gesture towards Islamists, a 1980 amendment elevated the *shari'a* to the status of *the* chief (but still not exclusive) source of legislation, yet was determined by the constitutional court as non-applicable to legislation passed prior to its ratification.[61] While constitutional amendments in the Sadat era seemed to favor modernist-apologetic demands, they fell short of unequivocally subjecting society to the divine laws; more importantly, these amendments did not result in what al-Ghazali, al-Qaradawi, and 'Imara considered to be the minimum level of social reform required for society to be considered as truly adhering to Allah's laws having, for example, failed to make alcohol and interest-based loans illegal.

There was another reason for contemporary modernist-apologists to assert the Islamic credentials of their political thought. An emerging body of anti-modernist texts, some influenced by *wahhabi* thought, rejected the notion that Islam and democracy are compatible at all, suggested that electoral politics and legislatures deny the sovereignty of Allah, and implied that in their quest to demonstrate the vitality of Islam through syntheses, the modernist-apologists unintentionally undermine Islam's integrity.[62] The anti-modernists demanded, in essence, the same thing modernist-apologists called for: a society governed by Islam. But their theories drew from a strong belief that the democratic process, in its essence, negates Islam, and that efforts to reshape it in an Islamic manner are the equivalent of calling wine water, which, as the Prophet warned, does not transform wine into water. These accusations encouraged contemporary modernist-apologists to stress that their envisioned *shura* regime is, first and foremost, Islamic, and that its democratic components are derived from and limited by the *shari'a*.

Raised in a society where state institutions were not *shari'a*-based and conflicted with Allah's laws as they understand them, al-Ghazali, al-Qaradawi and 'Imara recognized that the possibility of conflict between the decisions of elected assemblies and the revelation cannot be ignored. Their visions of the Islamic state thus introduced mechanisms that would ensure the compatibility of democratic decisions with revelation. Diverse structures were offered, some detailed, some vague, which came close to providing a conclusive answer as to who will have the final say in the ideal Islamic state. However, they fell short of establishing the precise structure and function of the body or individual tasked with deciding what constitutes an infringement of the *shari'a*. Thus, just as their predecessors, the contemporary modernist-apologists also avoided committing themselves to either a regime in which the ultimate power resides with the people or to a regime in which it resides with non-elected religious officials.

Muhammad al-Ghazali

Al-Ghazali's first comprehensive theorizing on political regimes is found in a book entitled *Islam and Political Despotism*. According to its introduction, al-Ghazali based his treatise on lectures he gave to Muslim Brothers incarcerated with him in al-Tur prison after the 1949 crackdown on the movement.[63] This statement was confirmed by al-Qaradawi.[64] In this book, al-Ghazali, shaken by the first *mihna*, or great trial of the Brothers (i.e., the regime's crackdown on the movement), asserted that Western imperialism was the source of political oppression in Egypt and scathingly attacked the West in general. He left little doubt of his conviction that the liberal democratic form of government is, by its nature, unsustainable, noting (in a critique reminiscent of al-Kawakibi's half a century earlier), that elected legislatures cannot remove rulers from power. Hitler's rise to dictatorial power through popular vote and his subversion of the popularly elected *Reichstag* in 1933 served as one example.[65] Al-Ghazali argued that the West had tried repeatedly to introduce systems that safeguard freedoms and had always failed.[66] Yet, his disenchantment with Western liberalism did not lead him to reject democratic ideals altogether. Rather, al-Ghazali strove to persuade his audience that Islam, and Islam alone, provided human beings in the past with a political system that secured their freedom and could do so in the future.[67] Acknowledging the impact al-Banna's assassination and the subsequent imprisonment of Muslim Brothers activists had on him, he argued that despotism is a serious offense according to the teachings of Islam. Only the nation can legitimize a ruler, and the ruler must abide by its will and manifest its spirit; he must fully recognize that power is a responsibility rather than luxury.[68]

As in foundational modernist-apologetic texts, al-Ghazali's book did not present a detailed structure of his envisioned regime. But he did make clear something early modernist-apologists did not: that a Muslim leader is beholden to the results of the practice of *shura*, i.e., that an "enlightened monarch" is illegitimate from an Islamic standpoint. This statement constitutes the most original contribution of his work. Al-Ghazali supported it with two arguments. First, *shura* cannot be expected to effectively direct leaders to the right path, unless they abide by its results; second, the Prophet and his righteous successors applied *shura*, and always accepted the opinions of those with whom they consulted.[69]

Another point highlighted by al-Ghazali was that there are clear limits to *shura*. All that has been revealed must be accepted without reservation; consultation should be applied only where there is room for *ijtihad*. Al-Ghazali cited a tradition to support the binding nature of *shura* and demonstrate that revelation overrides public opinion. It is wrong, wrote al-Ghazali, to justify despotism based on the example of the Prophet's refusal to accept his companions' opinion with regard to signing an agreement with the infidels of Mecca at Hudaybiyya in 628 AD. Indeed, the Prophet had told Abu Bakr and 'Umar that he would always accept an opinion on which the two consented, but this statement was only applicable to issues on which Allah had not issued His clear verdict. In Hudaybiyya, Allah had done so. After the people of Mecca refused to allow Muhammad and the 1,400 individuals who accompanied him to do the 'umra (the small pilgrimage), the Prophet was of the opinion that war should be waged, while the companions held that a peace accord should be signed. Then, things changed. The Prophet's camel suddenly stopped, and Muhammad interpreted this as a sign from Allah that he should accept the terms of the people of Mecca in order to preserve the sanctity of Allah's shrine. The companions, at that point, changed their minds and stood against an agreement, but that did not matter because once a revelation had been given, *shura* was no longer applicable.[70]

Thus, the equation is simple: the people's will is binding on all matters except where revelation exists. But who shall have the final say in cases where the content or application of a particular revelation is debated? Should it be reserved for the people, for their leader, or for religious scholars? Al-Ghazali did not address this question directly. Nevertheless, an analogy he made suggests the type of answer he had in mind: only qualified experts should decide some issues. In the past, he wrote, the clergy sentenced to death a scientist who observed that the earth was round. That was wrong; scientific truths should not be subjected to majority rule, just as religious truths should not be subjected to petty negotiations.[71] The irony of alluding to the troubled relations between Church and science in Christian societies in arguing that some religious "truths" must be accepted without debate escaped al-Ghazali. He did not address the possibility that "truths," whether scientific or religious, can be debated between experts, and, as an obvious result of neglecting to do so, did not find a need to suggest who should be authorized to distinguish between the permissible and the prohibited and how the political decision-making process should be structured.

Little was written by al-Ghazali on Islam and democratic theory during the 1960s and the 1970s, years in which he was more preoccupied with communism as a theoretical challenge. But this changed in the 1980s, as did his evaluation of the Western system of government. Whereas the young al-Ghazali, a survivor of the Palace's persecution of the Brothers under a liberal constitution, advocated for democracy but did not prioritize the issue and made his contempt for Western democracies evident, the elder al-Ghazali described the absence of democracy in the Muslim world as a fundamental weakness and humiliation that must be corrected, and his hostility to Western electoral politics gave way to more favorable interpretations. With the victory of the liberal democratic West in the Cold War, liberal democracy reemerged in the Arab world as a viable alternative to the failed ruling regimes, rather than a system unique to the West. Responding to global and regional transformations, al-Ghazali began to explicitly praise certain aspects of Western democracy and call for their technical adaptation in the Arab world. His brief visits to Muslim communities in the West during the 1970s and 1980s may have contributed to his sense of urgency that democracy is a core issue, not a peripheral one. In his book published in the mid-1980s, for example, al-Ghazali spoke of his "sadness and heartbreak [that] since the establishment of the State of Israel, elections there were never forged, while we [Muslims] are masters of creating [fake election] results, as the world knows well."[72] This sentiment did not imply, though, that he was at peace with the influence of Western ideologies on the Muslim world. On the contrary, al-Ghazali contextualized his desire for meaningful electoral democracy within his broader call to purify Muslim societies from the encroachment of the Western "cultural attack." Thus, he was lobbying for competitive electoral democracy and individual rights *as part* of his struggle to Islamize society, and was keen to demonstrate that the two objectives are in fact one.

In October 1990, four decades after authoring *Islam and Political Despotism*, al-Ghazali published another treatise focusing on Islam's ideal of government, *The Crisis of Shura*. The book's release coincided with Iraq's occupation of Kuwait and Operation Desert Shield, as well as the collapse of Communism in Eastern Europe. Within Arab societies and outside of them, the discourse on the "crisis of democracy in the Arab world" intensified. Al-Ghazali's central argument was similar to the one he introduced in the late 1940s: true Islam is the rival of despotism, as it binds rulers to *shura* and guarantees basic freedoms. But the book went further. Couched criticism of Western democracy gave way to clear expressions of admiration of certain practices and lament over their absence in Arab societies. At the same time, he emphasized the distinction between the Islamic ideal of government and the Western ideal.

Al-Ghazali spared no words in describing the poor state of Arab political culture and its desperate need for reform in comparison to the West. He recalled the time he observed, reading about General de Gaulle's ceding of power after suffering electoral defeat, that an Arab general would never have ceded power after such a defeat and would have remained in office until the people learned to respect him. Hearing this remark, a friend corrected al-Ghazali, saying that had it been an Arab country, either there would have been no elections, or they would have been rigged to ensure the general's victory. Al-Ghazali accepted the correction.[73]

The Muslims, he wrote, should learn from the political experience of the West. Western democracies established dignified principles that guide their political practices, and Muslims should adopt many of these. If the Western method of *shura* prevents despotism and protects critics of the government from harm, then clearly it is corrupt politicians, and not Allah and his Prophet, who benefit from opposing that method.[74] Having witnessed the persecution, varying in its severity, of the Muslim Brothers for more than 50 years, al-Ghazali's approach to Egypt's liberal past shifted from one of contempt to one of nostalgia. His new, revised opinion argued that while elections in monarchical Egypt were rigged, and while the 1923 constitution was repeatedly amended, freedoms were safeguarded, the regime treated citizens with respect, science and culture flourished, and religious associations, including the Muslim Brothers, were strong nevertheless. With the perspective of history, it is thus regrettable that the Brothers did not protect the liberal constitution more fiercely; religious activists in Egypt, wrote al-Ghazali, had learned the value of freedom the hard way. He added that it was his firm belief that were it impossible to fabricate the will of the people, then atheist ideologies would have never triumphed in Egypt.[75]

Al-Ghazali's newfound appreciation for the political achievements of the West was joined to other apologetic narratives. He emphasized that Islam had laid down democratic and liberal principles long before Western societies had done so. With time, and as the Muslim world stagnated and neglected its religious duties, Western societies developed more sophisticated practices of *shura* that fit the needs of more complex societies. But none of the principles the West adheres to are more sublime than those adhered to by the Muslim *umma* in the seventh century. An example he recalled was an interview with President Kennedy, who was asked by American journalists if his wife's trip to Europe was financed by her or by the government. This example of free speech and accountability reminded al-Ghazali of a conversation between the second Khalifa, 'Umar, and Salman al-Farisi, one of the Prophet's companions. Al-Farisi questioned the Khalifa's long clothing, noting that all other members of the *umma* could afford only short ones. In response, 'Umar asked his son, 'Abdallah, to speak to the people. 'Abdallah confessed to giving his father, being the tall man that he was, some of his own clothing. Muslims, concluded al-Ghazali, were given freedom of speech as a gift from Heaven; the West only reached this level of freedom through bloodshed.[76]

In *The Crisis of Shura*, al-Ghazali was careful to stress that, despite their similarities, *shura* is not synonymous with Western democracy. The latter, he wrote, serves as its own reference whereas the former's exclusive reference is Allah and is guided and restricted by His laws. Al-Ghazali put forward in this work a similar thesis to the one he had presented four decades earlier: where there is no revelation, *shura* must be implemented and the results of consultation are binding; where there is revelation, it must be adhered to regardless of public opinion. In the United States, alcohol was banned and then permitted, and in England, the House of Commons and the House of Lords caved to "dirty pressures" and legalized homosexuality—but, unlike Westerners, Muslims know that human beings cannot prohibit the permissible or permit the prohibited. Applied within its limits, *shura* does not affect faith, rituals and the *halal* and *haram*, and thus the argument that considering the people as the source of power impugns the sovereignty of Allah is nothing more than a game of words, displaying a level of ignorance that only serves despots.[77] The latter statement indicates al-Ghazali was aware of the emergence of counter-arguments being made by anti-modernist Islamic scholars, who questioned the credibility of the modernist-apologetic synthesis of *shura* and democracy.

Recognizing the limits of human legislation is the key difference between legitimate and illegitimate *shura*. But who shall have the final word as to where these boundaries lie? While *The Crisis of Shura* more thoroughly addressed structural details than his earlier works, al-Ghazali still failed to provide a clear, comprehensive answer. The book avoided any systematic treatment of interpretative authority and, moreover, displayed an ill-founded certainty that in an ideal Muslim society the limits of the permissible and the prohibited would always be recognized through consensus. An example is al-Ghazali's analysis of Abu Bakr's decision to wage a war-to-the-death against the *murtaddun* despite the reservations of the other companions.[78] The analysis disproved the argument that Abu Bakr did not abide by the results of *shura*. The real meaning of Abu Bakr's decision, according to al-Ghazali, is that the first successor of the Prophet adhered to *shura* on all matters that were not clearly revealed, and ignored it when it contradicted revelation. Suggesting that in any case lasting divisions over revealed, conclusive verses are unlikely between the truly devout, al-Ghazali emphasized that while 'Umar disagreed with Abu Bakr at first, he was quick to recognize the meaning of revelation (al-Ghazali found this example useful already in Islam and Political Despotism).[79] The narrative of Abu Bakr's insistence on abiding by the revelation clearly marks the limits of *shura* as interpreted by al-Ghazali. But it did not resolve the question of who shall have the authority to pass the final verdict in modern societies. According to al-Ghazali's own words, no ruler in contemporary times has Abu Bakr's qualities, and, if this is the case, potential disagreements over interpretations of the revelation are all the more likely.

One of al-Ghazali's comments provided a promising, albeit partial and passing, answer as to how a crucial aspect of interpreting and applying the revelation should be decided. He noted that nothing should be defined as *maslaha mursala*—the unattested safeguarding of a principle objective of the Lawgiver, which can potentially suspend a revealed law—without the consent of the nation.[80] Considering that *maslaha mursala* is the most effective means of accommodating prohibitions to changing circumstances, entrusting its determination to the voting public (or their elected officials)—rather than with the leader or the religious scholars—gives the public the final say on an important aspect of defining and accommodating *halal* and *haram*. Here, an overlap between majoritarian decisions and legitimate interpretations of the *shari'a* is suggested. Yet, al-Ghazali did not elaborate further on this idea, nor did he specify whether his intention was that the nation should hold, through its representatives or by some other means, the ultimate authority to decide on *all* questions regarding the prohibited and the permissible, or whether a distinction would be drawn between decisions regarding the determination of *maslaha* and other *shari'a*-related matters. His statements in subsequent years did little to dispel the ambiguity. For example, in a public debate between Islamists and so-called secularists, held during Cairo's international book fair on January 8, 1992 (in which 'Imara participated as well, with 3,000 attendees), al-Ghazali said that in Islam the government should be based "half" on revelation and "half" on rational consideration of *maslaha*[81]—a curious arrangement considering that the determination of *maslaha* is a means to affect the application of revealed laws rather than a process that is independent of the revelation. Nevertheless, one way or the other, he never clearly articulated the division of authority in an Islamic state.

Yusuf al-Qaradawi

Al-Qaradawi offered more specific ideas on the structure of the ideal Islamic regime, but his texts still did not establish whether unelected religious scholars would have a final say on political decisions, though they came extremely close. He first comprehensively addressed the relation between *shura* and democracy in the early 1970s. As progressive Pan-Arabism became ideologically bankrupt, and the Islamist idea gained currency, al-Qaradawi, who in his academic and political exile in Qatar had already gained some repute as the author of a textbook on religious law, began to gain notoriety also as an author of apologias. His explanation for the failings of the Arab world was simple and unoriginal: a massive Western cultural attack shrewdly destroyed faith and subordinated the Arabs without resorting to military force by causing them to neglect Islam as an all-encompassing system and to substitute faith with imported, artificial Western ideologies—liberal democracy and socialism. Given that the problem was the neglect of Islam, the solution was also simple: to purify Muslim societies from all corrupting Western influences, and reestablish Islam as the exclusive reference for all aspects of life. Yet, it was not al-Qaradawi's intention to abandon or discard all that the West had brought to the Muslim world. Rather, what is beneficial and compatible with Islam should be embraced, and what is not should be rejected.

Departing from this point, al-Qaradawi established his concept of democracy with an Islamic reference. His 1971 treatise *Imported Solutions and How They Have Taken over Our Nation* described liberal democracy as a system that is based on a number of concepts that contradict Islam, including secularism, capitalism, territorial-nationalism, excessive personal freedoms—particularly with regard to gender relations—and man-made legislation that replaces Allah's laws. Liberal democracy is the product of historical conditions that are unique to the West—the tyranny of the Church, which caused societies to abandon religion altogether, and instead sanctify science, individualism and territorial-nationalism. It can never succeed because it distances itself from Allah and is devoid of a spiritual foundation. True Muslims cannot accept it because their religion is a comprehensive system that governs all aspects of life.[82]

Loyal to modernist-apologetic teachings, and to those of Hasan al-Banna in particular, al-Qaradawi admitted that there is one positive aspect of liberal democracy: the existence of representative councils, whose members are elected in free and universal elections and check the power of the executive branch. As in the West, he argued, the nation is the source of authority in the ideal Islamic state. However, there is a crucial difference that distinguishes the two systems from each other: politics in the Islamic state are limited by the boundaries of *shari'a*. Thus, the legislator cannot permit the prohibited and prohibit the permissible, and parliamentary candidates must be religiously devout, moral and experts on public affairs.[83]

"Imported Solutions" did not detail which authority would be responsible for establishing whether a piece of legislation breaches Allah's laws, or which authority would be responsible for establishing which candidates are religious enough to run for office. Some of the ambiguity was dispelled in a subsequent book, *The Islamic Solution: Duty and Necessity*, published in 1974. As in "Imported Solutions," on which he admittedly relied, the main theme was the need to relinquish imported socio-political systems and adopt the Islamic system in totality, allowing it to govern all aspects of life. The language of the book was more combative, describing secularism and nationalism as "germs" that have contaminated the Muslim body,[84] and declaring that in the Islamic state, punishments such as amputating the hands of thieves or stoning individuals who commit adultery would be applied.[85] The need for the socio-political order to not only be in full accord with Islam, but also to be dubbed as Islamic, rather than as democratic, socialist, or capitalist, was emphasized. Al-Qaradawi posited that only if the Islamic solution is defined as Islamic will Muslims show pride in Allah's guidance, demonstrate that they are led by Islam and nothing else, and ensure that the principles of Islam are not subject to change or subordination to other principles.[86]

An Islamic order, according to al-Qaradawi, was an elected one. A legislature, he wrote, is only legitimate if elected in free elections; relying on Q. 3:159 and 42:38, he added that the legislature must apply *shura* before deciding on any matter on which there is no decisive text and which affects the public. He based his opinion that this kind of *shura* is binding, rather than merely consultative, not only on verses from the Quran and on traditions, but also on rational-pragmatic considerations. A *shura* that is not binding will be merely a façade and allow the rule of one despotic opinion, a situation that devastated Muslim societies in the past. Furthermore, an opinion reached by many is more likely to be correct than an opinion reached by one person, and when the majority participates in the development of a policy, the commitment of the public to that policy is greater and its self-esteem increases.[87]

The Islamic Solution described how the *shar'i* legitimacy of legislative decisions would be ensured in greater detail than any previous—and in fact, any later—modernist-apologetic treatise, indirectly criticizing Sadat's 1971 constitutional gesture to Islamists as insufficient. The book stipulated that the constitution in an Islamic state should include the following: the *shari'a* is the exclusive reference for all laws, in all aspects of life; any existing law that contradicts a decisive revelation or the consensus of the nation should be annulled; and, most importantly, a higher council of religious scholars, well-versed in the *shari'a* and in contemporary affairs, will be appointed, and tasked with examining new legislation, which it will approve or reject based on its compatibility with Islamic law.[88]

In introducing the latter condition, al-Qaradawi suggested that establishing *shari'a* as the benchmark for the legitimacy of democratic decisions requires the creation of a mechanism that will pass judgment on legitimate and illegitimate legislation. He made clear that such a mechanism will exist in his envisioned regime and be controlled by religious scholars. But he did not clarify who will possess the authority to establish the regulations according to which the council of religious scholars will function, and who will elect or select its members. Neither did he explain how disputes between the council and other authorities would be resolved. As suggested above, these seemingly technical details mark the difference between a theocratic and a non-theocratic regime. And while it is reasonable to understand from *The Islamic Solution* that al-Qaradawi had religious experts who are independent of the whims and corruption of public opinion in mind, the detailed political structure he presented was careful not to pledge that the nature of the panel holding a de facto monopoly over political decisions would be such.

In the late 1980s, like al-Ghazali, al-Qaradawi did not remain indifferent to the global wave of democratic revolutions that passed over the Arab world. In January 1990, safely in exile in Qatar, he published an "open letter" to the Egyptian President calling for the annulment of emergency laws, and warning that in a world where big tyrants fall, little tyrants would not stand a chance.[89] Al-Qaradawi of the 1990s was an ideological force to be reckoned with. While he did not hold any official position in the Muslim Brothers, having rejected offers to lead it, al-Qaradawi had, since the 1970s, established himself as a voice for gradualist, pragmatic, mainstream Islamism, and his interpretation of the legitimacy of electoral politics had practical implications for the future of the Brothers in Egypt. *On the Religious Law of the State in Islam*, which was first published in 1997, is his most systematic treatise on the relation between Islam and democracy. Its publication coincided with al-Qaradawi's efforts to distinguish *wasatiyya* as a socio-juristic doctrine, and to gain recognition as the leader of that doctrine.

In the book, al-Qaradawi was more far appreciative of the positive aspects of the Western political model than he was in his early writings—and more apologetic than before in suggesting that the Islamic model of *shura* constitutes the perfected and original version of the Western one. Western democracies, he wrote, have made fine achievements in safeguarding freedoms and it is the duty of Muslim states to learn from them.[90] (In a book published three years later on the challenges facing the Islamic nation at the turn of the twentieth century, he described democracy and personal freedoms as two of the greatest achievements of the century, pointing to Nixon's resignation and Clinton's impeachment trial as examples of Western leaders' lack of immunity.[91] In a post 9/11 exchange with a Switzerland-based Egyptian scholar, which he ultimately published in yet another book, he emphasized that the Arab world desires freely elected parliaments and meaningful oppositions, and noted that throughout his career he maintained that at its core, democracy is very close to the spirit of Islam).[92]

While emphasizing certain merits of liberal democracies, al-Qaradawi was adamant that learning from the Western experience should in no way suggest implanting something external to Islam. In *On the Religious Law of the State in Islam* he wrote that Islam preceded the West in introducing the freedoms of religion, speech and science, which the West boasts of as its own creation.[93] The ideal Islamic system is based on the best foundations of Western democracy, but is not its duplicate. Both systems require that the leader be elected, accountable and subject to removal, but while Western democracy has no limits—it has the authority to legitimize alcohol, allow men to transform into women, and to even renounce democracy itself—the Islamic society is constrained by the values of Islam and *shari'a* when applying *shura*, and must never permit the prohibited or prohibit the permitted.[94] In line with his view from the 1970s, he called for the establishment of a panel composed of religious scholars, possessing the authorities of a high court, that would ensure laws and regulations do not contradict Islam. He also called for adopting a constitutional amendment that would clearly state that any law or regulation contradicting conclusive *shar'i* law is invalid.[95]

Al-Qaradawi presented one of the main arguments against the modernist-apologetic concept of government as articulated by a number of Arab liberal thinkers (see below, C), according to which a *shari'a*-based state would effectively be an oppressive regime governed by the whims of religious scholars. Relying, in part, on 'Abduh's polemic with Farah Antun,[96] he offered three main counter-arguments as to why his political vision would not lead to the establishment of a theocracy. First, Islam did not establish the rule of religion but destroyed it. It created a regime based on choice and voluntary allegiance (*bay'a*) in which everyone, including the ruler, must equally abide by the revealed laws, and no one, including the ruler, may annul or suspend those laws. A Muslim commanded by his ruler to breach Islamic law may, and in fact must, reject that command.[97] Second, in the Islamic state, as opposed to the Christian one, there are no clergymen who can claim to speak God's word; each and every Muslim is a man of religion, and those specializing in religious studies are no different than professors of philosophy or law in other cultures. The separation of church and state is a Western exception, the result of the despotic nature of Christianity, and, as such, is irrelevant to Muslims.[98] Third, an Islamic state should not be confused with a religious state because Islam is much more comprehensive than a mere religion. For example, the Islamic education to be implemented in the future Islamic state would not be limited to religious studies but also include rational, physical, moral, military, economic, political, scientific, cultural and other studies.[99] Concerned that the Iranian Islamic revolution had become a deterrent, he argued that most Muslims are Sunnis and not Shi'ites, and the two have different concepts of leadership. He also hinted that the Iranian revolution had gone astray because the religious scholars who led it monopolized politics.[100]

Compelling as they are, when read in context al-Qaradawi's arguments are also confused and self-contradictory. They encourage reaching a conclusion contrary to his own, namely that the implementation of his envisioned form of government will create a regime in which the personal inclinations and preferences of religious scholars override all other opinions, and religious beliefs will be imposed on the public.

First, notwithstanding the differences between Shi'i and Sunni Islam, the development of the Iranian revolution serves as a warning of the dangers inherent in a society ruled by individuals who believe their ideals are loyal to an ultimate, undeniable, revealed truth. There is no shortage of similar warnings in human history. The differentiation between Islam as a comprehensive system and Islam as a "religion" is artificial and contradicts al-Qaradawi's own core ideological belief

that directives derived from revelation must govern all aspects of life. The observation on the different political roles religious scholars have in Muslim and Christian societies is correct, as there was never something like a pope in Islam, but this
is also misleading. Muslim religious scholars have enjoyed privileged positions that
affect political decisions throughout history. One feature of this position was that
theories of political legitimacy (as developed by preeminent theologians and jurists
such as Abu Hamid al-Ghazali[101] and Ibn Taymiyya[102]) established that the ability
to oppose or revolt against an unjust ruler who has breached Islamic law should be
determined by the application of "*fiqh al-muwazanat*" ("the jurisprudence of balances"), a religio-juristic mechanism that weighs the benefits and harms of actions
in relation to the primary objectives of the Lawgiver. By invoking this theory,
religious scholars made rebelling against a corrupt leader extremely difficult to
religiously legitimize, as one would have to be assured of its success before com-
mencing it, and subjected any such action to religio-legal evaluations by those most
proficient in evaluating *maslaha*, that is, the religious scholars themselves. This
classic concept of legitimacy and opposition was endorsed by al-Qaradawi in a
separate discussion in his treatise[103] (as it was by other mainstream Islamists,
including al-Banna[104]).

According to *On the Religious Law of the State in Islam*, the Islamic regime will be
one of choice rather than imposition. But elsewhere in the book al-Qaradawi
emphasized that the state is only legitimate to the extent that it applies Islamic
law.[105] Thus, the old modernist-apologetic paradox of freedom had not been resolved:
in the Islamic state, Islam must be chosen rather than imposed, but individuals only
have the right to choose Islam, as any other reference is illegitimate.

As part of adopting a more favorable approach to Western democracy, *On the
Religious Law of the State in Islam* broke from the teachings of Hasan al-Banna and
advocated for a multiparty system. Al-Qaradawi strongly defended this position,
arguing that its foundations are rooted in the times of the righteous *khulafa'*, as well as
in the reality of contemporary Muslim societies, and comparing the number of
parties in politics to the number of schools in Islamic law. But he also cautioned
that embracing a plurality of political parties does not imply embracing disputes and
contradictions, and that such plurality can only be sanctioned if the people stand as
one in regard to crucial issues such as Muslim existence, Muslim faith, Muslim law
and the Muslim nation.[106] Where should the line be drawn between a plurality
that is welcomed and one that is resented, and who should be the one drawing it?
And, if Islam is the benchmark for any political activity, what will be the fate of
non-Muslim political parties? Al-Qaradawi did not address these questions, leaving
the door open to a version of Iranian parliamentary elections in which candidates
are screened in accordance with their religious credentials by a panel directly and
indirectly controlled by the Supreme Leader.

Al-Qaradawi's idea of establishing a judicial panel of religious scholars tasked
with scrutinizing the *shar'i* legitimacy of laws suggests he remained conscious of the
possibility that even devout legislators in an ideal Islamic state could err in their
understanding of Allah's revealed words. In 1997, he wrote little on the structure

and constitution of this panel of religious scholars—even less, in fact, than he wrote in 1974—but nevertheless conveyed, in a way similar to al-Ghazali's, his conviction that decisive *shar'i* laws are a strict, unequivocal, clearly distinguishable category.[107] Thus, al-Qaradawi implied that, regardless of how the panel is composed or who sits on it, the result is certain to be the same, and the danger of the whimsical rule of religious scholars does not exist.

One example, drawn from al-Qaradawi's own writings, will suffice to demonstrate how far-fetched this notion is. In *On the Religious Law of the State in Islam*, al-Qaradawi cited interest-based loans as an example of the universal nature of prohibitions in Islam.[108] The Quran strictly prohibits usury, or *riba* (Q. 2:275–9, 3:130, 4:161, 30:39), and indeed, for most of his career, al-Qaradawi reiterated the impermissibility of charging and paying interest as a decisive text that does not allow room for juristic discretion except in the most exceptional cases. He referred to usury time and again to demonstrate that there are clear boundaries to *ijtihad*. In his first major work, *The Permissible and Prohibited in Islam*, he stressed the moral and social importance of this prohibition and argued that only a "true necessity" (the highest rank of *maslaha*) and not a "need" (the second highest rank) could legitimize the paying of interest.[109] He again articulated, in a book published in 1988 on the need for the renewal of religion, his unequivocal belief that *ijtihad* on usury not only breaches a decisive text but is unnecessary.[110] He maintained the same position in the mid-1990s while formulating a broader approach to *maslaha,* pointing to interest (along with alcohol and pork) as examples of prohibitions that are based on decisive textual evidence, and thus should not be subject to *ijtihad*. He rejected the opinion that in the modern economic system paying interest has become a necessity that justifies the suspension of prohibitions, explaining that there is no benefit in usurious transactions and that, in any case, people should not ignore Allah's guidance when judging what their *maslaha*s are.[111]

Despite all of the above, in October 1999, a Dublin-based voluntary juristic panel headed by al-Qaradawi, The European Council for Fatwa and Research, permitted Muslims in Europe to take mortgages under certain conditions, based on considering the "need" to own a home as a "necessity" in the European context.[112] The decision, and the juristic methodology applied in order to reach it, stirred fierce debates, including among jurists who are generally sympathetic to al-Qaradawi's views. The debate, still on-going, serves as a clear demonstration that "decisive" and "indecisive" *shar'i* laws are not a simple matter; in evaluating certain circumstances, some jurists may find that the suspension of a specific revealed command is justified, whereas other jurists may find that it is not.

In the context of our discussion, the most instructive aspect of this controversy is the explanation al-Qaradawi provided for changing his mind on the matter. He attributed his change of heart and decision to the tenderness and confidence that come with old age.[113] For a jurist of al-Qaradawi's stature this is a rare admission that the subjective inclinations of the interpreter impact the juristic result no less than the literal meaning of the text or the external, "objective" circumstances. His self-reflection illuminates and highlights why the composition and structure of a juristic panel authorized to pass judgment on legislation are not a mere technicality. Different jurists may come up with different decisions on the application of the prohibited and the permissible based solely on differences in their personal cir- cumstances. Thus, determining "who the interpreter is" matters a great deal once revelation is established as the foundation for constitutional interpretation.

Muhammad 'Imara

The more philosophically inclined and theoretically sophisticated of the con- temporary Egyptian modernist-apologists, it is perhaps not surprising that Muhammad 'Imara's first independent study on the system of government in Islam, authored in 1977, focused on, and denounced, the argument that a *shari'a*-based regime could only be theocratic. As 'Abduh, whose works he edited and relied on extensively on this subject, 'Imara considered the infallibility of the religious authority and the divine right of kings as the qualities that render a regime theo- cratic. He argued that whereas in Christian societies kings claimed to rule through divine right and popes were declared infallible, in Islam, the Prophet was infallible only on issues on which he received a revelation, and his successors were required to apply Allah's *shari'a* and could not amend it. According to 'Imara, the regime in Islam is revelation-based, but it is not a theocracy because the revelation is a fixed text which nevertheless allows a great deal of discretion, and those delegated with interpreting and implementing it cannot claim to do so based on divine inspiration and derive their authority to rule from the consent of the people.[114]

The idea that in a revelation-based system political leaders and religious scholars can abuse their power and impose arbitrary decisions only if they claim to have a divine right or divine inspiration is fanciful – and 'Imara's own overview of Muslim history provides ample evidence for that.[115] His apologia about the non-theocratic nature of the ideal Islamic regime did not provide assurances against the potential monopolization of the interpretation and implementation of the revelation. While he clarified what an Islamic regime should not be, he did not provide a clear answer as to how it would precisely function in a modern state, and, more parti- cularly, express the terms according to which its political authorities would engage with the *shari'a*.

This central aspect was treated by 'Imara, albeit never in a systematic or exhaustive way, in later works in which he wrote extensively on the similarities and differences between Islam's ideal of government and liberal democracy. Most were published beginning in the mid-1980s and reflected, as did the works written by al-Ghazali and al-Qaradawi, an approach that recognized the great appeal of liberal democracy as a desired universal system of government and the need for it to be addressed in a sympathetic and nuanced way.

'Imara's principal musings on Islam and democracy, articulated during the "third wave of democratization," resembled those of al-Ghazali and al-Qaradawi in their essence: Islam offers all the positive aspects of participatory politics, without any of their negative aspects. *Shura* is the democracy of the Muslims and of Islam, its philosophy of government. The nation has the right to elect its leadership and to dismiss it if it is corrupt, exploitative or failing. It has the freedom to legislate within the limitations of the permissible and prohibited. The mechanisms for exercising *shura* can be developed by the nation, accommodating changing circumstances.[116] 'Imara emphasized that Islam preceded the West in establishing the concepts of political rights and human rights, and that human rights and political rights in Islam are not merely rights, but necessities (i.e., the highest rank of *maslaha*) ordained by Allah, which human beings cannot deny.[117] The latter concept aggravated all the more the guilt he felt for living in a reality in which certain religious scholars legitimize despotic regimes while at the same time Westerners, whose political reference is not revelation, benefit from democracy.[118]

'Imara spared no effort in trying to convince his readers that one can find examples of democratic and liberal political norms and practices in Islamic history. He argued, for example, that in telling Abu Bakr and 'Umar that he would accept their mutual opinion even if his differed, the Prophet Muhammad established the rule of the majority as a *shar'i* principle.[119] Some of 'Imara's narrated parallelisms are hardly convincing. For example, he argued that pluralism and individual, as well as popular, opposition are not only permitted in Islam in principle, but had also been part of Muslim political life throughout Islamic history, establishing precedents that can be followed by contemporary Muslims. Such is the case of Sa'd b. 'Ubada b. Dulaym, a member of the Ansar (the citizens of Madina who supported the Prophet Muhammad), who believed he should succeed the Prophet and, having failed to garner support for his ambition, refused to swear allegiance to Abu Bakr and remained firm in his dissent, but no one forced him to change his mind. According to 'Imara, b. 'Ubada's determined quest for power resembles presidential races in the West in which the loser remains in opposition and refuses to swear allegiance to the winner. This argument is mistaken in two ways: the loser in Western presidential races is expected to consent to the will of the majority, but nevertheless has an opportunity to compete for the people's confidence in another round of elections. In general, 'Imara's presentation of opposition as an Islamic norm and an integral part of early Islamic society is dismissive of the firm juristic agreement that developed regarding the undesirability of rebellions and the highly restrictive conditions in which a despot may be challenged.[120]

Readers of 'Imara's writings on democracy and Islam will be left with no doubt that he believed *shari'a* should serve as the exclusive, all-encompassing basis for politics (even his reluctant willingness to allow secular organizations to participate in the political process is based on *shar'i* justifications and on the certainty of their defeat).[121] He recognized that having revelation as the reference constitutes the core difference between his political theory and the liberal one; much of the discussion in two of his books, *On the Islamic Political System* and *The Clash of Western and Islamic Concepts*, as well as in other works, revolves around this issue. Western democracy and *shura*, he argued, are similar in some ways and contradictory in others. Western constitutionalism and elected assemblies are worthy developments as mechanisms of *shura*; thus, they are acceptable from the Islamic point of view.

However, whereas in the West the people are the primary and exclusive reference for legislation, in Islam, Allah is the primary and exclusive reference, and the role of the people is to construct a system of government and enact laws based on what He has stipulated as the permissible and prohibited. 'Imara attributed this difference to the impact Aristotelian philosophy has had on Western thought since the renaissance, arguing that it denied an active role for the creator in the world.[122]

However, the question of authority remains open. How can one ensure that elected representatives never breach the laws of the Lawgiver? In the book that most systematically presented his belief in the modernist-apologetic doctrine as the means to acquire independence from Western cultural domination, 'Imara argued that the ideal Islamic regime is something which lies between limitless liberalism and totalitarianism; it is a "guided democracy," in which Islam is accepted as the permanent reference and basic Islamic norms are adhered to. Within this frame-work, pluralism is allowed with regard to certain legislations and to the choice of political mechanisms.[123]

But who will be the "guide" in the "guided democracy?" 'Imara's most specific structural idea suggested that an elected council tasked with exercising *ijtihad* and legislating should be established. This council—mentioned by him in different texts in passing remarks, but not detailed in a systematic way—will safeguard the primary objectives of the *shari'a* and its decisions would override those of other authorities in case of a conflict between them.[124] Whereas al-Qaradawi separated the legislature from the panel of experts that would examine the *shar'i* legitimacy of legislation, 'Imara implied that the legislature can supervise itself; representatives would be individuals knowledgeable in both contemporary affairs and Islamic law, and would be responsible for enacting legislation that accommodates changing circumstances while ensuring that the laws enacted do not breach the prohibited and permissible.[125] This is a sophisticated structure, already intimated by al-Ghazali. It purports to resolve the conflict between the rule of *shari'a* and the rule of the people by suggesting that the two can actually be one. But vital questions remain unanswered. What guarantees would be in place to ensure that the legislative council abides by the one guiding rule that it cannot alter—to never breach the prohibited and permissible? Would non-Muslims be permitted to participate in its processes of *ijtihad* and legislation? And who is to decide whether candidates are sufficiently proficient in the *shari'a*?

The more the discussion becomes specified, the more confusing it becomes. In both *On the Islamic Political System* and *The Clash of Western and Islamic Concepts*, 'Imara presented (in similar, albeit not identical words) the unique features of the Islamic legislative council in support of his argument that his envisioned Islamic regime provides a greater separation of powers than the Western one. In the West, he correctly observed, the ruling parliamentary faction elects the government and, thus, there is no real separation between the executive and the legislature. The Islamic regime, on the other hand, allows the existence of four, rather than three, powers, separating the legislative authority from the authority that elects the executive and oversees its actions. Because the *shari'a* is divine, and the Islamic legislative authority would abide by it and would hold the authority to override all other powers, there is certainty that the rule of law would prevail and society would be free from the rule of despotism and human lusts.[126] This conclusion is puzzling. It is not clear what made 'Imara confident that the legislative council's representatives would be more correct than other officials in interpreting the revelation. If it is because they would be elected and would represent the will of the people, *vox populi, vox Dei*, then one can only wonder what convinced 'Imara that members of one council he proposed (the legislative-*ijtihadi*) would be better qualified to protect the *shari'a* than members of another council (the one that nominates the leadership and supervises it). If it is because those members are academically confirmed experts in religious law, then the theocracy which 'Imara promised to avoid throughout his career may be created. But whichever of the two is the one he had in mind, the supreme position intended for the legislative-*ijtihadi* council appears to endorse an unchecked, total rule of one authority that would speak in the name of Allah rather than allow greater checks and balances as he suggested.

The Egyptian Muslim Brothers

One could argue that the Egyptian modernist-apologists discussed above should not be judged too harshly for neglecting to offer an unequivocal, specific plan for the division of authorities in their envisioned Islamic state. After all, is it not conceivable that they believed that, as theorists, it was not their place to dwell too much on the details? Is it not possible that the obscure language, use of passive phrasings ("a council should be elected") and lack of commitment to a specific structure, speaks of their desire to leave something for politicians or the public to decide, rather than of an effort to skirt unraveling contradictions between the revelation and the people as ultimate references? The answers to these questions can only be guessed. It is instructive, however, to note that in the case of the most direct descendent of the largely Egyptian-based modernist-apologetic political thought, the Egyptian Muslim Brothers, even detailed political documents failed to dispel the clouds of theocracy.

As noted by Harnisch and Mecham, since the mid-1980s, members of the Egyptian Muslim Brothers have consistently professed their commitment to an electoral democratic system of government as both a strategic-political and ideological choice, while emphasizing that democratic decisions must not breach the boundaries of Islamic law. In 1984, for the first time since 1945, the movement participated in the elections for the people's assembly (in alliance with the New Wafd), gaining 59 of 454 possible seats,[127] and has since maintained its support for democratic elections as the means of choosing the government.

This commitment to democracy, which solidified even further during the 1990s, implied that the modernist-apologetic legacy, particularly as it was formulated by al-Ghazali and al-Qaradawi, had triumphed over other Islamist conceptualizations of government—a triumph that was far from certain only a decade earlier. However, one long-lingering question remained unresolved: precisely how would the *shari'a* be protected from transgressions in a democratic regime? The on–going ambiguity raised doubts among critics of the movement as to the sincerity of its democratic commitment.[128] Different ideas introduced by modernist-apologetic scholars were endorsed by different factions of the movement. Some among the movement's younger generation argued that the elected representatives themselves could ensure the compatibility of legislation with Allah's revelation—i.e., alluding to the constitution of an illiberal democracy; others, among the movement's old guard, envisioned a panel of religious scholars—i.e., suggesting a plan for a theocratic regime in which political power is monopolized by a religious establishment.[129]

On August 25, 2007, the Brothers' blueprint for their political program was leaked. The document offered a comprehensive vision for an Egypt that would be both Islamic and democratic, and was the most detailed plan for governance the movement had ever authored. It claimed that *shura* is the essence of democracy and a means for the nation to accomplish what is in its interest, and presented a long list of promises for democratic practices and values that will be practiced. To note only a few, the Brothers pledged a government elected by the people, political plurality and freedom of the press. In the third sub-section of its third section on policies and strategies, the program directly addressed the balance of power between religious and democratic authorities. According to this, the freely elected parliament will legislate by majority rule in accordance with the *shari'a* on all issues on which the Quran did not explicitly legislate. It will seek in all matters the advice of an independent committee of senior religious scholars, who will be elected in free elections by other religious scholars. A law governing the qualifications for participating in electing the committee of senior religious scholars will also be enacted.[130]

While oriented more toward the theocratic model than a democratic one, the draft platform did not commit to either. It shied away from explicitly untangling the web that the luminaries of modernist-apologetic thought also never fully settled. Who will be the final authority defining which issues were explicitly determined by the Quran? What will be the division of authority between the council of religious scholars and the Supreme Court? What mechanisms will resolve differences of opinion between senior scholars and the parliament, should such arise on different issues? Will the council, once established, have the authority to veto legislation that effect its structure?

As Brown and Hamzawy noted, critics of the draft program, including those within the Brothers' ranks and among intellectuals sympathetic to its quest for legitimacy, were quick to recognize that it opened a wide door for a theocracy, and suggested that it should be reconsidered.[131] Running for the first (and last) post-revolutionary free parliamentary elections, the platform of the Freedom and Justice Party, the political party founded by the Brothers, made a specific effort to dispel those concerns and explicitly noted that Egypt would not become a theocracy. The platform included no mention of a council of religious scholars, an omission signifying a shift in the balance of power toward the younger generation, and recognition of the need to broaden the appeal of a movement running for competitive elections in a post-revolutionary society. It stated that the "Islamic democratic state" would have *shari'a* as its constitutional reference, but vested the authority to pass judgment on the constitutionality of legislation with the supreme constitutional court.[132]

In power, the Brothers passed a new constitution, which was partially responsible for stirring the agitation that led to their downfall. In some ways, it was far more democratic than the 2007 draft program and even the 2011 platform. Most importantly, while it stipulated that the codes of the *shari'a* are the principal source for legislation, it maintained the existing hierarchy rather than elevating the *shari'a* to the status of an *exclusive* source (article 2). However, it also introduced a mechanism that was absent in the 2011 platform, requiring that the senior scholars of al-Azhar be consulted on all matters pertaining to Islamic law, and that al-Azhar will maintain absolute autonomy (article 4).[133]

While not mentioning whether those senior scholars would be given veto power over legislation, the latter article had yet again left the door open to the possible future rule of religious scholars, who would potentially be controlled directly or indirectly by the Brothers' leadership. The numerous rivals of the Brothers were certain where to the movement is destined to lead Egypt should it only be given the time and the opportunity. The short-lived reign of the movement ended in a way that, tragically, proved right the pragmatic arguments of anti-democratic former members such as Muhammad Qutb, who three decades earlier had warned of the futility of Islamizing society through electoral participation.[134] Unlike the arguments of some critics, a "rule of a religious group" or "reign of terror" did not characterize the Brothers' brief period in power. It was fear of theocracy, rather than actual theocracy, which fueled the speedy return to authoritarianism, and legitimized it, at least in the eyes of some Egyptians. In a sense, the Brothers paid the price for adhering to an intellectual legacy that avoided clearly answering a question that could not be avoided in the world of practical politics.

Tunisia and the post-Islamist debate

The standard-bearer of revelation-based political theory in Tunisia has been, since the 1980s, al-Nahda (renaissance), established by Rashid al-Ghannushi (b. 1941), one of the more prolific non-Egyptian modernist-apologetic thinkers and a long-time intellectual ally of al-Qaradawi. Recent developments in al-Ghannushi's, and al-Nahda's, views on the relation between revelation and democracy and religion and politics, have been described in academic literature as part of a broader, and recent, phenomenon of "post-Islamism," which include also Recep Tayyip Erdoğan's ruling Justice and Development Party (AKP) in Turkey, as well as several Islamic political parties in Pakistan, Malaysia, Indonesia and other Muslim states. Post-Islamism is defined as the embrace, by Islamic parties, of pragmatic policies and the abandonment of the desire to establish *shari'a* as the primary reference for politics and law.[135] The following discussion analyzes whether an ideological disparity has indeed developed between al-Nahda and the Egyptian Muslim Brothers.

It also examines whether Tunisian modernist-apologetic political thought has introduced a new theory on the relation between revelation and democracy.

Al-Ghannushi, a Pan-Arab nationalist who converted to Islamism in the late 1960s, established, in 1981, the Islamic Tendency Movement that called for the Islamizing of Tunisia in terms similar to those of the Egyptian Muslim Brothers.[136] He shone as both a political and ideological authority, two roles that among the Egyptian Brothers had largely divided since the death of al-Banna. In 1987, Tunisia's President, Habib Bourgiba, characterized him as the most dangerous threat to the regime and al-Ghannushi was sentenced to life imprisonment. A year later, in 1988, shortly after he was pardoned by the new President, Zayn al-'Abidine b. 'Ali, al-Ghannushi founded al-Nahda, which competed in the April 1989 parliamentary elections and emerged as the only viable opposition to b. 'Ali's newly established regime.[137] Shortly after the elections, b. 'Ali's appeasement policy towards al-Nahda ended, and al-Ghannushi was forced to flee into exile in London. He returned to Tunisia in January 2011, after massive demonstrations led to the resignation of b. 'Ali and sparked the wave of revolutions and civil wars across the Middle East known as the "Arab Spring." Yet, upon his return, al-Ghannushi sought no political role for himself. In October 2011, al-Nahda won the first post-revolutionary free elections with 89 of 217 sits in the Constituent Assembly. Short of an absolute majority and seeking to establish social consensus, it formed a "troika" coalition with two center-left parties. One of al-Nahda's leaders, former journalist and political prisoner Hamdi Jibali, was appointed Prime Minister.[138]

In his years as a political dissident, al-Ghannushi expressed his commitment to electoral democracy and to liberal freedoms, principles he argued are grounded in Islam, and presented his political movement as Tunisia's chief Islamic and chief democratic opposition.[139] However, as the Egyptian modernist-apologetic scholars, his statements from the 1970s through the 1990s and 2000s suggested that revelation should serve as the ultimate reference for political actions, human legislation should not conflict with Allah's decrees, and religious scholars may have the final verdict on legislation. In 1979 he stated that Islam strongly rejects the Western separation between religion and state because it regards the state as a servant to religion. He argued that the Quran clearly establishes (4:65, 5:44) that religion has authority over political and social life.[140] In an article published in 1994, he defined his desired regime as an Islamic regime that has the *shari'a* as its reference, in which *shura* is applied, and in which all decisions are in line with Allah's decrees. He legitimized prospective participation in the creation of a regime that was not grounded in revelation, to the extent that the establishment of an Islamic regime would not be feasible, by arguing that it was the duty of a Muslim to advance whatever primary objectives of the *shari'a* that were within his or her power to advance. Still, he emphasized that the ultimate goal must remain the establishment of an Islamic regime, whether in the short or long term.[141] Commenting on Tunisia's 1988 constitution, he stated that two amendments would suffice in order to make it consonant with al-Nahda's political stance:

a   all laws must be compatible with *shariʻa*;
b   the authority to decide whether laws comply with the *shariʻa* will reside with
    an Islamic Council.[142]

Al-Ghannushi's intimate knowledge of Western societies and Western philosophy added a layer of originality and sophistication to his observations on the
essentiality of revelation-based politics. For example, in an analysis of Israeli society,
published in 1993, he suggested that the stability of its democratic system was due
to the broad agreement between rival political factions about the Jewish character
of the state, implying that the Islamizing of Arab societies is a prerequisite for a
sustainable democratization process.[143] In a commentary on Western democracies,
published in 2000, he predicted their downfall and deterioration to anarchy due to
their secular nature and the absence of a civilizing metaphysical legal reference,
such as the one that Islam offers.[144] In a treatise published in 2008 on human rights
in Islam he asserted that Islam does not allow theocratic rule and suggested the
divine source of human rights in Islam renders them more credible and meaningful
than human rights in the West, which are hypocritical and privilege a minority of
the strongest.[145]

   Shortly after al-Nahda became the first political party whose agenda is rooted
in the modernist-apologetic tradition to ever assume power in an Arab state, al-
Ghannushi released his most extensive work on Islam and politics, *Democracy and
Human Rights in Islam*. At the time of the book's publication, in the winter of
2012, al-Ghannushi and other al-Nahda leaders repeatedly promised that the party
had no desire to impose Islamic law or adopt a theocratic, Iranian-styled model of
government. Still, analysts and secular Tunisians expressed concerns that their
statements were merely tactical and did not reflect a "real" post-Islamist transformation. They suggested al-Nahda was merely responding to opportunities created by a new political context, and had not given up its ambition to establish a
revelation-based society.[146] Al-Ghannushi's book was an indirect reply to these
allegations.

   The lion's share of al-Ghannushi's book echoed the modernist-apologetic
legacy, including his previous writings. Al-Ghannushi rejected the separation of
state and religion,[147] and described a Muslim state as a state in which the leader was
freely elected by the people and was supervised by them, a rule of law prevailed
and citizens were not discriminated against based on their gender or beliefs. He
suggested that the only difference between the mechanisms of contemporary liberal
democracies and those of the Muslim state is that the latter has *shariʻa* as its reference. Throughout the book he presented Islam, properly understood, as the most
suitable ideology to safeguard the exercise of democracy. He argued that the
absence of political freedom that characterized much of Muslim history represented
a gap between the ideal and reality that should, and can, be amended.[148]

   To these long-held modernist-apologetic ideas, al-Ghannushi added two arguments on the relation between revelation and democracy that constitute an audacious contribution to the modernist-apologetic tradition. First, he argued that

because there is no Church that monopolizes the interpretation of the revelation in Islam, the application of Allah's laws is facilitated through consensus or majority vote. Thus, he argued, Allah's rule is, in fact, the people's rule.[149] While, as demonstrated in this chapter, several other modernist-apologists came very close to arguing for an essential and complete overlap between decisions taken by demo-cratic majorities and legitimate interpretations of the revelation, none—including the younger al-Ghannushi—have done so in such a decisive way that it leaves no space for interventions by unelected religious scholars. Second, al-Ghannushi asserted in his book that al-Nahda would accept the people's decision even if it loses the elections and the Communist party wins them. If this happened, he wrote, the party would have to reexamine its agenda and work harder to win the people's confidence; it would interpret its defeat not as a choice against Islam, but as a choice against a specific *ijtihad*, i.e., an interpretation of the revelation that represents a human effort rather than an undeniable truth.[150] With this argument, al-Ghannushi assuaged, in the most straightforward of words, concerns that al-Nahda's support for electoral democracy was a ruse and could disappear if it ever lost power.

Thus, in his first major work published in the aftermath of the revolution, al-Ghannushi did something the contemporary Egyptian luminaries of modernist-apologetic thought avoided: he unequivocally committed to the legitimacy of any electoral and parliamentary majority. However, his book did not present a new theory that reconciles, in a coherent way, his continued commitments to both revelation and democracy. His depictions of *shari'a* as the political reference and of majority rule as the binding political principle were introduced in different parts of the book as separate categories, and little attention was given to potential contra-dictions that may arise between them. His legitimization of a non-Islamic electoral victory was not grounded in religio-legal justifications, but through the argument that it was not just or moral to ask secular political parties to accept al-Nahda's victories, if al-Nahda did not accept theirs.[151] He did not explain how a revelation-based reference for democratic politics could, in theory, tolerate the reign of the Communist party, or any other atheist party for that matter, whose ideology denies revelation altogether. In a similar vein, al-Ghannushi's discussion on the revelation-based legitimacy of majorities as representatives of *ijtihad* overlooked the difference between two potential situations: legislation enacted through majority vote as a result of fallacious *ijtihad*, and legislation enacted through majority vote with no regard for Islamic decrees. If, for example, a parliamentary majority misapplies the mechanism of *maslaha* to legitimize the selling of alcohol, then, as suggested by al-Ghannushi in his book, it can credibly be argued, from a religio-legal point of view, that the premise of this legislation is nevertheless the revelation. But if alco-hol were to be legalized by a majority that did not recognize the truth or authority of the revelation in any way (e.g., a Communist majority) then that decision could not be credibly described as a form of *ijtihad*.

Al-Nahda's time in sharing power met with strong resistance, particularly from secularists who feared the party sought the gradual Islamizing of the country. In January 2014, amidst political turmoil caused in part by assassinations of secular politicians, the party, still leading the government as the largest faction in parliament, conceded power to a government of technocrats, and Tunisia's new constitution was approved. Unlike the constitution that was passed under the Muslim Brothers government in Egypt, which, as analyzed above, left ambiguous space for future interventions of non-elected religious scholars in parliamentary decisions, the new Tunisian constitution did not even introduce *shari'a* as a source of legislation. It merely declared (Article 1) that Islam is the religion of the state and that the state guarantees freedom of conscience and belief and the neutrality of mosques from partisanship (Article 6). The Preamble and Article 6 described Islam as a religion of tolerance, openness and moderation.[152] In the October 2014 elections, al-Nahda finished second, just behind a secular coalition. Al-Ghannushi argued that his party's voluntary concession of power even before its electoral defeat, and the approval, with its support, of the 2014 constitution's text, demonstrate that al-Nahda's commitment to democracy is not a ruse. He suggested al-Nahda is the Islamic version of Europe's Christian democratic parties.[153] A year and a half later, he further asserted his new post-ideological position before his party's congress by calling for religion to be kept apart from political struggles. He emphasized that practical programs, rather than ideologies and slogans, are what matter to a modern state.[154]

The evolution of al-Ghannushi's theory on the relation of revelation and politics made it easier for al-Nahda to concede power voluntarily and embrace a constitution with no place for *shari'a*. It represents an ideological disparity that emerged between the Egyptian Muslim Brothers and Tunisian Islamists. Still, comparative analysis of the Egyptian and Tunisian experiences should not overlook how specific political opportunities and limitations affected political opinions and practices. While winning in 2011 more votes than any other single political party, al-Nahda was confronted by a majority of secularist left-leaning parties and independents. At first, it did not give up on the ambition to establish a revelation-based political system. In February 2012, a draft constitution attributed to al-Nahda was leaked; Clause 10 stated the *shari'a* should be established as a main source of legislation and Clause 20 stated that freedom of speech does not pertain to the sacred. A majority of the party's parliamentary members at the time believed that *shari'a* must be part of the new constitution. It was only after al-Nahda's secularist coalition partners made clear that they would never accede to this stance that al-Ghannushi, immediately followed by his party's executive committee, agreed in March 2012 to accept a constitution that was not revelation-based, albeit without making clear whether he no longer sees a revelation-based constitution as a political goal.[155] In contrast to al-Nahda, the Egyptian Muslim Brothers won in 2011, along with another revelation-based political party (the *salafi* al-Nur), more than two-thirds of the seats in the parliament, and in 2012 they won, albeit narrowly, the first free presidential election. These two electoral victories were interpreted by the Brothers, perhaps understandably, as a public mandate to advance the decades-long revelation-based agenda of the movement. Even so, the constitution the Egyptian Brothers passed fell short of committing to the movement's core historical demand by not explicitly requiring all legislation be in line with *shar'i* norms.

Attempts to discern the "real intentions" behind the actions and statements of political movements are somewhat naïve; they are underlined by the false assumption that the actions of politicians are always guided by clear-cut ideological roadmaps which they either disclose or conceal. The only thing that can be said with certainty when comparing the Tunisian experience to the Egyptian is that al-Ghannushi and al-Nahda introduced to the modernist-apologetic ideological spectrum, and then applied, an unequivocal commitment to respect secular majorities, albeit without presenting a new systematic theory that coherently reconciles the commitments to both revelation and democracy, and without having the opportunity to constitutionally establish the primacy of revelation through a parliamentary majority.

C. Criticizing the Modernist-Apologists: The Secularist Paradox

In the intellectual sense, at least, it is lamentable that the Muslim Brothers' spell in power in Egypt was so brief. A more enduring reign would have forced the movement in the long, if not the short, run to detail its modernist-apologetic theory. It would have compelled the Egyptian Brothers to clearly define the practical structure and power-balances of a *shari'a*-based democracy. However, though the political materialization of their ideal was so decisively struck down in Egypt and in the Arab world at large for the time being, it should not be confused as a death blow to the popular appeal of the promise of a politics that offers all the advantages of both doubt-based and revelation-based societies. If Egypt's generals were certain of the Brothers future defeat at the ballot box, they would have not hastened to end their country's experiment with competitive, pluralistic politics. In historical retrospect, not being given a fair chance to rule after winning power in democratic elections may, in the end, keep the promise of a *shari'a*-based democratic system alive.

That it was never really put to the test is one reason why the modernist-apologetic political ideal has maintained such broad appeal in Egypt. Another is the weakness of the theoretical challenges this concept encountered over the course of the past century from intellectuals and activists who strove to separate the state from religion. Individuals in this tradition, starting with 'Ali Abd al-Raziq at the beginning of the twentieth century and ending with Faraj Fuda and Nasr Abu Zayd at its close, were personally familiar not only with the modernist-apologetic agenda but also with the individuals and movements representing it, and were deeply troubled by the implications of revelation-grounded politics. However, they did not put forward a coherent liberal alternative.

To discredit the possibility of a revelation-based democracy does not, in itself, discredit the foundation of the modernist-apologetic theory, according to which it is the divine will that the *shari'a* should serve as the exclusive reference for politics in a Muslim society. To do so, two lines of argumentation, two counter-theories so to speak, can be employed. One is the substantive liberal view of politics as a field of continuous competition in an open society between different agendas and priorities in which no specific belief, principle or opinion is immune from challenge, with the only exception being that the principle of free competition itself must be safeguarded at all times. To hold this point of view, individuals must not necessarily deny the truth of a revelation or of all revelations; but they must be tolerant to the possibility that the revelation in which they believe may not be true, and must allow other beliefs equal opportunities. The substantive liberal view makes protecting the struggle to find truth, as opposed to protecting a certain truth, its foundational objective.

The other line of argumentation is to reject the notion of revelation-based politics based on the revelation itself. Unlike the substantive liberal argument, this argument is not external to the scared text, but is derived from it. It accepts a certain revelation as the ultimate truth, which cannot be denied, and, as such, holds that anything commanded by the revelation—including anything regarding politics—must be adhered to. However, it also holds that a correct reading of the revelation teaches that the revelation allows, or even requires, a separation between the religious sphere and the political sphere; or, that a correct reading of history suggests that in order for the true spirit of revelation to be maintained its separation from politics is essential.

While the two lines of argumentation lead to the same result in terms of the desired political structure, they provide different premises for the debate on whether religion and politics should be separate. The substantive liberal point of view is indifferent to theological or religio-juristic arguments on the role of religion in politics. Its position of fundamental neutrality on the metaphysical negates the relevancy of such arguments. The revelation-based point of view, on the other hand, cannot be dismissive of religious arguments. Because this position grounds its opposition to revelation-based politics on a revelation, the credibility of its theorizing must endure the test of religious polemics. In accordance with its own terms, it can claim legitimacy only to the extent that it can prove itself to be religiously legitimate. It thus denies revelation a place in politics, applying logic that inadvertently reaffirms revelation as the ultimate arbitrator on constitutional matters.

In the Egyptian religio-political discourse, and in academic scholarship, the Egyptian intellectuals and activists who theorized against the synthesis of state and religion are commonly referred to as "secularist." Indeed, in terms of their objective—to discredit shari‘a as the constitutional reference—they deserve this label. However, the more well-known opponents of the modernist-apologetic school refuted the notion that Islam had set an ideal for government based not on liberal theories but on revelation-based arguments. They have done so, possibly, for two reasons that are not mutually exclusive: as faithful Muslims, it was important for them to assure themselves and their audience that their political conceptualizations do not negate the position of the Quran and the traditions as a final truth; and, as actors in a political discourse that did not tolerate any challenge to the Quran and the traditions as the ultimate truth, they calculated (and if so, erroneously) that revelation-based argumentations would meet less resistance from religious circles.

Commenting on the non-secular nature of Egyptian secular-liberal thought, Daniel Brown noted the irony that secularists legitimized secularism based on the assumption that the Prophet was a good secularist.[156] Still, Brown, as others who used the label "secularists" for those who invoked the revelation as a means to legitimize secularism, did not fully appreciate the historical implication of this observation. The most significant books that countered the modernist-apologetic promise for an Islamic democracy have done so from a point of view that embraced the revelation as the ultimate reference. Thus, a confident liberal theory, a conscious argument for a politically doubt-based society, had not developed in Egypt, and the polemic about the role of religion in politics remained restricted to a field in which the modernist-apologetics feel most comfortable: that of selective exegesis and hermeneutics.

In this sense, the works that were most detested by the modernist-apologists have actually served them well. 'Ali 'Abd al-Raziq's treatise on the foundations of government in Islam, a cornerstone for later revelation-based refutations of revelation-based politics,[157] is a good example. 'Abd al-Raziq (1888–1966), son of a distinguished political and intellectual family, an al-Azhar graduate, a *qadi* and a lecturer in the foundations of *fiqh*, stated that the Prophet Muhammad was a religious messenger but not a political one and that Islam does not require any specific system of government. He based this assertion on a number of arguments: it is impossible to find either in the Quran or the traditions any evidence that Islam has a political character;[158] while the Prophet introduced many laws on a range of issues, from warfare to commerce, all these laws were religious laws intent on safeguarding religious *maslahas*, and had nothing to do with the political and legal foundations of states;[159] had the Prophet established a state, or stipulated the laws governing its establishment, he would have been active in foundational aspects of a state, such as appointing judges, and would have set the precise mechanisms for *shura*;[160] and, while it is reasonable that the world could adopt one religion, it is inconceivable and could not be Allah's will that the world would adopt one government and be grouped into a single political union.[161]

As noted by Hourani, al-Raziq's treatise was written in the context of the debate over the necessity of a Caliphate, which had arisen in the Muslim world following the abolition of the Caliphate in Turkey in 1924.[162] But the work that led an al-Azhar committee to investigate al-Raziq's religious credentials, ultimately costing him his job as a *qadi*, also constituted a rebuke of a formidable body of literature that conceptualized an Islamic system of government, and argued that certain aspects of modernity and Islamic traditions are compatible. Rida was enraged by al-Raziq, declaring his treatise an attempt by the enemies of Islam to divide and weaken it.[163] Because his work continued to be circulated, al-Raziq continued to be deemed a challenge also by contemporary modernist-apologists. 'Imara dedicated an entire book to the controversy ignited by al-Raziq's treatise and to refuting his ideas.[164] Al-Ghazali lamented that al-Raziq did not publicly renounce his grave errors before he died, in a patronizing and offensive article which included a gratuitous description of al-Raziq's private medical information.[165]

Yet, when read closely, the gap between al-Raziq's ideas and those of the modernist-apologists is not as radical as it may appear at first. Regardless of whether one accepts or rejects his work, as an argument for the separation of state and religion it is susceptible to criticism. First, al-Raziq accepted, in principle, that the revelation is the ultimate authority in all aspects of life, and denied it a political role based on his understanding that it was devoid of one. Thus, he departed from the modernist-apologists only in terms of his understanding of how the revelation should be interpreted. Second, his distinction between religious laws and political ones is very weak. A logical conclusion to draw from his work is that the revelation is binding on issues such as waging war or charging interest. If one accepts this conclusion, how can one argue that the revelation has no political implications?

The next in the generational line of individuals who became famous (and infamous) for challenging the modernist-apologetic political synthesis was Khalid Muhammad Khalid (1920–1996), another al-Azhar graduate and author of works on Muslim history and theology. The book he published in 1950, *From Here We Start*, constituted a direct attack against those who wish for a "religious state" in which *shari'a* is the exclusive source for legislation (Khalid, who broke from the Muslim Brothers shortly before the publication of his book,[166] did not explicitly mention the movement). In what could only be interpreted as an attack on the core of the modernist-apologetic argument, he warned that a *shari'a*-based regime is a reactionary plan that would bring society back to the fold of oppressive theocracy. He suggested that just as Christians had ultimately rebelled against a Church that monopolized politics, so would Muslims, should a religious state be reestablished.[167]

Khalid's arguments against revelation-based politics combined his interpretation of the Prophet's message with his own pragmatic considerations. As al-Raziq, he wrote that Muhammad was a Prophet rather than a king. The Prophet's message was not of a political nature, and his participation in politics was based on necessity and did not establish specific norms or structures that must be followed.[168] Religious scholars and politicians have different roles—the former, to guide people to good virtues, the latter, to take care of the worldly interests of the population—and one cannot take the place of the other; the state has the power to force compliance, but there is no compulsion in religion.[169] Should a religious state be established, it would not be governed by Allah's book and the example of His Prophet, but by the personal-inclinations, ambitions and self-interests of its rulers. Such a state would demand blind and absolute obedience from its subjects in the name of unity, and would not permit freedom of speech and opposition.[170]

In this book and in a subsequent one authored also in the early 1950s, *Democracy—Always*, Khalid further undermined the modernist-apologetic theory by challenging the notion that Islam provides a set of social laws that have precedence over civilian laws.[171] Such a blatant attack on all the foundations of modernist-apologetic thought, published at a time when the Brothers were fighting for survival and anticipating a change of fortune, could not have remained unanswered—and indeed, one of al-Ghazali's first works, published only a few months after the publication of Khalid's treatise, was dedicated to refuting it. Like al-Raziq's work, Khalid's was easy prey from a modernist-apologetic point of view in that it sought to change the paradigm of revelation-based politics without challenging the premise on which that paradigm relied. To rebuke Khalid's idea, one only needed to persuasively demonstrate that his interpretation of the Prophet's role, or of the implications of Muslim history, is incorrect—and that is precisely what al-Ghazali, a personal friend of Khalid, aimed to do.[172] Khalid's book remained an example in modernist-apologetic thought, along with al-Raziq's, of the decline of Islam and its subordination to the West in Egypt.[173] But Khalid's story ended well from the modernist-apologetic perspective: in 1981 he wrote *The State in Islam* in which he rescinded his earlier theory and acknowledged the unity of state and religion in Islam.[174]

The third generation in the historical chain of revelation-based refutations of revelation-based politics surfaced at a time when the modernist-apologetic ideal had gained more appeal in Egypt. The story of Faraj Fuda (1945–1992) is revealing with regard to the implications this transformation had. A professor of agronomy by profession, Fuda was an outspoken politician and an intellectual who withdrew from the New Wafd party in 1984 in protest at their alliance with the Muslim Brothers and established a new party, *al-Mustaqbal* (the Future).[175] He based his case for the separation of religion and politics on a different line of argumentation than that of al-Raziq and Khalid, but one that is, nevertheless, just as vulnerable to criticism. His reading of Muslim history suggested that even during times when the regime was religious, such as in the days of the four righteous successors, it witnessed conflicts and political assassinations. He argued that given that establishing an ideal religious regime is nothing but wishful thinking, the separation of religion from politics would benefit both (removing religion from the state itself was not desired, as he emphasized the importance of religious studies in schools, for example).[176] Second, Fuda noted that the revelation allows great freedom with regard to many worldly affairs, setting general principles only. He did not specify what these principles are, but made clear just how wide the interpretive possibilities are in the political sphere. For example, some scholars found in revelation evidence for the capitalist nature of Islam, and some for the socialist nature of Islam; some found evidence to support the peace treaty with Israel, and some found evidence to oppose it. In Fuda's view, having the revelation as the reference for politics would result in the creation of a regime that claims a divine right, controls public opinion, and delegitimizes dissenting opinions that are legitimate according to the interpretive space allowed by the revelation itself.[177]

In June 1992, two members of a Qutbist-Islamist group, al-Jama'a al-Islamiyya, assassinated Fuda. Appearing as an expert witness in their trial in June 1993, Muhammad al-Ghazali defended their action, arguing that Fuda's call for a society not governed by the *shari'a* qualified him as a *murtadd*, a Muslim who has renounced Islam, a crime punishable by death. According to al-Ghazali, since the regime did not kill Fuda, it was just for individuals to do so. Al-Ghazali's testimony stirred a storm; in his eulogy of al-Ghazali, al-Qaradawi praised him for standing his ground on the matter despite heavy pressures from the government to change it.[178] While they were careful not to say so explicitly, al-Ghazali's and al-Qaradawi's opinions amounted to legitimizing future attacks on anyone who would impugn their belief in the unity of state and religion.

Fuda enraged the modernist-apologists so much because, more than any other Egyptian of his day, he exposed, in a direct manner, the potential despotic implications of a revelation-based democratic political system, doing so at a time when revelation-based democracy had become a core aspect of the modernist-apologetic agenda. However, his theoretical premise was not as distant from that of the modernist-apologists as he and his rivals believed. Both agreed that Islam set general principles on how human beings should conduct their affairs. They diverged only in that whereas the modernist-apologists were certain that the accommodating nature of the revelation allows democratic politics to prosper in a revelation-based regime, Fuda was certain that to protect the right of Muslims to interpret the revelation in the spirit of freedom it allows, the revelation itself must not serve as the political reference. He never reconciled his principal opinion that the revelation does set certain general guidelines on worldly affairs with his pragmatic opinion that it should not affect those worldly affairs.

Another refutation of modernist-apologetic political theorizing brings us to the tragedy of Nasr Abu Zayd. His opposition to the modernist-apologetic view of Islam and democracy, part of his broader effort to liberate the Quran from imposed interpretations, reasserted and combined the main arguments of the above-mentioned scholars, and demonstrated just how difficult it is for liberal thinkers to deny revelation the role of a binding reference. Like Fuda, Abu Zayd recognized that having the revelation as a "focal point of gravity" subjects the political community to the ideological inclinations of those who interpret it;[179] like al-Raziq, he argued that the Quran did not introduce a system of government and, thus, that Muslims are allowed to choose any system of government they wish. Specifically, he argued that *shura* cannot be characterized as a democratic system because, historically speaking, it is a pre-Islamic authoritarian method of consultation.[180] While the first argument denied revelation a role in politics based on a pragmatic concern that such a role would lead to despotism, the second accepted revelation as a reference, and suggested that politics should not be modeled in accordance with its scheme simply because it does not have one.

Abu Zayd's troubles began in 1992 when his promotion was debated by an academic committee at the University of Cairo. One of the reports on the quality of his studies accused him of heresy; subsequently, not only was his promotion denied, but his life was threatened and a group of lawyers filed a case to force his divorce from his wife on the grounds that he was a *kafir*. The case was initially dismissed on procedural grounds by a Giza Court of First Instance. But a higher Appellate Court in Cairo, citing, among others, the second clause of the constitution, which established *shari'a* as the primary reference, ruled in June 1995 that Abu Zayd's marriage must end because of his blasphemy. The decision was upheld in August 1996 by Egypt's Supreme Court.[181]

Fearing for his life, Abu Zayd was forced into exile in the Netherlands, and though he testified to his faith in Islam, he was never able to return to Egypt. Ironically, the story of a man who sought to liberate Egyptian society from the specter of revelation-based politics and law was a clear example of the potential despotic implications of revelation-based politics and law. That he and those before him who dared speak their mind about how the political implications of the revelation should be understood met with such intolerance, in a society that did not even have revelation as an exclusive reference, was not a good indication for the prospects of pluralism, should the modernist-apologists ever have their way in Egypt.

Notes

1 Alexis de Tocqueville, *Democracy in America*, translated and edited by Harvey C. Mansfield and Delba Winthrop (Chicago: University of Chicago Press, 2000), 419–20.
2 Arnold Toynbee, *Civilization on Trial* (London, New York and Toronto: Oxford University Press, 1948), 184–212.
3 For example, Charles Issawi, "Economic and Social Foundations of Democracy in the Middle East," *International Affairs*, 32:1 (January 1956), 27–41.
4 Bernard Lewis, "A Historical Overview: Islam and Liberal Democracy," *Journal of Democracy*, 7:2 (April 1996), 54–56.
5 Elie Kedourie, *Democracy and Arab Political Culture* (Washington, DC: The Washington Institute for Near East Policy, 1992), 5–9.
6 Gudrun Krämer, "Islamist Notions of Democracy," *Middle East Report*, no. 183 (July-August 1993), 4.
7 David Bukay, "Can There be an Islamic Democracy?" *Middle East Quarterly*, 14:2 (Spring 2007), 78.
8 Ibid., 79.
9 Ibid., 77–78.
10 Bassam Tibi, "Islamist Parties and Democracy: Why They Can't be Democratic," *Journal of Democracy*, 19:3 (July 2008), 44–45.
11 John L. Esposito and John O. Voll, *Islam and Democracy* (New York and Oxford: Oxford University Press, 1996), 193.
12 Ahmad S. Moussalli, *The Islamic Quest for Democracy, Pluralism and Human Rights* (Gainesville: University Press of Florida, 2001), 160.
13 Ibid., 165.
14 Raghid El-Solh, "Islamist Attitudes Towards Democracy: A Review of the Ideas of al-Ghazali, al-Turabi and 'Amara," *British Journal of Middle Eastern Studies*, 20:1 (1993), 63.
15 Karl R. Popper, *The Open Society and Its Enemies* (London: Routledge, 1969, first published 1945), 124.
16 Azizah Y. al-Hibri, "Islamic Constitutionalism and the Concept of Democracy," *Case Western Reserve Journal of International Law*, 24:1 (Winter 1992), 16–19.
17 Bernard Lewis, *The Muslim Discovery of Europe* (New York and London: W.W Norton & Company, 1982), 212–16.
18 Florian Riedler, *Opposition and Legitimacy in the Ottoman Empire* (London: Routledge, 2011), 26–41; Hanioğlu M. Şükrü, *A Brief History of the Late Ottoman Empire* (Princeton, NJ: Princeton University Press, 2008), 103–04.
19 For an evaluation of the Ottoman constitution and parliament: Robert Devereux, *The First Ottoman Constitutional Period: A Study of the Midhat Constitution and Parliament* (Baltimore, MD: Johns Hopkins Press, 1963); Nathan J. Brown and Adel Omar Sharif,

"Inscribing the Islamic Shari'a in Arab Constitutional Law," in Yvonne Yazbeck Haddad and Barbara Freyer Stowasser (eds), *Islamic Law and the Challenges of Modernity* (Walnut Creek, CA: Altamira, 2004), 59–60; and, Stanford J. Shaw and Ezel Kural Shaw, *History of the Ottoman Empire and Modern Turkey*, vol. 2 (Cambridge: Cambridge University Press, 1977), 174–89.

20 Ibid., 213–14.
21 Jacob M. Landau, *Parliaments and Parties in Egypt* (Tel Aviv: Israel Publishing House, 1953), 7.
22 Ami Ayalon, *Language and Change in the Arab Middle East: The Evolution of Modern Political Discourse* (New York: Oxford University Press, 1987), 110–26.
23 Landau, *Parliaments and Parties in Egypt*, 7–22.
24 Elie Kedourie, *Afghani and Abduh: An Essay on Religious Unbelief and Political Activism in Modern Islam* (London: Frank Cass, 1966), 23–27.
25 Albert Hourani, *Arabic Thought in the Liberal Age, 1798–1939* (London and New York: Oxford University Press, 1962), 116–17.
26 For an analysis and translation of al-Afghani's "al-Hukuma al-Istibdadiyya": L.M Kenny, "al-Afghani on Types of Despotic Government," *Journal of the American Oriental Society*, 86:1 (January–March 1966), 19–27. The text was reprinted by Rashid Rida with minor modifications: "Al-Hukuma al-Istibdadiyya," *al-Manar*, 3:25, 3:26 (November 4, November 14, 1900), 577–82, 601–7.
27 Nikki R. Keddie, *Sayyid Jamal ad-Din "al-Afghani": A Political Biography* (Berkeley: University of California Press, 1972), 10.
28 Jamal al-Din al-Afghani, "al-Haq wal-Akthariyya," in Muhammad 'Imara (ed.), *al-A'mal al-Kamila li-Jamal al-Din al-Afghani* (al-Mu'assasa al-Misriyya al-'ama lil-T'alif wal-Nashr, 1968), 428–29.
29 Jamal al-Din al-Afghani, "Misr wal-Hukm al-Niyabi," in ibid., 473–74.
30 Jamal al-Din al-Afghani, "Misr wal-Misriyyin wal-Sharq," in ibid., 477–79.
31 Muhammad 'Abduh, "Fi al-Shura wal-Istibdad," in Muhammad 'Imara (ed.), *al-A'mal al-Kamila lil-Imam Muhmmad 'Abduh* (Beirut: al-Mu'assasa al-'Arabiyya lil-Dirasat wal-Nashr, 1972, Vol. 1), 350–51. The essay was first published in *al-Waqa'i' al-Misriyya*, no. 1279, December 12, 1881.While it is not signed, 'Imara convincingly explains why 'Abduh is its author: ibid., 221–22.
32 Ibid., 353.
33 Ibid., 353–54.
34 Ibid., 354–55.
35 Muhammad 'Abduh, "Fi al-Shura," in ibid., 357–61. The essay was first published in *al-Waqa'i' al-Misriyya*, no. 1280, December 13, 1881.
36 Muhammad 'Abduh, "al-Shura wal-Qanun," in ibid., 362–65. The essay was first published in *al-Waqa'i' al-Misriyya*, no. 1290, December 25, 1881.
37 Ibid., 362–63, 365.
38 Jacob M. Landau, *Parliaments and Parties in Egypt*, 28–54.
39 'Abd al-Rahman al-Kawakibi, "Kitab Taba'i al-Isti'bad wa-Masari' al-Istibdad," in Muhammad 'Imara (ed.), *al-A'mal al-Kamila li-'Abd al-Rahman al-Kawakibi*(al-Hay'a al-Misriyya al-'ama lil-Ta'lif wal-Nashr, n.d.), 337–38.
40 Ibid., 338–40.
41 Ibid., 342–48.
42 Ibid., 420.
43 Ibid., 434–36.
44 Ibid., 348.
45 Ibid., 365.
46 'Abd al-Rahman al-Kawakibi, "Umm al-Qura," in Muhammad 'Imara (ed.), *al-A'mal al-Kamila li-'Abd al-Rahman al-Kawakibi* (al-Hay'a al-Misriyya al-'ama lil-Ta'lif wal-Nashr, n.d.), 153, 156.
47 'Abd al-Rahman al-Kawakibi, "Kitab Taba'i al-Isti'bad wa-Masari' al-Istibdad," 348.
48 Ibid., 339.

49 Ibid., footnote 2.
50 Ibid., 348.
51 Muhammad Rashid Rida, "Al-Umma wa-Sultat al-Hakim al-Mustabid," *al-Manar*
9:12 (February 13, 1906), 905–06.
52 Muhammad Rashid Rida, *al-Khilafa* (Cairo: al-Zahra' lil-I'lam al-'Arabi, 1994), 82.
53 Ibid., 18–23.
54 Ibid., 38–39.
55 Ibid., 39.
56 Richard P. Mitchell, *The Society of the Muslim Brothers* (New York, Oxford and Toronto:
Oxford University Press, 1993), pp. 14–15, 18.
57 Hasan al-Banna, "Risalat al-Mu'tamar al-Khamis" (February 1939), in *Majmu'at
Rasa'il al-Imam al-Shahid Hasan al-Banna* (Cairo: Dar al-Tawzi' wal-Nashr al-Islamiyya,
2006), 357.
58 Ibid., 359–60.
59 Ibid., 360.
60 A landmark in the resurrection of liberal democracy as a universally applicable system
of government was the conference on the Crisis of Democracy in the Arab Homeland,
organized by the Centre for Arab Unity Studies in Cyprus in November 1983. Some
participants expressed a loss of faith in political rhetoric that claimed that lack of
democratization was due to the poor state of social progress or security concerns. For
the proceedings of the conference, see Ibrahim Sa'd al-Din, *Azamat al-Dimuqratiyya fi
al-Watan al-'Arabi* (Beirut: Markaz Dirasat al-Wahda al-'Arabiyya, 1987). In the early
1990s the liberal discourse was further developed, primarily in forums and publications
of the same Centre. In April 1990, the Centre organized a conference in Cairo titled
"The Future of Democracy in the Arab Homeland." The head of its office in the
Egyptian capital, Wahid 'Abd al-Majid, argued in the opening lecture that with the
collapse of the Soviet bloc, the argument that there exist different models for
democracy, rather than merely the Western one, is no longer valid. He called for the
initiation of an Arab movement for democracy similar to that of the Polish Solidarity
Movement: "Hawla Mustaqbal al-Dimuqratiyya fi al-Watan al-'Arabi," *al-Mustaqbal
al-'Arabi*, 8:138 (1990), 80–93.
61 Clark B. Lombardi, "Constitutional Provisions Making Sharia 'A' or 'The' Chief
Source of Legislation: Where Do They Come from? What Do They Mean? Do They
Matter?," University of Washington School of Law, *Legal Studies Research Paper* no.
2014–01 (2013), 754–58; Brown and Sherif, "Inscribing the Islamic Shari'a in Arab
Constitutional Law," 64–75.
62 One example is a lively polemic that was published in 1985 in the opinion columns of
the Saudi-owned Arab daily, *al-Sharq al-Awsat*, as to whether *shura* is the Islamic equivalent of democracy. Muhsin 'Abd al-Hamid, one of several participating scholars who
cautioned against equating the two, explained that every civilization has a point of view, or
an ideology, which is based on interrelated principles. According to al-Hamid, generously narrowing a broader chronological progression, the comparison between *shura*
and democracy draws on the tradition of the 1950s. Back then, many scholars,
including Islamist scholars, attempted to find an Islamic equivalent for Western terms
because they did not comprehend, at that time, the dangers posed to their civilization
by making such comparisons. He argued that Islam does respect human dignity and
does, in fact, distinguish a role for people in running the affairs of society and
encourages the airing of opposing views. However, though there are some similarities
between democracy and *shura*, the two still contradict each other. In a democratic
system, religion and state are separated, and it is impossible to outlaw political parties
that oppose Islamic principles, as Islam ordains; furthermore, people are granted the
personal freedom to commit immoral acts. The Islamic system of government and
the Western one must not and should not be confused: Muhsin 'Abd al-Hamid,
"al-Farq al-Jawhari bayna Nizam al-Shura wa-Mustalah al-Dimuqratiyya," *al-Sharq
al-Awsat*, March 15, 1985, 14. Joining the polemic in *al-Sharq al-Awsat*, Muhammad

Mahmud Mandura, an Egyptian teaching at Saudi Arabia's King Saud University, wrote that Islam prohibits conversion to other religions, interest-based loans, mixing of men and women, prostitution, and homosexuality. All of these are legal in the West, where personal freedoms, rather than God's word, are sacred. Thus, *shura* cannot be compared to democracy: Muhammad Mahmud Mandura, "al-Dimuqratiyya Mabda' Yukhalifu al-Islam," *al-Sharq al-Awsat*, March 19, 1985, 14. Fikri al-Jaziri, another scholar participating in the same debate, noted that abortions, forbidden according to religious law, are legal in the United States because women wanted them to be so; democracy, as opposed to *shura*, is a system of government that grants complete sovereignty to human beings, forgetting that sovereignty and basic legislation are for Allah only. Thus, according to al-Jaziri, democracy, though it may be a nice word, should not be rejected because it is foreign or flawed, but because its very essence contradicts Islam. Fikri al-Jaziri, "Al-Dimuqratiyya laysa hiya al-Shura," *al-Sharq al-Awsat*, March 4, 1985, 14.

63   Muhammad al-Ghazali, *al-Islam wal-Istibdad al-Siyasi* (Cairo: Dar al-Kutub al-Haditha, 1961), 3.
64   Yusuf al-Qaradawi, *Ta'rikhuna al-Muftara 'alayhi* (Cairo: Dar al-Shuruq, 2008), 61.
65   Muhammad al-Ghazali, *al-Islam wal-Istibdad al-Siyasi*, 57–58.
66   Ibid., 70–72.
67   Ibid., 59–60, 73–4.
68   Ibid., 56.
69   Ibid., 57.
70   Ibid., 51–53.
71   Ibid., 55.
72   Muhammad al-Ghazali, *al-Ghazw al-Thaqafi Yamtaddu fi Fagharina* (Cairo: Dar al-Shuruq, second printing, 1998, the writing of the book dates to the mid-1980s), 41, see also 94.
73   Muhammad al-Ghazali, *Azmat al-Shura fi al-Mujtama'at al-'Arabiyya wal-Islamiyya* (place of publication and name of publisher not mentioned: October 1990), 41.
74   Ibid., 69.
75   Ibid., 70–72.
76   Ibid., 36.
77   Ibid., 45–46; on al-Ghazali's understanding of the limits of *shura* and the duty to abide by the decisive laws also: Khalid Muhsin (ed.), *Misr bayna al-Dawla al-Islamiyya wal-Dawla al-'Almaniyya* (Cairo: Markaz al-I'lam al-'Arabi, 1992), 26–28.
78   Al-Ghazali, *Azmat al-Shura*, 43.
79   Al-Ghazali, *al-Islam wal-Istibdad al-Siyasi*, 57.
80   Al-Ghazali, *Azmat al-Shura*, 46–47.
81   Muhsin, *Misr bayna al-Dawla al-Islamiyya wal-Dawla al-'Almaniyya*, 29.
82   Yusuf al-Qaradawi, *al-Hulul al-Mustawrada wa-Kayfa Jannat 'ala Ummatina* (Beirut: Mu'assasat al-Risala, 1974, first published 1971), 52, 112, 120–27.
83   Ibid., 77–78.
84   Yusuf al-Qaradawi, *al-Hall al-Islami: Farida wa-Darura* (Beirut: Mu'assasat al-Risala, 1974), 88.
85   Ibid., 47.
86   Ibid., 116–18.
87   Ibid., 226.
88   Ibid., 82–84.
89   Yusuf al-Qaradawi, "Risala Maftuha ila Ra'is al-Jumhuriyya," *al-Sha'b*, January 16, 1990, 12.
90   Yusuf al-Qaradawi, *Min Fiqh al-Dawla fi al-Islam* (Cairo: Dar al-Shuruq, 2001, first published 1997), 39.
91   Yusuf al-Qaradawi, *Ummatuna bayna Qarnayn* (Cairo: Dar Al-Shuruq, 2002, first published 2000), 22–23.
92   Yusuf al-Qaradawi, *Nahnu wal-Gharb: As'ila Sha'ika wa-Ajwiba Hasima* (Cairo: Dar al-Tawzi' wal-Nashr al-Islamiyya, 2006), 158–59.

93   Al-Qaradawi, *Min Fiqh al-Dawla fi al-Islam* 39, 49.
94   Ibid., 35–7. See also *Ummatuna bayna Qarnayn*, 26.
95   Al-Qaradawi, *Min Fiqh al-Dawla fi al-Islam*, 30–31, 141–42.
96   Ibid., 73–74
97   Ibid., 58.
98   Ibid., 30, 76.
99   Ibid., 58.
100   Ibid., 71–72.
101   Abu Hamid al-Ghazali, *Fada'ih al-Batiniyya* (Cairo: al-Dar al-Qawmiyya lil-Tiba'a wal-
      Nashr, 1964), 191–94; for analysis: Michael Cook, *Commanding Right and Forbidding
      Wrong in Islamic Thought* (Cambridge: Cambridge University Press, 2000), 432–33,
      440–41; Hamilton Gibb, "Constitutional Organization," in Majid Khadduri and
      Herbert J. Liebesny (eds.), *Law in the Middle East*, vol. 1: Origin and Development of
      Islamic Law (Washington DC: The Middle East Institute, 1955), 19–20; Khaled Abou
      El Fadl, *Rebellion and Violence in Islamic Law* (Cambridge: Cambridge University Press,
      2001), 10–11.
102   Taqi al-Din Ibn Taymiyya, *al-Siyasa al-Shar'iyya fi Islah al-Ra'i wal-Ra'iyya* (Egypt: Dar
      al-Kitab al-'Arabi, 1969), 161; for analysis: Askar H. al-Enazy, *The Creation of Saudi
      Arabia: Ibn Saud and British Imperial Policy, 1914–1927* (London and New York:
      Routledge, 2010), 13–15; Muhammad Rawas, *Mawsu'at Fiqh Ibn Taymiyya*, vol. 1
      (Beirut: Dar al-Nafa'is, 1998), vol. 1, 285–300; Abou El Fadl, *Rebellion and Violence in
      Islamic Law*, 273–74.
103   Al-Qaradawi, *Min Fiqh al-Dawla fi al-Islam*, 118–26.
104   Al-Banna, "Risalat al-Mu'tamar al-Khamis," 252–53.
105   Al-Qaradawi, *Min Fiqh al-Dawla fi al-Islam*, 33.
106   Ibid., 151–60.
107   Ibid., 37.
108   Ibid., 51.
109   Yusuf al-Qaradawi, *al-Halal wal-Haram fi al-Islam* (Cairo: Matkabat Wahaba, 2004, first
      published 1960), 230–33.
110   Yusuf al-Qaradawi, *Min Ajl Sahwa Rashida* (Cairo: Dar al-Shuruq, 1988, accessed
      August 2, 2012: http://www.mlazna.com), 44–45.
111   Yusuf al-Qaradawi, *al-Ijtihad fi al-Shari'a al-Islamiyya* (Kuwait: Dar al-Qalam, 1996),
      160–61, 179.
112   For the full text of the *fatwa* see Imam Muhammad Imam, "Fatwa Tujizu Shira' al-Manazil
      bi-Qard Ribawi lil-Muslimin fi Ghayr Bilad al-Islam," *al-Sharq al-Awsat* (October 3,
      1999), 25; Yusuf al-Qaradawi, "Shira' Buyut al-Sukna fi al-Gharb 'an Tariq al-Bunuk,"
      in *Fi Fiqh al-Aqalliyyat al-Muslima* (Cairo: Dar al-Shuruq, 2007, first published 2001),
      174–79. For an English translation, Anas Usama al-Tikriti and Shakir Nasif al-'Ubaydi
      (trans.) *Fatwas of European Council for Fatwa and Research* (Cairo: Islamic INC, 2002),
      160–68.
113   Al-Qaradawi, *Fi Fiqh al-Aqalliyyat al-Muslima*, 169–70.
114   Muhammad 'Imara, *al-Dawla al-Islamiyya bayna al-'Almaniyya wal-Sulta al-Diniyya*
      (Cairo: Dar al-Shuruq, 1988), 26–60.
115   Ibid., 19–21.
116   Muhammad 'Imara, *al-Islam wa-Huquq al-Insan—Darurat, La Huquq* (Jedda: Maktabat
      Bustan al-Marfa, 2004–5), 36–37, 60–61, and, Muhammad 'Imara, *Hal al-Islam Huwa
      al-Hall? Limadha wa-Kayfa?* (Cairo: Dar al-Shuruq, 1995), 81.
117   'Imara, *al-Islam wa-Huquq al-Insan*, 13–15, 38–40, and, *Hal al-Islam Huwa al-Hall*, 77–78.
118   'Imara, *al-Islam wa-Huquq al-Insan*, 35–37.
119   Muhammad 'Imara, *Fi al-Nizam al-Siyasi al-Islami* (Cairo: Maktabat al-Imam al-Bukhari,
      n.d.), 63–64; and without the implication that in saying so the Prophet Muhammad
      established the rule of the majority as a *shar'i* principle, *Ma'rakat al-Mustalahat: bayna
      al-Gharb wal-Islam* (Nahdat Misr lil-Tiba'a wal-Nashr wal-Tawzi', n.d.), 121.
120   'Imara, *al-Islam wa-Huquq al-Insan*, 101–04.

121 'Imara, *Hal al-Islam Huwa al-Hall*, 90–91.

122 'Imara, *Fi al-Nizam al-Siyasi al-Islami*, 45, 66, 75–80; *Ma'rakat al-Mustalahat: bayna al-Gharb wal-Islam*, 4–5, 119–21, 125–26; "al-Shura al-Islamiyya wal-Dimuqratiyya al-Gharbiyya," *Majalat al-Dimuqratiyya* (published by al-Ahram), December 20, 2012, accessed April 20, 2015: http://democracy.ahram.org.eg/News; *Hal al-Islam Huwa al-Hall*, 84–85. In the latter book he quoted the aforementioned words of Hasan al-Banna about the compatibility of Islamic norms and certain Western political norms.

123 Muhammad 'Imara, *al-Istiqlal al-Hadari* (October 6th, City: Nahdat Misr lil-Tiba'a wal-Nashr wal-Tawzi', 2007), 198. On his notion of pluralism within a unifying Islamic framework see also: Muhammad 'Imara, *al-Islam wal-Ta'addudiyya* (Cairo: Dar al-Rashad, 1997), 164–78.

124 'Imara, *Fi al-Nizam al-Siyasi al-Islami*, 45, 47; *Ma'rakat al-Mustalahat: bayna al-Gharb wal-Islam*, 122.

125 Ibid., 122.

126 'Imara, *Fi al-Nizam al-Siyasi al-Islami*, 79–80; *Ma'rakat al-Mustalahat: bayna al-Gharb wal-Islam*, 126.

127 Chris Harnisch and Quinn Mecham, "Democratic Ideology in Islamist Opposition? The Muslim Brotherhood's 'Civil State'," *Middle Eastern Studies*, 45:2 (2009), 190.

128 Ibid., 196.

129 Ibid., 197.

130 "Barnamaj Hizb al-Ikhwan al-Muslimin," 7, 13–24, accessed February 10, 2010: www.islamonline.net/arabic/Daawa/2007/08/ikhwan.pdf.

131 Nathan J. Brown and Amr Hamzawy, *The Draft Party Platform of the Egyptian Muslim Brotherhood: Foray into Political Integration or Retreat into Old Positions?* Carnegie Endowment Middle East Series, no. 89 (January 2008), 4. See the comments of 'Isam al-Aryan, one of the leaders of the movement's younger generation: "Misr: al-'Aryan Yantaqidu Barnamaj 'al-Ikhwan," *al-Hayat*, October 13, 2007, 1.

132 Election Program—Freedom and Justice Party (2011), accessed May 3, 2015: www. scribd.com/doc/73955131/FJP-Program-En.

133 Constitution of Egypt, December 2012, accessed August 18, 2015: www.sis.gov.eg/ newvr/theconistitution.pdf.

134 More inclined to the Saudi *salafi* point of view on democracy as the absolute opposite of Islam, Muhammad Qutb (1919–2014, brother of Sayyid, in academic exile in Saudi Arabia from 1972 until his death) held that participation in secular political systems would contradict the very essence of the Islamic call and undermine its credibility because, regardless of how such participation is justified, it would legitimize a *jahili* order: Muhammad Qutb, *al-Tatawwur wal-Thabat fi Hayat al-Bashar*, (Beirut and Cairo: Dar al-Shuruq, 1985), 248; *Waqi'una al-Mu'asir* (Cairo: Dar al-Shuruq, 2006), 441–42. In the aftermath of Brothers' overthrow in 2013, it is fascinating that Qutb's rejection of electoral participation was not only principled, but also pragmatic. He held it to be naïve to think that a parliamentary majority alone would secure the Islamic revolution. Politics, he wrote in 1986, are about power, not about majorities and justice. Thus, without the existence in Egyptian society of a solid "base" committed to Islam, even if a parliament that is one hundred percent Muslim were elected and even if that parliament endorsed the complete application of Allah's laws, that parliament would be dissolved by a military coup and its members would be thrown to prison. Ibid., 40, 42.

135 For example, Nader Hashemi, "Why Islam (Properly Understood) Is the Solution: Reflections on the Role of Religion in Tunisia's Democratic Transition," *The American Journal of Islamic Social Sciences*, 30:4 (2013), 143–44; Vali Nasr, "The Rise of 'Muslim Democracy'," *Journal of Democracy*, 16:2 (April 2005), 14–16.

136 For al-Ghannushi's biography see: Azzam S. Tamimi, *Rachid al-Ghannouchi: A Democrat within Islamism* (Oxford: Oxford University Press, 2001), 4–71.

137 Mark J. Gasiorowski, "The Failure of Reform in Tunisia," *Journal of Democracy*, 3:4 (October 1992), 92; on Bourgiba's approach to al-Ghannushi: Derek Hopwood, *Habib*

Bourgiba of Tunisia: The Tragedy of Longevity (New York: St. Martin's Press, 1992), 102–3; on b. 'Ali's approach to al-Nahda: Jacob Abadi, *Tunisia Since the Arab Conquest: The Saga of a Westernized Muslim State* (Reading: Ithaca, 2013), 507–13.

138 Laura K. Landolt and Paul Kubicek, "Opportunities and Constraints: Comparing Tunisia and Egypt to the Coloured Revolutions," *Democratization*, 21:6 (2014), 992; Valentine M. Moghadam, "What is Democracy? Promises and Perils of the Arab Spring," *Current Sociology*, 61:4 (2013), 400.

139 For example in his interviews given in: Yasir al-Za'atra, *Hiwar ma'a al-Shaykh Rashid al-Ghannushi* (Manshurat Filastin al-Muslima, 1996), 40–3; see also Khaled Elgindy, "The Rhetoric of Rashid Ghannushi," *Arab Studies Journal*, 3:1 (Spring 1995), 110–14; John L. Esposito and James P. Piscatori, "Democratization and Islam," *Middle East Journal*, 45:3 (Summer 1991), 427–40.

140 Muhammad Elihachmi Hamdi, *The Politicisation of Islam* (Boulder, CO: Westview Press, 1998), 90–91.

141 Rashid al-Ghannushi, "Hukm Musharakat al-Islamiyyin fi Nizam Ghayr Islami," in 'Azzam al-Tamimi (ed.), *Musharakat al-Islamiyyin fi al-Sulta* (London: Liberty for the Muslim World, 1994), 12–23.

142 Stefano Maria Torelli, "The 'AKP Model' and Tunisia's al-Nahda: From Convergence to Competition?" *Insight Turkey*, 14:3 (2012), 76.

143 Rashid al-Ghannushi, "al-Usuliyya al-Waraqa Allati La'iba biha 'Arafat," *Filastin al-Muslima* (October 1993), 44–45.

144 Rashid al-Ghannushi, "Secularism in the Arab Maghreb," in Azzam Tamimi and John L. Esposito (eds), *Islam and Secularism in the Middle East* (London: Hurst & Company, 2000), 115–23.

145 Rashid al-Ghannushi, *Huquq al-Insan fi al-Islam wa-Athruha 'ala Suluk al-Muslim al-Iqtisadiyya* (Dublin: al-Majlis al-'Urubbi lil-Ifta' wal-Buhuth, July 2008), 3–6.

146 Francesco Cavatorta and Fabio Merone, "Moderation through Exclusion? The Journey of the Tunisian Ennahda from Fundamentalist to Conservative Party," *Democratization*, 20:5 (2013), 858–61; Laura K. Landolt and Paul Kubicek, "Opportunities and Constraints: Comparing Tunisia and Egypt to the Coloured Revolutions," *Democratization*, 21:6 (2014), 993; Nadia Marzouki, "From Resistance to Governance: The Category of Civility in the Political Theory of Tunisian Islamists," in Nouri Gana (ed.), *The Making of the Tunisian Revolution: Contexts, Architects, Prospects* (Edinburgh: Edinburgh University Press, 2013), 208.

147 Rashid al-Ghannushi, *al-Dimuqratiyya wa Huquq al-Insan fi al-Islam* (Beirut: al-Dar al-'Arabiiya lil-'Ulum Nashirun; Duha, Markaz al-Jazeera lil-Diraasat, 2012), 10–11, 109–10.

148 Ibid., 14–22, 63, 109.

149 Ibid., 70–71.

150 Ibid., 99, 132–33.

151 Ibid., 99.

152 For the text of the Tunisian Constitution (accessed April 5, 2016): www.constitutep roject.org/constitution/Tunisia_2014.pdf.

153 "Rashid Al-Ghannushi: Nuridu an Nakun Namudhajan lil-Dimuqratiyya al-'Arabiyya," December 23, 2014, accessed April 15, 2015: www.noonpost.net/content/ 4786; for the original German text of the interview by Daniel Bax und Tsafrir Cohen: "Wir wollen ein Vorbild für die arabische Demokratie sein," accessed April 15, 2015: https://de.qantara.de/inhalt/interview-mit-rachid-ghannouchi-wir-wollen-ein-vorbild-fue r-die-arabische-.

154 *Al-Jazeera*, "Tunisia's Ennahda Distances Itself from Political Islam," May 21, 2016, accessed May 25, 2016: www.aljazeera.com/news/2016/05/tunisia-ennahda-dista nces-political-islam-160520172957296.html.

155 Marzouki, "From Resistance to Governance: The Category of Civility in the Political Theory of Tunisian Islamists," 217–18.

156 Daniel W. Brown, *Rethinking Tradition in Modern Islamic Thought* (Cambridge: Cambridge University Press, 1996), 66–67.

157 For this evaluation, as well as the depiction of al-Raziq as the first Islamic scholar to endorse secularism: Fauzi M. Najjar, "The Debate on Islam and Secularism in Egypt," *Arab Studies Quarterly*, 18:2 (Spring 1996), 1.

158 'Ali 'Abd al-Raziq, *al-Islam wa-Usul al-Hukm* (Beirut: Manshurat Dar al-Haya, 1966), 151.

159 Ibid., 171.

160 Ibid., 122.

161 Ibid., 153. For an English translation of a portion of the book that contains some of the abovementioned ideas: "Message Not Government, Religion Not State," in Charles Kurzman (ed.), *Liberal Islam: A Sourcebook* (New York and Oxford: Oxford University Press, 1998), 29–36.

162 Hourani, *Arabic Thought in the Liberal Age, 1798–1939*, 183–88. On the affair, also: Meir Hatina, "On the Margins of Consensus: The Call to Separate Religion and State in Modern Egypt," *Middle Eastern Studies*, 36:1 (January 2000), 38–42.

163 Hourani, *Arabic Thought in the Liberal Age, 1798–1939*, 189.

164 Muhammad 'Imara, *al-Islam wa-Usul al-Hukm li-'Ali 'Abd al-Raziq* (Beirut: al-Mu'assasa al-'Arabiyya lil-Dirasat wal-Nashr, 1972), for his critical approach of the book: 43–52.

165 Muhammad al-Ghazali, "Hadha Dinuna," *al-Sha'b*, no. 895, November 15, 1994, 12.

166 Rachel M. Scott, "The Role of 'Ulama' in an Islamic Order: The Early Thought of Muhammad al-Ghazali (1916–96)," *The Maghreb Review*, 32:2–3 (2007), 151.

167 Khalid Muhmmad Khalid, *Min Huna Nabda'* (Dar al-Fikr al-Arabi, 1952, sixth printing), 146–47.

168 Ibid., 152–53.

169 Ibid., 164–65.

170 Ibid., 160–62.

171 Ibid., 156–57; Khalid Muhammad Khalid, *al-Dimuqratiyya. Abadan* (Egypt: Dar al-Fikr al-'Arabi, 1953, second printing), 140–48.

172 Muhammad al-Ghazali, *Min Huna Na'lam* (Cairo: Dar al-Kutab al-Haditha bil-Qahira, n.d., fifth printing, first published 1950).

173 Al-Qaradawi, *Ummatuna bayna Qarnayn*, 92–93.

174 Hatina, "On the Margins of Consensus: The Call to Separate Religion and State in Modern Egypt," 52–53. On al-Ghazali's appreciation of Khalid's change of mind: Muhammad al-Ghazali, "Hadha Dinuna," *al-Sha'b*, no. 895, November 15, 1994, 12.

175 Hatina, "On the Margins of Consensus: The Call to Separate Religion and State in Modern Egypt," 55.

176 Faraj Fuda, *Qabla al-Suqut* (Alexandria: Dar wa-Matabi' al-Mustaqbal, 2004, first published 1985), 7–14.

177 Ibid., 50–56.

178 Yusuf al-Qaradawi, *al-Shaykh al-Ghazali Kama 'Araftuhu: Rihlat Nisf Qarn* (Al-Munsura: Dar al-Wafa' lil-Tiba'a wal-Nashr wal-Tawzi', 1995), 270–75.

179 Nasr Abu Zayd, *Reformation of Islamic Thought: A Critical Historical Analysis* (Amsterdam: Amsterdam University Press, 2006), 98–99.

180 Ibid., 96.

181 On Abu Zayd's approach to the Quran, Muhammad 'Imara's response to his approach, and the legal case against his marriage: Fauzi M. Najjar, "Islamic Fundamentalism and the Intellectuals: The Case of Nasr Hamid Abu Zayd," *British Journal of Middle Eastern Studies*, 27:2 (November 2000), 177–200. On his rejection of the Quran as a reference for politics, and specifically his criticism of Islamist modernist views, as well as the legal challenge against his marriage, also: George N. Sfeir, "Basic Freedoms in a Fractured Legal Culture: Egypt and the Case of Nasr Hamid Abu Zayd," *The Middle East Journal*, 52:3 (Summer 1998), 402–14.

CONCLUSION

In almost every lecture I give on the crisis of democracy in Arab societies, just before I begin presenting contesting theories on the matter, someone in the audience shouts out, "It's because they are Muslims. Islam and democracy don't go hand in hand." Often, someone else makes another contribution: "What gives us"—by us the West is implied—"the right to think that democracy is the best system and should be a universal system?"

In my response I ask the audience to shift their attention from the Muslim world and reflect on the Korean peninsula. Seventy years ago there was only one Korean people with no democratic heritage at all. Cold War battles divided the peninsula arbitrarily into what evolved to be a liberal-democratic South Korea and what evolved to be the largest concentration camp in history, North Korea. The former, a doubt-based society and a pluralistic democracy, has become a scientific, technological, financial and cultural powerhouse. The latter, a horrifyingly disturbed version of revelation-based society ruled by a totalitarian regime based on a personality cult, is home to a starved, oppressed and brainwashed population. The Korean example demonstrates that freedom is not predestined or genetic. Heritage and traditions cannot predict its existence or absence. Human societies have the capacity to develop to be democratic just as they have the capacity to develop to be Stalinist, and, as the most recent example of Indonesia teaches us, Muslim societies are no exception to this rule. There is nothing in "Islam" that prevents Muslim societies from democratizing. What people make of Islam, however, can have that effect. Where the interpretation of Islam encourages the establishment of a revelation-based regime, in which unelected religious scholars monopolize the interpretation of religion, democracy cannot prevail. Where the main opposition forces call for the creation of revelation-based societies, democracy is less likely to prevail. And it is possible for democracy to fail even without such opposition.

There are good arguments for the advantage of democracies over tyrannies; there are good arguments for the universality of democracy. But the intention of this book was not to make the case for either. Its outlook was inward rather than external. It examined the coherence of an Islamic approach that finds its roots primarily in late nineteenth century Egypt, and was passed down, loyally, through several generations. The modernist-apologists, whether a century ago or in contemporary times, recognized the dire state of science and politics in their societies, and identified the absence of reason and freedom as a cause. Determined to protect the status of revelation as an inerrant, all-encompassing, legally binding reference in the modern world, they invoked a historical distinction between Islam and Christianity, and introduced interpretive mechanisms, to argue for the ability of a Muslim revelation-based society to be free from arbitrary interventions of religious scholars in science or in politics. In short, to be revelation-based, yet enjoy all the benefits that Western societies enjoyed as a result of their transformation into doubt-based social orders.

This study demonstrated that there are considerable limitations to the latter statement. First, the insistence of modernist-apologists on a revelation-based social order draws from the argument that the truth of God, His Prophet and His final message to humanity can, and should, be rationally ascertained. Their texts state that they believe the Quran should be embraced as the inerrant and legally binding word of God in full freedom, through the application of reason—because a sound, unbiased logical historical and linguistic inquiry proves it to be so. But this statement is compromised by what always follows it: an unmitigated conviction that an open-minded rational study that seeks the honest truth can only lead to one result, the acceptance of Islam's foundations. Although the logic the modernist-apologists apply is cyclical, and the historical evidence they provide is unsubstantiated, they do not consider alternative views on the revelation as legitimate positions in an unending pluralistic discursive exchange. The freedom to reason and the freedom to doubt exist, in their minds, only to the extent that they lead to an inevitable conclusion that proves their dogmas to be correct.

The major lacuna in works authored by modernist-apologists is their neglect of the problems of scientific certainty and political reference. A crucial aspect of their promise for a revelation-based social order that is free from arbitrary theocratic interventions in empirical investigations of the natural world is the reintroduction and contextualization of an interpretation mechanism that allows the allegorizing of the literal meaning of revealed passages to accommodate new, proven scientific theories, models and facts. Yet neither the early modernist-apologists nor contemporary ones have defined what constitutes a proven scientific theory, model or fact, or who should have the authority to determine what has, in fact, been proven. A crucial aspect of their promise for a revelation-based social order that is free of arbitrary theocratic interventions in political decisions is their suggestion that in a *shura* regime an elected parliament, representing the free will of the people, would be permitted to legislate in any way it saw fit on any issue, except, that is, if it were to legislate against revealed laws. Yet even when coming close to doing so, the modernist-apologists, almost without exception, fell short of determining precisely who should have the authority to interpret the laws given by Allah, or who should elect those in authority. The one scholar who did eventually commit unequivocally to the people's authority, the founder of Tunisia's al-Nahda party, Rashid al-Ghannushi, failed to offer a systematic explanation on how this commitment is reconciled with his commitment to a revelation-based political order.

Modernist-apologetic treatments of science betrayed that they take for granted the existence of scientific certainties, while their treatment of politics betrayed that they take for granted the existence of decisive, absolutist and unanimously agreed-upon divine laws. The histories of science and of Islamic law, including modernist-apologists' engagements with both fields, demonstrate these assumptions to be false. In any society governed by modernist-apologetic norms, it is inevitable that on some issues, and most likely on the more sensitive and controversial ones, different interpretations will arise, forcing the question as to who has the power to decide what constitutes legitimate science or politics to be raised. If the ultimate authority is composed of unelected religious scholars, then theocracy, so vehemently denied by the modernist-apologists, is nevertheless established.

Indeed, although they usually avoid saying so explicitly, modernist-apologetic writings hint that they see confirmed religious scholars—rather than elected politicians, experienced scientists and others—filling the role of ultimate arbitrators on questions of legitimacy. There is much in their writings to suggest why giving that power to religious scholars, even those who are modernist and pragmatically inclined, can gravely impede the ability to think, study and conduct research independent of theocratic interventions. The case of modernist-apologetic treatments of the theory of evolution is but one example. Whereas early modernist-apologetic treatments of the theory invoked allegorizing to argue for the potential reconcilability between the Quran and Darwinism, even pointing to the theory as demonstration of Islam's truth, contemporary modernist-apologists have rejected the theory as premeditated falsehood and heresy that must be shunned from Muslim societies. This shift to de-legitimization was not based on developments in faculties for life sciences. It was inspired by the writings of American fundamentalist Creationists.

It is tempting to judge the modernist-apologists based on specific views on topical issues. In theoretical terms, though, whether they are supportive or hostile to certain sciences or political programs has no bearing on the coherence of their claim to have established a concept of a revelation-based society in which the natural world can be studied with complete freedom from arbitrary theocratic interventions, and in which politics are regulated by similar freedom. Theocracy, the type of regime detested in modernist-apologetic writings, is not necessarily a backward, intolerant political regime. As defined also by the modernist-apologists, it is, simply put, a regime in which religious scholars are the ultimate arbiters of truth and legitimacy, and have the authority to arbitrarily impose their individual views. While the modernist-apologists convincingly established a concept of revelation that allows space for innovative science and competitive politics, they have failed to establish a coherent concept for society governed by revelation and enjoying all the benefits of doubt-based social orders. They would have been successful, at least in theoretical terms, in a world where everyone understands, continuously, the words of God and the phenomena of the natural world in a similar way. But such a world is fanciful.

The quest to see revelation as an exclusive, legally binding reference has been fiercely criticized throughout the twentieth century by liberal Arab intellectuals, who interpreted it as an effort to monopolize culture and politics using a religious premise. However, some aspects of the alternatives introduced by the more well-known voices for the separation of religion and science and religion and politics reveal the continuous broad traction the concept of revelation as an overriding premise has, and the difficulty in debating it. In addressing political structures, Arab liberal thinkers identified the potential despotic implications of establishing a revelation as an exclusive reference, and determined that religion and politics must be separated. However, aware of the place revelation occupies among the majorities in their respective societies, and unwilling to directly challenge it, paramount liberal texts were careful to legitimize their de-politicization of the revelation through an interpretation of the revelation itself. In doing so, they maintained revelation as the premise of constitutional debates and, contrary to their ideological ambitions, further asserted its status as a binding reference.

Arab Liberal texts against religious interventions in scientific inquiries established an artificial break between contemporary modernist-apologetic views and earlier ones, failing to recognize that the latter, no less than the former, were champions of the idea that revelation should have overriding authority over any human activity. Al-Afghani, 'Abduh and their immediate disciples were described as precursors of a liberal trend, and their works as a stepping stone on which efforts to advance reason and freedom should build. In social climates intolerant to secularism, liberals cannot be too picky about their intellectual allies. The agenda introduced by the early modernist-apologists against religious conservatism and for the pursuit of science and participatory politics has spared their works the kind of scrutiny that would have exposed its inherent conflict with the agenda of Muslims who wish to see a separation of religion, science and politics.

The underlying promise of the modernist-apologetic approach is hardly resistible. It argues that the ease of mind that unmitigated faith in the guidance of an all-encompassing, legally binding revelation provides does not compromise, in Islam and in Islam only, progress in science and politics. It suggests that for Muslims—or, more correctly, for Muslims who correctly interpret their religion—faith and reason, tradition and modernity, and past and future are not conflicting but complementary concepts. To generations of Muslims that found solace in revelation, whose identity was defined by belief in its inerrancy and overriding authority, the modernist-apologetic approach has offered a structured alternative to religious conservatism on the one hand, and secular ideologies on the other. It is understandable why not only Muslims, but also observers of Muslim societies, viewed the approach to be a desirable solution to the lingering ideological tensions in Arab societies and politics.

The success of the early modernist-apologists in establishing their approach as mainstream did not have a parallel in the Christian experience. In their struggles with the tensions between revelation and reason and freedom, Christian theologians and religious establishments did not develop a defense of the inerrancy of their revelation that demonstrated its adaptability to modern scientific and political concepts. At the beginning of the great scientific revolution, the Catholic Church made it clear that it would not accommodate scientific advances that undermined its dogmas, or individuals that challenged its overriding authority over human thought. Galileo's *Letter to the Grand Duchess* of 1615, which proposed a method of reconciliation between scientific facts and revealed passages, was ignored by the Catholic Church. His advocacy of the Copernican model was oppressed. Three centuries later, while heliocentrism was legitimized, the Church still insisted on its authority on scientific, philosophical and literary matters and censored thousands of works. Rising in the nineteenth century, Protestant liberal Christian theology, responding to higher criticism of the Bible and to fascinating new scientific discoveries, damaged, to varying degrees, the inerrant status of the revelation and even its centrality to faith. The response of Protestant Churches who sought to defend the inerrancy and primacy of the Bible did not come in the form of an innovative method of accommodating modernity. Instead, the fundamentalists applied literalism and invented counter pseudo-sciences, stating that scientific findings must be wrong if they contradicted revealed passages.

Literalist and dogmatic stubbornness among Christians greatly increased the persuasiveness and appeal of secularist demands to completely separate religion from science and politics in the West. The sophisticated ideas introduced by Muslim modernist-apologists greatly decreased the appeal of secularist demands in Arab societies. This book demonstrated that, while appealing, the modernist-apologetic approach failed to coherently establish the possibility of a revelation-based society that enjoys all the benefits of a doubt-based, rationalist and modern society.

It was about time, wrote Yusuf al-Qaradawi not long ago, that the debate on Islam as a theocratic system, a debate that had already begun in Muhammad 'Abduh's days, came to an end once and for all. But perhaps the time is not ripe; perhaps it is time for something radically different—a Copernican revolution in our understanding of that debate, its roots and its implications.

BIBLIOGRAPHY

'Abd al-Fattah, Nabil. *Taqrir al-Hala al-Diniyya fi Misr*, vol. 2. Cairo: Markaz al-Dirasat al-Siyasiyya wal-Istratijiyya bil-Ahram, 1998.

'Abd al-Hamid, Muhsin. "Al-Farq al-Jawhari bayna Nizam al-Shura wa-Mustalah al-Dimuqratiyya," *al-Sharq al-Awsat*, March 15, 1985, 14.

'Abd al-Raziq, 'Ali. *Al-Islam wa-Usul al-Hukm*. Beirut: Manshurat Dar al-Haya, 1966.

'Abd al-Raziq, 'Ali. "Message Not Government, Religion Not State," in Charles Kurzman (ed.), *Liberal Islam: A Sourcebook*, 29–36. New York and Oxford: Oxford University Press, 1998.

Abdel Baki, Magdy. *True Religion—Unequivocal Evidence*. Engineering House Press, n.d.

'Abduh, Mahmud. *Muhammad al-Ghazali: Da'iya al-Nahda al-Islamiyya*. Beirut: Markaz al-Hadara li-Tanmiyyat al-Fikr al-Islami, 2009.

'Abduh, Mahmud. "Risalat al-Tawhid," in Muhammad 'Imara (ed.), *al-A'mal al-Kamila lil-Imam Muhmmad 'Abduh*, vol. 3, 351–476. Beirut: al-Mu'assasa al-'Arabiyya lil-Dirasat wal-Nashr, 1972.

'Abduh, Muhammad. *Al-Islam Din al-'Ilm wal-Madaniyya*. Beirut: Manshurat Dar Maktabat al-Haya, 1989.

'Abduh, Muhammad. "Al-Shaykh Rashid Rida," in Muhammad 'Imara (ed.), *al-A'mal al-Kamila lil-Imam Muhammad 'Abduh*, vol. 3, 131–132. Beirut: al-Mu'assasa al-'Arabiyya lil-Dirasat wal-Nashr, 1972.

'Abduh, Muhammad. "Al-Qada' wal-Qadr," in Muhammad 'Imara (ed.), *al-A'mal al-Kamila lil-Imam Muhammad 'Abduh*, vol. 3, 481–483. Beirut: al-Mu'assasa al-'Arabiyya lil-Dirasat wal-Nashr, 1972.

'Abduh, Muhammad. "Al-Shura wal-Qanun," in Muhammad 'Imara (ed.), *al-A'mal al-Kamila lil-Imam Muhammad 'Abduh*, vol. 1, 362–366. Beirut: al-Mu'assasa al-'Arabiyya lil-Dirasat wal-Nashr, 1972.

'Abduh, Muhammad. "Bismarck wal-Din," in Muhammad 'Imara (ed.), *al-A'mal al-Kamila lil-Imam Muhammad 'Abduh*, vol. 3, 489–491. Beirut: al-Mu'assasa al-'Arabiyya lil-Dirasat wal-Nashr, 1972.

'Abduh, Muhammad. "Fi al-Shura," in Muhammad 'Imara (ed.), *al-A'mal al-Kamila lil-Imam Muhammad 'Abduh*, vol. 1, 357–361. Beirut: al-Mu'assasa al-'Arabiyya lil-Dirasat wal-Nashr, 1972.

'Abduh, Muhammad. "Fi al-Shura wal-Istibdad," in Muhammad 'Imara (ed.), *al-A'mal al-Kamila lil-Imam Muhammad 'Abduh*, vol. 1, 350–356. Beirut: al-Mu'assasa al-'Arabiyya lil-Dirasat wal-Nashr, 1972.

'Abduh, Muhammad. "Hadith bayna al-Filusuf al-Inglizi Spencer wa-bayna al-Ustadh al-Imam," in Muhammad 'Imara (ed.), *al-A'mal al-Kamila lil-Imam Muhmmad 'Abduh*, vol. 3, 492–494. Beirut: al-Mu'assasa al-'Arabiyya lil-Dirasat wal-Nashr, 1972.

'Abduh, Muhammad. "Kitab Ta'rikh al-Ahdath al-'Urabiyya," in Muhammad 'Imara (ed.), *al-A'mal al-Kamila lil-Imam Muhammad 'Abduh*, vol. 1, 475–560. Beirut: al-Mu'assasa al-'Arabiyya lil-Dirasat wal-Nashr, 1972.

'Abduh, Muhammad. "Tabi'at al-Din al-Masihi" (his response to Farah Antun), in Muhammad 'Imara (ed.), *al-A'mal al-Kamila lil-Imam Muhammad 'Abduh*, vol. 3, 259–281. Beirut: al-Mu'assasa al-'Arabiyya lil-Dirasat wal-Nashr, 1972.

'Abduh, Muhammad. *The Theology of Unity*, translated by Ishaq Musa'ad and Kenneth Cragg. London: George Allen & Unwin, 1966.

'Abduh, Muhammad. "Tufan No'ah … Hal Amma al-Ard Kulha?" in Muhammad 'Imara (ed.), *al-A'mal al-Kamila lil-Imam Muhmmad 'Abduh*, vol. 3, 511–513. Beirut: al-Mu'assasa al-'Arabiyya lil-Dirasat wal-Nashr, 1972.

Abu Ghanima, Ziyad. *Al-'Ilm Yatabarra'u min Nazariyyat Darwin: Akbar Jarimat Tazwir 'Ilmi fi al-Ta'rikh: Dirasat Watha'iqiyya*. Amman: Dar 'Ammar, 1989.

Abu Zayd, Nasr. *Reformation of Islamic Thought: A Critical Historical Analysis*. Amsterdam: Amsterdam University Press, 2006.

Al-Afghani, Jamal al-Din. "Al-Haq wal-Akthariyya," in Muhammad 'Imara (ed.), *al-A'mal al-Kamila li-Jamal al-Din al-Afghani*, 424–429. Al-Mu'assasa al-Misriyya al-'ama lil-T'alif wal-Nashr, 1968.

Al-Afghani, Jamal al-Din. "Al-Nushu' wal-Irtiqa'," in Muhammad 'Imara (ed.), *al-A'mal al-Kamila li-Jamal al-Din al-Afghani* (n.d.), 249–253.

Al-Afghani, Jamal al-Din. *Al-Radd 'ala al-Dahriyyin*. Cairo: Dar al-Karnak, n.d.

Al-Afghani, Jamal al-Din. "Al-Radd 'ala Raynan," n.d., accessed October 21, 2015: http://nachaz.org/index.php/fr/textes-a-l-appui/histoire/53-2012-07-18-01-32-26.html.

Al-Afghani, Jamal al-Din. "Al-Siyasa wal-'Ulum fi al-Qur'an," in Muhammad 'Imara (ed.), *al-A'mal al-Kamila li-Jamal al-Din al-Afghani* (n.d.), 266–270.

Al-Afghani, Jamal al-Din. "Misr wal-Hukm al-Niyabi," in Muhammad 'Imara (ed.), *al-A'mal al-Kamila li-Jamal al-Din al-Afghani*, 472–475. Al-Mu'assasa al-Misriyya al-'ama lil-T'alif wal-Nashr, 1968.

Al-Afghani, Jamal al-Din. "Misr wal-Misriyyin wal-Sharq," in Muhammad 'Imara (ed.), *al-A'mal al-Kamila li-Jamal al-Din al-Afghani*, 476–479. Al-Mu'assasa al-Misriyya al-'ama lil-T'alif wal-Nashr, 1968.

Al-Afghani, Jamal al-Din. "Ra'ihi fi Madhhab al-Nushu' wal-Irtiqa'," in Muhammad al-Makhzumi (ed.), *Khatirat Jamal al-Din al-Afghani*, 181–187. Beirut: al-Matba'a al-'Ilmiyya, 1931.

Al-'Aqqad, 'Abbas Mahmud. *Al-Ustadh al-Imam Muhammad 'Abduh*. Cairo: Maktabat Misr, 1960.

Al-Azm, Sadek Jalal and Abu Fakhr. "Trends in Arab Thought: An Interview with Sadeq Jalal al-Azm," *Journal of Palestine Studies* 27:2 (Winter 1998), 68–80.

Al-Azm, Sadik Jalal. "Islam and the Science-Religion Debates in Modern Times," *European Review*, 15:3 (2007), 283–295.

Al-'Azm, Sadiq Jalal. *Naqd al-Fikr al-Dini*. Beirut: Dar al-Tali'a lil-Tiba'a wal-Nashr, November 1969.

Al-Banna, Hasan. *Al-Salam fi al-Islam*. Manshurat al-'Asr al-Hadith, June 1971, originally published in al-Shihab, December 13, 1947.

Al-Banna, Hasan. *Mudhakkirat al-Da'wa wal-Da'iya*. Cairo: Dar al-Kitab, n.d.

Al-Banna, Hasan. "Da'watuna fi Tawr Jadid" (August 1942), in *Majmu'at Rasa'il al-Imam al-Shaid Hasan al-Banna*, 473–506. Cairo: Dar al-Tawzi' wal-Nashr al-Islamiyyah, 2006.

Al-Banna, Hasan. "Risalat al-Minhaj" (September 1938), in *Majmu'at Rasa'il al-Imam al-Shaid Hasan al-Banna*, 249–270. Cairo: Dar al-Tawzi' wal-Nashr al-Islamiyya, 2006.

Al-Banna, Hasan. "Risalat al-Mu'tamar al-Khamis" (February 1939), in *Majmu'at Rasa'il al-Imam al-Shahid Hasan al-Banna*, 328–378. Cairo: Dar al-Tawzi' wal-Nashr al-Islamiyya, 2006.

Al-Banna, Hasan. "Risalat bayna al-Ams wal-Yawm" (1943), in *Majmu'at Rasa'il al-Imam al-Shahid Hasan al-Banna*, 507–530. Cairo: Dar al-Tawzi' wal-Nashr al-Islamiyya, 2006.

Al-Banna, Hasan. "Risalat nahwa al-Nur" (October 1936), in *Majmu'at Rasa'il al-Imam al-Shahid Hasan al-Banna*, 153–180. Cairo: Dar al-Tawzi' wal-Nashr al-Islamiyya, 2006.

Al-Dajawi, Yusuf. "Sahib al-Manar: wal-Salat wal-Salam 'ala al-Rasul Sala Allah 'Alayhi wa-Salam: Ba'd al-Adhan," *Nur al-Islam*, 3:5 (September 1932), 330–340.

Al-Ghannushi, Rashid. "al-Usuliyya al-Waraqa Allati La'iba biha 'Arafat," *Filastin al-Muslima* (October 1993), 44–45.

Al-Ghannushi, Rashid. "Hukm Musharakat al-Islamiyyin fi Nizam Ghayr Islami," in 'Azzam al-Tamimi (ed.), *Musharakat al-Islamiyyin fi al-Sulta*, 13–24. London: Liberty for the Muslim World, 1994.

Al-Ghannushi, Rashid. *Huquq al-Insan fi al-Islam wa-Athruha 'ala Suluk al-Muslim al-Iqtisadiyya*. Dublin: al-Majlis al-'Urubbi lil-Ifta' wal-Buhuth, July 2008.

Al-Ghannushi, Rashid. *Al-Dimuqratiyya wa-Huquq al-Insan fi al-Islam*. Beirut: al-Dar al-'Arabiyya lil-'Ulum Nashirun; Duha, Markaz al-Jazeera lil-Diraasat, 2012.

Al-Ghazali, Abu Hamid. *Fada'ih al-Batiniyya*. Cairo: al-Dar al-Qawmiyya lil-Tiba'a wal-Nashr, 1964.

Al-Ghazali, Abu Hamid. *The Incoherence of the Philosophers*, translated by Michael Marmura. Provo, UT: Brigham Young University, 2000.

Al-Ghazali, Muhammad. *Al-Da'wa al-Islamiyya fi al-Qarn al-Hali*. Cairo: Dar al-Shuruq, 2000.

Al-Ghazali, Muhammad. *Al-Ghazw al-Thaqafi Yamtaddu fi Fagharina*. Cairo: Dar al-Shuruq, second printing, 1998, the writing of the book dates to the mid-1980s.

Al-Ghazali, Muhammad. *Al-Islam al-Muftara 'alayhi: bayna al-Shuyu'iyyin wal-Ra'smaliyyin*. Cairo: Maktabat Wahaba, fifth printing, 1960, first published 1950.

Al-Ghazali, Muhammad. *Al-Islam fi Wajh al-Zahf al-Ahmar*. Beirut: Al-Maktaba al-'Asriyya, 1966, accessed 3 May 2012: www.al-mostafa.com.

Al-Ghazali, Muhammad. *Al-Islam wal-Awda' al-Iqtisadiyya*. Cairo: Dar al-Kitab al-'Arabi, third printing, 1952, first published 1947.

Al-Ghazali, Muhammad. *Al-Islam wal-Istibdad al-Siyasi*. Cairo: Dar al-Kutub al-Haditha, 1961.

Al-Ghazali, Muhammad. *Al-Islam wal-Manahij al-Ishtirakiyya*. Cairo: Dar al-Kutub al-Haditha, fourth printing, 1960, first published 1949.

Al-Ghazali, Muhammad. *Al-Sunna al-Nabawiyya bayna Ahl al-Fiqh wa-Ahl al-Hadith*. Cairo: Dar al-Shuruq, 1989.

Al-Ghazali, Muhammad. *Azmat al-Shura fi al-Mujtama'at al-'Arabiyya wal-Islamiyya*. Place of publication and name of publisher not mentioned, October 1990.

Al-Ghazali, Muhammad. "Hadha Dinuna," *al-Sha'b*, no. 491, April 24, 1989, 12.

Al-Ghazali, Muhammad. "Hadha Dinuna," *al-Sha'b*, no. 538, March 20, 1990, 12.

Al-Ghazali, Muhammad. "Hadha Dinuna," *al-Sha'b*, no. 540, April 3, 1990, 12.

Al-Ghazali, Muhammad. "Hadha Dinuna," *al-Sha'b*, no. 645, April 21, 1992, 12.

Al-Ghazali, Muhammad. "Hadha Dinuna," *al-Sha'b*, no. 771, August 31, 1993, 12.

Al-Ghazali, Muhammad. "Hadha Dinuna," *al-Sha'b*, no. 895, November 15, 1994, 12.

Al-Ghazali, Muhammad. "Hadha Dinuna," *al-Sha'b*, no. 944, May 9, 1995, 12.

Al-Ghazali, Muhammad. *'Ilal wa-Adwiya*. Doha: 1984.

Al-Ghazali, Muhammad. *Kayfa Nata'amalu ma'a al-Qur'an?*Al-Jiza: Nahdat Misr lil-Tiba'a wal-Nashr wal-Tawzi', seventh printing, July 2005.

Al-Ghazali, Muhammad. *Ma'a Allah: Dirasat fi al-Da'wa wal-Du'a*. Al-Jiza: Nahdat Misr lil-Tiba'a wal-Nashr wal-Tawzi', 2005.

Al-Ghazali, Muhammad. *Min Huna Na'lam*. Cairo: Dar al-Kutab al-Haditha bil-Qahira, n.d., fifth printing, originally published 1950.

Al-Ghazali, Muhammad. *Mustaqbal al-Islam Kharij Ardihi: Kayfa Nufakkiru fihi?* (Cairo: Dar al-Shuruq 1997, originally published 1984).

Al-Ghazali, Muhammad. *Nahwu Tafsir Mawdu'i li-Suwar al-Qur'an al-Karim*. Cairo: Dar-al-Shuruq, 1992.

Al-Ghazali, Muhammad. *Nazarat fi al-Qur'an*. Nahdat Misr lil-Tiba'a wal-Nashr wal-Tawzi', 2005.

Al-Ghazali, Muhammad. *Qadha'if al-Haqq*. Damascus: Dar al-Kalam, 1991.

Al-Ghazali, Muhammad. *Raka'iz al-'Iman bayna al-'Aql wal-Qalb*. Kuwait: Maktabat al-Amal, 1967.

Al-Ghazali, Muhammad. *Sirr Ta'akhkhur al-'Arab wal-Muslimin*. Al-Jiza: Nahdat Misr, March 2005, originally written 1985.

Al-Ghazali, Muhammad. *Zalam min al-Gharb*. Cairo: Dar al-Kitab, n.d.

Al-Haddad, Muhammad. "Al-Nass al-Haqiqi wal-Kamil lil-Munazara bayna Raynan wal-Afghani," n.d., accessed October 21, 2015: http://nachaz.org/index.php/fr/textes-a-l-app ui/histoire/53-2012-07-18-01-32-26.html

Al-Hayat. "Misr: al-'Aryan Yantaqidu Barnamaj 'al-Ikhwan'," October 13, 2007, 1.

Al-Hazmi, Manea H. *Dialogue with an Atheist*. Alexandria: Conveying Islamic Message Society, n.d.

Al-Jaziri, Fikri. "Al-Dimuqratiyya Laysa Hiya al-Shura," *al-Sharq al-Awsat*, March 4, 1985, 14.

Al-Jisr, Husayn. *Al-Risala al-Hamidiyya fi Haqiqat al-Diyana al-Islamiyya wa-Haqqiyyat al-Shari'a al-Muhammadiyya*. Cairo and Beirut: Dar al-Kitab al-Misri, Dar al-Kitab al-Lubnani, 2012, originally published 1888.

Al-Jundi, 'Abd al-Halim. *Al-Imam Muhammad 'Abduh*. Cairo: Dar al-Ma'arif, 1979.

Al-Kawakibi, 'Abd al-Rahman. "Kitab Taba'i al-Isti'bad wa-Masari' al-Istibdad," in Muhammad 'Imara (ed.), *al-A'mal al-Kamila li-'Abd al-Rahman al-Kawakibi*, 328–438. Al-Hay'a al-Misriyya al-'Amma lil-Ta'lif wal-Nashr, n.d.

Al-Kawakibi, 'Abd al-Rahman. "Umm al-Qura," in Muhammad 'Imara (ed.), *al-A'mal al-Kamila li-'Abd al-Rahman al-Kawakibi*, 125–324. Al-Hay'a al-Misriyya al-'Amma lil-Ta'lif wal-Nashr, n.d.

Al-Manar. "Abuna Adam wa-Madhhab Darwin, min Bab Intiqad al-Manar," 8:23 (January 26, 1906), 920.

Al-Manar. "Al-Dalil 'ala Wujud Allah Ta'ala," 7:4 (May 2, 1904), 138–140.

Al-Manar. "Al-Hukuma al-Istibdadiyya," 3:25, 3:26 (November 4, November 14, 1900), 577–582, 601–607.

Al-Manar. "Al-Ilhad fi al-Madaris al-'Almaniyya," 14:7 (July 26, 1911), 544–548.

Al-Manar. "Al-Juyush al-Gharbiyya al-Ma'nawiyya: fi al-Futuhat al-Sharquiyya," 1:17 (July 13, 1898), 299–308.

Al-Manar. "Al-Maqal al-Thalith 'Ashar: al-Buhayta al-Sabi'a Ma Samaha Tatbiq al-Qur'an 'ala Madhhab Darwin," 33(1):1 (March 3, 1933), 58–64.

Al-Manar. "Al-Rihla al-'Urubiyyya" (part 6), 23(2):8 (October 20, 1922), 635–640.

Al-Manar. "Al-Umma wa-Sultat al-Hakim al-Mustabid," 9:12 (February 13, 1907), 905–906.

Al-Manar. "Bab al-Munazara wal-Murasala: al-Duktur Shibli Afandi Shumayyil," 12(1):8 (September 14, 1909), 632–637.

Al-Manar. "Bab Tafsir al-Quran al-Karim–Surat al-Nisa'," 12:7 (August 16, 1909), 481–498.

Al-Manar. "Kitab Yusr al-Islam wa-Usul al-Tashri' al-'amm," 29:1 (March 22, 1928), 63–70.

Al-Manar. "Manafi' al-'Urubbiyyin wa-Madharuhum fi al-Sharq," 10:3 (May 12, 1907), 192–199.

Al-Manar. "Nazariyyat Darwin wal-Islam," 30:8 (March 1, 1930), 593–600.

Al-Muqtataf. "Charles Darwin," 7:1 (June 1882), 1–6.

Al-Muqtataf. "Al-Madhhab al-Darwini," 7:2, 7:3 (July and August 1882), 65–72, 121–127.

Al-Mustaqbal al-'Arabi, "Hawla Mustaqbal al-Dimuqratiyya fi al-Watan al-'Arabi," 8:138 (1990).

Al-Nabulsi, Shakir. *Al-Libaraliyyun al-Judud: Jadal Fikri*. Cologne: Manshurat al-Jamal, 2005.

Al-Nabulsi, Shakir. "Limadha Yu'adi Rijal al-Din al-'Almaniyya?" *al-Hiwar al-Mutamadin*, no. 1508, April 2, 2006, accessed August 1, 2015: http://www.ahewar.org/debat/show.art.asp?aid=61203.

Al-Nadwi, Abu al-Hasan. *Madha Khasara al-'Alam bi-Inkhitat al-Muslimin*. Cairo: Maktabat al-'iman, 1994.

Al-Qaradawi, Yusuf. *Al-Halal wal-Haram fi al-Islam*. Cairo: Matkabat Wahaba, 2004, first published 1960.

Al-Qaradawi, Yusuf. *Al-Hall al-Islami: Farida wa-Darura*. Beirut: Mu'assasat al-Risala, 1974.

Al-Qaradawi, Yusuf. *Al-Hulul al-Mustawrada wa-Kayfa Jannat 'ala Ummatina*. Beirut: Mu'assasat al-Risala, 1974, first published 1971.

Al-Qaradawi, Yusuf. *Al-Ijtihad fi al-Shari'a al-Islamiyya*. Kuwait: Dar al-Qalam, 1996.

Al-Qaradawi, Yusuf. *Al-Khasa'is al-'Ama lil-Islam*. Cairo: Maktabat Wahba, August 1977.

Al-Qaradawi, Yusuf. *Al-Mubashshirat bi-Intisar al-Islam*. Beirut: Mu'assasat al-Risala, 2000.

Al-Qaradawi, Yusuf. *Al-Sahwa al-Islamiyya bayna al-Jumud wal-Tatarruf*. Cairo: Dar al-Shuruq, 2005.

Al-Qaradawi, Yusuf. *Al-Sahwa al-Islamiyya min al-Murahaqa ila al-Rushd*. Cairo: Dar al-Shuruq, 2008, first printed 2002.

Al-Qaradawi, Yusuf. *Al-Sahwa al-Islamiyya wa-Humum al-Watan al-'Arabi al-Islami*. Cairo: Dar al-Shuruq, 2006.

Al-Qaradawi, Yusuf. *Al-Shaykh al-Ghazali Kama 'Araftuhu: Rihlat Nisf Qarn*. Al-Munsura: Dar al-Wafa' lil-Tiba'a wal-Nashr wal-Tawzi', 1995.

Al-Qaradawi, Yusuf. *Al-Siyasa al-Shar'iyya fi Daw' Nusus al-Shari'a wa-Maqasidiha*. Beirut: Mu'assasat al-Risala, 2001.

Al-Qaradawi, Yusuf. *Bidayat al-Khalq wa-Nazariyyat al-Tatawwur*, transcript of a discussion in the television program "al-Shari'a wal-Hayat", February 25, 2009, accessed December 20, 2013: www.aljazeera.net/programs/pages/af1ea016-4280-4a0d-838f-8ca05f31c8df.

Al-Qaradawi, Yusuf. *Fi Fiqh al-Aqalliyyat al-Muslima*. Cairo: Dar al-Shuruq, 2007, first published 2001.

Al-Qaradawi, Yusuf. *Fiqh al-Wasatiyya al-Islamiyya wal-Tajdid: Ma'alim wa-Manarat*. Cairo: Dar al-Shuruq, 2010.

Al-Qaradawi, Yusuf. *Kayfa Nata'amalu ma'a al-Qur'an al-'Azim*. Cairo: Dar al-Shuruq, 2000.

Al-Qaradawi, Yusuf. *Khitabuna al-Islami fi 'Asr al-'Awlama*. Cairo: Dar al-Shuruq, 2009, first printed 2004.

Al-Qaradawi, Yusuf. *Hajat al-Bashriyya ila al-Risala al-Hadariyya li-Ummatina*. Cairo: Maktabat Wahaba, 2004.

Al-Qaradawi, Yusuf. *Malamih al-Mujtama' al-Muslim Alladhi Nanashuduhu*. Beirut: Mu'assasat al-Risala, 1996.

Al-Qaradawi, Yusuf. *Min Ajl Sahwa Rashida* (Cairo: Dar al-Shuruq, 1988, accessed August 2, 2012: http://www.mlazna.com).

Al-Qaradawi, Yusuf. *Min Fiqh al-Dawla fi al-Islam*. Cairo: Dar al-Shuruq, 2001, first published 1997.

Al-Qaradawi, Yusuf. *Nahnu wal-Gharb: As'ila Sha'ika wa-Ajwiba Hasima*. Cairo: Dar al-Tawzi' wal-Nashr al-Islamiyya, 2006.

Al-Qaradawi, Yusuf. "Pokemon Games," posted December 30, 2003, accessed December 10, 2013: www.onislam.net/english/ask-the-scholar/arts-and-entertainment/cinema-thea tre-and-tv/174701.html?TV=.

Al-Qaradawi, Yusuf. "Risala Maftuha ila Ra'is al-Jumhuriyya," *al-Sha'b*, January 16, 1990, 12.

Al-Qaradawi, Yusuf. "Shira' Buyut al-Sukna fi al-Gharb 'an Tariq al-Bunuk," in *Fi Fiqh al-Aqalliyyat al-Muslima*, 154–191. Cairo: Dar al-Shuruq, 2007, first published 2001.

Al-Qaradawi, Yusuf. *Ta'rikhuna al-Muftara 'alayhi*. Cairo: Dar al-Shuruq, 2008.

Al-Qaradawi, Yusuf. *Taysir al-Fiqh lil-Muslim al-Mu'asir fi Daw' al-Qur'an wal-Sunna*. Beirut: Mu'assasat al-Risala, 2000.

Al-Qaradawi, Yusuf. *Thaqafat al-Da'iya*. Cairo: Maktabat Wahaba, 10th printing, 1996.

Al-Qaradawi, Yusuf. *Ummatuna bayna Qarnayn*. Cairo: Dar Al-Shuruq, 2002, first published 2000.

Al-Qaradawi, Yusuf. *Wujud Allah*. Casablanca: Dar al-Ma'rafa, n.d.

Al-Sharbasi, Ahmad. *Rashid Rida: Sahib al-Manar, 'Asruhu wa-Hayatuhu wa-Masadir Thaqafatihi*. n.p., 1970.

Al-Tahtawi, Rifa'a Rafi', *Takhlis al-Ibriz fi Talkhis Bariz*. The United Arab Republic—The Egyptian Region, n.d., originally published in 1834.

Al-Tikriti, Anas Usama and al-'Ubaydi, Shakir Nasif (trans.). *Fatwas of European Council for Fatwa and Research*. Cairo: Islamic INC, 2002.

Al-Tunisi, Khayr al-Din. *Aqwam al-Masalik fi Ma'rifat Ahwal al-Mamalik*. Al-Dar al-Tunisiyya lil-Nashr, n.d., originally published 1867.

Al-'Urwa al-Wuthqa. Paris: 28 March 1884.

Al-'Uthaymin, Muhammad b. Salih. "Hukm man Yad'a anna Sabab Takhaluf al-Muslimin Huwa Tamasukuhum bi-Dinihim," in *Fatawa al-Balad al-Haram*, 1069–1071. Cairo: al-Maktaba al-Tawfiqiyya, n.d.

Al-Za'atra, Yasir. *Hiwar ma'a al-Shaykh Rashid al-Ghannushi*. Manshurat Filastin al-Muslima, 1996.

Amir, 'Abas. *Al-Ma'na al-Qur'ani bayna al-Tafsir wal-Ta'wil*. Beirut: Mu'ssasat al-Intishar al-'Arabi, 2008.

Antun, Farah. *Ibn Rushd wa-Falsafatuhu*. Alexandria: Idarat al-Jami'a, January 1903.

Asad, Muhammad. *The Message of Quran* (Gibraltar: Dar al-Andalus, 1980), accessed July 20, 2015: https://www.usc.edu/schools/college/crcc/private/cmje/religious_text/The_Messa ge_of_The_Quran__by_Muhammad_Asad.pdf.

'Azzam, Abdallah. "Al-Saratan al-Ahmar," n.d., accessed January 1, 2014: http://www. moslim.se/maktaba/kotob/melal-saradan-azzam.htm.

"Barnamaj Hizb al-Ikhwan al-Muslimin," 7, 13–24, accessed February 10, 2010: http:// www.islamonline.net/arabic/Daawa/2007/08/ikhwan.pdf.

Bucaille, Maurice. *The Quran and Modern Science*. UKIM Dawah Centre International, 2014, first published 1993.

Constitution of Egypt, December 2012, accessed August 18, 2015: http://www.sis.gov.eg/newvr/theconstitution.pdf.

Fawzan, 'Abdallah b. Salih. "Mawqifuna min al-Hadara al-Gharbiyya," in *Fatawa al-Balad al-Haram*, 1072–1073. Cairo: al-Maktaba al-Tawfiqiyya, n.d.

Freedom and Justice Party, Election Program: Freedom and Justice Party (2011), accessed May 3, 2015: http://www.scribd.com/doc/73955131/FJP-Program-En.

Fuda, Faraj. *Qabla al-Suqut*. Alexandria: Dar wa-Matabi' al-Mustaqbal, 2004, first published 1985.

Hadm Nazariyyat al-Tatawwur fi 'Ishrin Su'alan on ar.Harunyahya.com (accessed December 10, 2014).

Ibish, Yusuf. *Rihlat al-Imam Muhammad Rashid Rida*. Beirut: al-Mu'assasa al-'Arabiyya lil-Dirasat wal-Nashr, 1971.

Ibn Taymiyya, Taqi al-Din. *Al-Siyasa al-Shar'iyya fi Islah al-Ra'i wal-Ra'iyya*. Egypt: Dar al-Kitab al-'Arabi, 1969.

Imam, Imam Muhammad. "Fatwa Tujizu Shira' al-Manazil bi-Qard Ribawi lil-Muslimin fi Ghayr Bilad al-Islam," *al-Sharq al-Awsat* (October 3, 1999), 25.

'Imara, Muhammad (ed.). *Al-A'mal al-Kamila li-'Abd al-Rahman al-Kawakibi*. Al-Hay'a al-Misriyya al-'ama lil-Ta'lif wal-Nashr, n.d.

'Imara, Muhammad (ed.). *Al-A'mal al-Kamila li-Jamal al-Din al-Afghani*. Al-Mu'assasa al-Misriyya al-'ama lil-T'alif wal-Nashr, 1968.

'Imara, Muhammad (ed.). *Al-A'mal al-Kamila lil-Imam Muhammad 'Abduh*, vol. 1. Beirut: al-Mu'assasa al-'Arabiyya lil-Dirasat wal-Nashr, 1972.

'Imara, Muhammad. *Al-Dawla al-Islamiyya bayna al-'Almaniyya wal-Sulta al-Diniyya*. Cairo: Dar al-Shuruq, 1988.

'Imara, Muhammad. *Al-Gharb wal-Islam: ayna al-Khata'? … Wa-ayna al-Sawab?* Cairo: Maktabat al-Shuruq al-Dawliyya, 2004.

'Imara, Muhammad. *Al-Ghazw al-Fikri Wahm am Haqiqa?* Beirut and Cairo: Dar al-Shuruq, 1997, first published 1989.

'Imara, Muhammad. *Al-Islam wa-Huquq al-Insan—Darurat, La Huquq*. Jedda: Maktabat Bustan al-Marfa, 2004–5.

'Imara, Muhammad. *Al-Islam wal-Ta'addudiyya*. Cairo: Dar al-Rashad, 1997.

'Imara, Muhammad. *Al-Islam wa-Usul al-Hukm li-'Ali 'Abd al-Raziq*. Beirut: al-Mu'assasa al-'Arabiyya lil-Dirasat wal-Nashr, 1972.

'Imara, Muhammad. *Al-Istiqlal al-Hadari*. October 6th City: Nahdat Misr lil-Tiba'a wal-Nashr wal-Tawzi', 2007.

'Imara, Muhammad. *Al-Qur'an Yatahada*. Cairo: Maktabat al-Imam al-Bukhari lil-Nashr wal-Tawzi', 2009.

'Imara, Muhammad. *Al-Shaykh Muhammad al-Ghazali: al-Mawqi' al-Fikri wal-Ma'arik al-Fikriyya*. Cairo: Dar al-Salam, 2009.

'Imara, Muhammad. "Al-Shura al-Islamiyya wal-Dimuqratiyya al-Gharbiyya," *Majalat al-Dimuqratiyya* (published by al-Ahram), December 20, 2012, accessed April 20, 2015: http://democracy.ahram.org.eg/News.

'Imara, Muhammad. *Fi al-Nizam al-Siyasi al-Islami*. Cairo: Maktabat al-Imam al-Bukhari, n.d.

'Imara, Muhammad. *Fi Fiqh al-Muwajaha bayna al-Gharb wal-Islam*. Cairo: Maktabat al-Shuruq al-Dawliyya, 2003.

'Imara, Muhammad. *Hal al-Islam Huwa al-Hall? Limadha wa-Kayfa?* Cairo: Dar al-Shuruq, 1995.

'Imara, Muhammad. "Hayatuhu," in Muhammad 'Imara (ed.), *al-A'mal al-Kamila li-'Abd al-Rahman al-Kawakibi*, 13–32. Al-Hay'a al-Misriyya al-'Amma lil-Ta'lif wal-Nashr, n.d.

'Imara, Muhammad. *Ma'rakat al-Mustalahat: bayna al-Gharb wal-Islam*. Nahdat Misr lil-Tiba'a wal-Nashr wal-Tawzi', n.d.

'Imara, Muhammad. *Rifa'a al-Tahtawi: Ra'id al-Tanwir fi al-'Asr al-Hadith*. Cairo: Dar al-Shuruq, 2009.

'Imara, Muhammad. *Shubuhat Hawla al-Islam*. Nahdet Misr, 2002.

Iqbal, Muzaffar. "Darwin's Shadow: Evolution in an Islamic Mirror," *Islam & Science*, 8:1 (Summer 2010 2010), 11–32.

Islamwise, *Science and Islam*.

Kassab, Akram. *Al-Manhaj al-Da'wi 'ind al-Qaradawi*. Cairo: Maktabat Wahba, 2006.

Khalas, Ibrahim. "Al-Tariq li-Khalq Insanuna al-'arabi al-Jadid," *Jaysh al-Sha'b*, no. 794 (April 25, 1967), 34.

Khalid, Khalid Muhmmad. *Al-Dimuqratiyya. Abadan*. Egypt: Dar al-Fikr al-'Arabi, , second printing, 1953.

Khalid, Khalid Muhmmad. *Min Huna Nabd'*. Egypt: Dar al-Fikr al-Arabi, sixth printing, 1952.

Khalil, Mahir. *Suqut Nazariyyat Darwin: fi Daw' al-Iktishafat al-'Ilmiyya al-Haditha*. Alexandria: al-Markaz al-'Arabi, 1986.

Kuhn, Thomas S. *The Structure of Scientific Revolutions*. Chicago: University of Chicago Press, 1970.

Mahfouz, Naguib. *The Cairo Trilogy, vol. 2: Palace of Desire*, translated by William Maynard Hutchins. New York: Knopf, 2001, first published in Arabic 1957.

Mandura, Muhammad Mahmud. "Al-Dimuqratiyya Mabda' Yukhalifu al-Islam," *al-Sharq al-Awsat*, March 19, 1985, 14.

Muhsin, Khalid (ed.). *Misr bayna al-Dawla al-Islamiyya wal-Dawla al-'Almaniyya*. Cairo: Markaz al-I'lam al-'Arabi, 1992.

Muntasir, Khalid. *Fubya al-'Ilm*. Cairo: Dar Akhbar al-Yawm, December 2008.

Muntasir, Khalid. "Hal bil-Adabi wa-Alfiyyat Ibn Malik sa-Yatafawwaq al-'Arab 'ala Isra'il?!" June 27, 2008, accessed April 10, 2014: www.elaph.com/Web/ElaphWriter/2008/6/343355.htm.

Muntasir, Khalid. "Hum Ikhtaru al-Kimiya wa-Ihna Ikhtarna al-Fustan al-Bumbay," October 10, 2011, accessed April 16, 2014: www.almasryalyoum.com/node/503303.

Muntasir, Khalid. "Isra'il Tataqaddamu bil-Fiziya' wa-Nahnu bil-Fuqaha'," March 26, 2009, accessed July 6, 2013: www.ahl-alquran.com/site/arabic/show_article.php?main_id=5053

Muntasir, Khalid. *Wahm al-'I'jaz al-'Ilmi*. Egypt: Dar al-'ayn lil-Nashr, 2005.

Naik, Zakir. *The Quran and Modern Science: Compatible or Incompatible?* Riyadh: Maktabat Dar-us-Salam, 2007.

Nasar, 'Ismat. "Taqdim," in Husayn al-Jisr, *al-Risala al-Hamidiyya fi Haqiqat al-Diyana al-Islamiyya wa-Haqqiyyat al-Shari'a al-Muhammadiyya*, 21–83. Cairo and Beirut: Dar al-Kitab al-Misri, Dar al-Kitab al-Lubnani, 2012, originally published 1888.

Nawfal, 'Abd al-Razzaq. *Al-Insan wal-Qird wa-Suqut Darwin*. Cairo: Matbu'at al-Sha'b, 1984.

Qutb, Muhammad. *Al-Tatawwur wal-Thabat fi Hayat al-Bashar*. Beirut and Cairo: Dar al-Shuruq, 1985.

Qutb, Muhammad. *Waqi'una al-Mu'asir*. Cairo: Dar al-Shuruq, 2006, written in 1986.

Qutb, Sayyid. *Fi Zilal al-Quran, Surah 23 (al-Mu'minun)*, English translation. accessed March 30, 2014: http://tafsirzilal.files.wordpress.com/2012/06/al-mukminun-eng.pdf.

Qutb, Sayyid. "Madha Khasara al-'Alam bi-Inkhitat al-Muslimin" (a review), *al-Risala*, 19: 947 (August 7, 1951), 965–967.

"Rashid Rida," Wikipedia entry, accessed July 12, 2015: https://en.wikipedia.org/wiki/Rashid_Rida.

Rawas, Muhammad. *Mawsu'at Fiqh Ibn Taymiyya*, vol.1. Beirut: Dar al-Nafa'is, 1998.

Renan, Ernest. "Ta'qib Raynan 'ala Radd al-Afghani," n.d., accessed October 21, 2015: http://nachaz.org/index.php/fr/textes-a-l-appui/histoire/53-2012-07-18-01-32-26.html

Rida, Muhammad Rashid. *Al-Khilafa*. Cairo: al-Zahra' lil-I'lam al-'Arabi, 1994.

Rida, Muhammad Rashid. *Al-Wahy al-Muhammadi*. Beirut: Mu'asassat 'Izz al-Din, 1986.

Sa'd al-Din, Ibrahim, et al. *Azamat al-Dimuqratiyya fi al-Watan al-'Arabi*. Beirut: Markaz Dirasat al-Wahda al-'Arabiyya, 1987.

Sidqi, Muhammad. "Al-Din fi Nazr al-'Aql al-Sahih" (fourth section), *al-Manar*, 8:19 (November 28, 1905), 737–744.

Yusuf, Muhammad 'Ali. *Masra' al-Darwiniyya*. Jedda: Dar al-Shuruq, 1983.

Secondary Sources in English and Other Languages

Abadi, Jacob. *Tunisia Since the Arab Conquest: The Saga of a Westernized Muslim State*. Reading, MA: Ithaca, 2013.

Abaza, Mona. "Two Intellectuals: The Malaysian S.N. Al-Attas and the Egyptian Moham-med 'Immara, and the Islamization of Knowledge Debate," *Asian Journal of Social Science*, 30:2 (2002), 354–383.

Abou El Fadl, Khaled. *Rebellion and Violence in Islamic Law*. Cambridge: Cambridge University Press, 2001.

Abu-Lughod, Ibrahim A. *Arab Rediscovery of Europe: A Study of Cultural Encounter*. Princeton, NJ: Princeton University Press, 1963.

Abu Rabi, Ibrahim M. *Intellectual Origins of Islamic Resurgence in the Modern Arab World*. Albany: State University of New York Press, 1996.

Adams, Charles C. *Islam and Modernism in Egypt: A Study of the Modern Reform Movement inaugurated by Muhammad 'Abduh*. New York: Russell & Russell, 1968, first published 1933.

Ajami, Fouad. *The Arab Predicament: Arab Political Thought and Practice since 1967*. Cambridge: Cambridge University Press, 1989.

Al-Enazy, Askar H. *The Creation of Saudi Arabia: Ibn Saud and British Imperial Policy, 1914–1927*. London and New York: Routledge, 2010.

Al-Hibri, Azizah Y. "Islamic Constitutionalism and the Concept of Democracy," *Case Western Reserve Journal of International Law*, 24:1 (Winter 1992), 1–27.

Al-Husry, Khaldun Sati. *Three Reformers: A Study in Modern Arabic Political Thought*. Beirut: Khayats, 1966.

Al-Ghannushi, Rashid. "Secularism in the Arab Maghreb," in Azzam Tamimi and John L. Esposito (eds), *Islam and Secularism in the Middle East*, 97–123. London: Hurst & Company, 2000.

Al-Khadar, 'Abd al-'Aziz. *Al-Sa'udiyya Sirat Dawla wa-Mujtama'*. Beirut: Arab Network for Research and Publishing, 2010.

Allen, Don Cameron. *The Legend of Noah*. Urbana: University of Illinois Press, 1963.

Asghar, Anila, Hameed, Salman and Farahani, Najme Kishani. "Evolution in Biology Textbooks: A Comparative Analysis of 5 Muslim Countries," *Religion and Education*, 41:1 (2014), 1–15.

Ayalon, Ami. *Language and Change in the Arab Middle East: The Evolution of Modern Political Discourse*. New York: Oxford University Press, 1987.

Ayubi, Nazih N. *Political Islam: Religion and Politics in the Arab World*. London: Routledge, 1991.

Ayyad, 'Abd al-Aziz Ahmad. *The Politics of Reformist Islam: Muhammad 'Abduh and Hasan al-Banna*. Ann Arbor, MI: University Microfilms International, 1991.

Baker, Raymond William. "Invidious Comparisons: Realism, Postmodern Globalism and Centric Islamic movements in Egypt," in John L. Esposito (ed.), *Political Islam—Revolution, Radicalism or Reform?* 115–133. Boulder, CO and London: Lynne Rienner, 1997.

Baker, Raymond William. *Islam without Fear: Egypt and the New Islamists.* Cambridge, MA: Harvard University Press, 2003.

Baran, Zeyno. *Torn Country: Turkey Between Secularism and Islamism.* Stanford, CA: Hoover Institution Press, 2010.

Barker, Eileen. "Let There Be Light: Scientific Creationism in the Twentieth Century," in John Durant (ed.), *Darwinism and Divinity: Essays on Evolution and Religious Belief,* 181–204. Oxford and New York: Basil Blackwell, 1985.

Bello, Iysa A. *The Medieval Islamic Controversy between Philosophy and Orthodoxy: Ijma' and Ta'wil in the Conflict between al-Ghazali and Ibn Rushd.* Leiden: E. J. Brill, 1989.

Berkman, Michael B., Pacheco, Julianna Sandell and Plutzer, Eric. "Evolution and Creationism in America's Classrooms: A National Portrait," *PLoS Biology,* 6:5 (May 2008), 920–924.

Brooke, John Hedley. *Science and Religion: Some Historical Perspectives.* Cambridge: Cambridge University Press, 1991.

Brown, Daniel W. *Rethinking Tradition in Modern Islamic Thought.* Cambridge: Cambridge University Press, 1996.

Brown, Nathan J. and Hamzawy, Amr. "The Draft Party Platform of the Egyptian Muslim Brotherhood: Foray into Political Integration or Retreat into Old Positions?" *Carnegie Endowment Middle East Series,* no. 89 (January 2008).

Brown, Nathan J. and Sherif, Adel Omar. "Inscribing the Islamic Shari'a in Arab Constitutional Law," in Yvonne Yazbeck Haddad and Barbara Freyer Stowasser (eds), *Islamic Law and the Challenges of Modernity,* 55–80. Walnut Creek: Altamira, 2004.

Bukay, David. "Can There be an Islamic Democracy?" *Middle East Quarterly,* 14:2 (Spring 2007), 71–79.

Burton, Elise K. "Evolution and Creationism in Middle Eastern Education: A New Perspective," *Evolution,* 65:1 (2011), 301–304.

Çarkoğlu, Ali. "Political Preferences of the Turkish Electorate: Reflections of an Alevi-Sunni Cleavage," in Ali Çarkoğlu and Barry Rubin (eds), *Religion and Politics in Turkey,* 131–150. London and New York: Routledge, 2006.

Cavatorta, Francesco and Merone, Fabio. "Moderation through Exclusion? The Journey of the Tunisian Ennahda from Fundamentalist to Conservative Party," *Democratization,* 20:5 (2013), 857–875.

Cesari, Jocelyne. *The Awakening of Muslim Democracy: Religion, Modernity, and the State.* New York: Cambridge University Press, 2014.

Cohn, Norman. *Noah's Flood: The Genesis Story in Western Thought.* New Haven, CT and London: Yale University Press, 1996.

Cole, Stewart G. *The History of Fundamentalism.* Westport, CT: Greenwood Press, 1971.

Commager, Henry Steele. *The Search for a Usable Past and Other Essays in Historiography.* New York: Alfred A. Knopf, 1967.

Cook, Michael. *Commanding Right and Forbidding Wrong in Islamic Thought.* Cambridge: Cambridge University Press, 2000.

Craig, William Lane and Smith, Quentin. *Theism, Atheism and Big Bang Cosmology.* Oxford: Clarendon Press, 1993.

Crecelius, Daniel. "The Course of Secularization in Modern Egypt," in Donald E. Smith (ed.), *Religion and Political Modernization,* 67–95. New Haven: Yale University Press, 1974.

Dagher, Zoubeida R. and BouJaoude, Saouma. "Science Education in Arab States: Bright Future or Status Quo?" *Studies in Science Education,* 47:1 (2011), 73–101.

Danner, Victor. "Western Evolutionism in the Arab World," *The American Journal of Islamic Social Science*, 8:1 (1991), 67–82.

Davidson, Lawrence. *Islamic Fundamentalism: An Introduction*. Westport, CT and London: Greenwood Press, 2003.

De Tocqueville, Alexis. *Democracy in America*, translated and edited by Harvey C. Mansfield and Delba Winthrop. Chicago: University of Chicago Press, 2000.

Devereux, Robert. *The First Ottoman Constitutional Period: A Study of the Midhat Constitution and Parliament*. Baltimore: Johns Hopkins Press, 1963.

Dorrien, Gary. *The Making of American Liberal Theology: Imagining Progressive Religion, 1805–1900*. Louisville: Westminster John Knox Press, 2001.

Dorrien, Gary. *The Making of American Liberal Theology: Idealism, Realism and Modernity 1900–1950*. Louisville: Westminster John Knox Press, 2003.

Ebert, Johannes. *Religion und Reform in der Arabischen Provinz*. Frankfurt am Main: Peter Lang, 1991.

Edis, Taner. "Modern Science and Conservative Islam: An Uneasy Relationship," *Science & Education*, 18:6–7 (2009), 885–903.

Eisenstadt, S. N. *Fundamentalism, Sectarianism and Revolution: The Jacobin Dimension of Modernity*. Cambridge: Cambridge University Press, 1999.

Elihachmi, Muhammad Hamdi. *The Politicisation of Islam*. Boulder, CO: Westview Press, 1998.

Elgindy, Khaled. "The Rhetoric of Rashid Ghannushi," *Arab Studies Journal*, 3:1 (Spring 1995), 101–119.

Elshakry, Marwa. "Global Darwin: Eastern Enchantment," *Nature*, 461:7268 (October 2009), 1200–1201.

Elshakry, Marwa. "Muslim Hermeneutics and Arabic Views of Evolution," *Zygon*, 46:2 (June 2011), 330–344.

El-Solh, Raghid. "Islamist Attitudes Towards Democracy: A Review of the Ideas of al-Ghazali, al-Turabi and 'Amara," *British Journal of Middle Eastern Studies*, 20:1 (1993), 57–63.

Esposito, John L. and Piscatori, James P. "Democratization and Islam," *Middle East Journal*, 45:3 (Summer 1991), 427–440.

Esposito, John L. and Voll, John O. *Islam and Democracy*. New York and Oxford: Oxford University Press, 1996.

Faksh, M.A. "Islamic Fundamentalist Thought: An Analysis of Major Theoretical Formulations," in Bryan S. Turner (ed.), *Islam: Critical Concepts in Sociology, vol. IV: Islam and Social Movements*, 164–185. London and New York: Routledge, 2003.

Faraj, Nadia. "The Lewis Affair and the Fortunes of al-Muqtataf," *Middle Eastern Studies*, 8:1 (January 1972), 73–83.

Finocchiaro, Maurice A. (ed. and translator). *The Galileo Affair: A Documentary History*. Berkeley, Los Angeles and London: University of California Press, 1989.

Freely, John. *Light from the East: How the Science of Medieval Islam Helped to Shape the Western World*. London: I. B. Tauris, 2015.

Freeman, Charles. *The Closing of the Western Mind: The Rise of Faith and the Fall of Reason*. New York: Vintage Books, 2005.

Furniss, Norman F. *The Fundamentalist Controversy, 1918–1931*. Hamdan, CT: Archon Books, 1963.

Gasiorowski, Mark J. "The Failure of Reform in Tunisia," *Journal of Democracy*, 3:4 (October 1992), 85–97.

Geymonat, Ludovico. *Galileo Galilei: A Biography and Inquiry into His Philosophy of Science*. New York: McGraw-Hill Book Company, 1965.

Gibb, Hamilton. "Constitutional Organization," in Majid Khadduri and Herbert J. Liebesny (eds), *Law in the Middle East, vol. I: Origin and Development of Islamic Law*, 3–27. Washington, DC: The Middle East Institute, 1955.

Gräf, Bettina and Skovgaard-Petersen, Jakob (eds), *Global Mufti: The Phenomenon of Yusuf al-Qaradawi*. London: Hurst & Company, 2009.

Grusin, Richard A. *Transcendentalist Hermeneutics: Institutional Authority and the Higher Criticism of the Bible*. Durban and London: Duke University Press, 1991.

Hale, William. "Christian Democracy and the AKP: Parallels and Contrasts," *Turkish Studies*, 6:2 (June 2005), 293–310.

Hallaq, Wael B. *A History of Islamic Legal Theories*. Cambridge: Cambridge University Press, 1997.

Hallaq, Wael B. *Authority, Continuity and Change in Islamic Law*. Cambridge: Cambridge University Press, 2001.

Hallaq, Wael B. (ed.). *The Formation of Islamic Law*. Aldershot: Ashgate, 2004.

Hallaq, Wael B. *The Origins and Evolution of Islamic Law*. Cambridge: Cambridge University Press, 2005.

Hameed, Salman. "Evolution and Creationism in the Islamic World," in Thomas Dixon, Geoffrey Cantor and Stephen Pumfrey (eds), *Science and Religion: New Historical Perspectives*, 133–152. Cambridge: Cambridge University Press, 2010.

Hameed, Salman. "Making Sense of Islamic Creationism in Europe," *Public Understanding of Science*, 24:4 (November 2014), 388–399.

Hameed, Salman. "Science and Religion: Bracing for Islamic Creationism," *Science*, 332:5908 (December 12, 2008), 1637–1638.

Harnisch, Chris and Mecham, Quinn. "Democratic Ideology in Islamist Opposition? The Muslim Brotherhood's 'Civil State'," *Middle Eastern Studies*, 45:2 (2009), 189–205.

Hashemi, Nader. "Why Islam (Properly Understood) Is the Solution: Reflections on the Role of Religion in Tunisia's Democratic Transition," *The American Journal of Islamic Social Sciences*, 30:4 (2013), 137–145.

Hatina, Meir. "On the Margins of Consensus: The Call to Separate Religion and State in Modern Egypt," *Middle Eastern Studies*, 36:1 (January 2000), 35–67.

Heilbron, John L. *Galileo*. Oxford and New York: Oxford University Press, 2010.

Helfont, Samuel. *Yusuf al-Qaradawi: Islam and Modernity*. Tel Aviv: Moshe Dayan Center, 2009.

Heper, Metin and Toktaş, Şule. "Islam, Modernity, and Democracy in Contemporary Turkey: The Case of Recep Tayyip Erdoğan," *The Muslim World*, 93:2 (April 2003), 157–185.

Hopwood, Derek. *Habib Bourguiba of Tunisia: The Tragedy of Longevity*. New York: St. Martin's Press, 1992.

Hourani, Albert. *Arabic Thought in the Liberal Age, 1798–1939*. London and New York: Oxford University Press, 1962.

Hourani, Albert. *Arabic Thought in the Liberal Age, 1798–1939*. Cambridge: Cambridge University Press, 1983.

Howard, Damian. *Being Human in Islam: The Impact of the Evolutionary Worldview*. London and New York: Routledge, 2011.

Hyman, Anthony. "Muslim Fundamentalism," *Conflict Studies*, 174, 1985.

Issawi, Charles. "Economic and Social Foundations of Democracy in the Middle East," *International Affairs*, 32:1 (January 1956), 27–42.

Jansen, Johannes J. G. *The Dual Nature of Islamic Fundamentalism*. Ithaca, NY: Cornell University Press, 1997.

Kaya, Veysel. "Can the Quran Support Darwin? An Evolutionist Approach by Two Turkish Scholars after the Foundation of the Turkish Republic," *The Muslim World*, 102:2 (April 2012), 357–370.

Keddie, Nikki R. *An Islamic Response to Imperialism: Political and Religious Writings of Sayyid Jamal al-Din "al-Afghani"*. Berkeley and Los Angeles: University of California Press, 1968.

Keddie, Nikki R. *Sayyid Jamal ad-Din "al-Afghani": A Political Biography*. Berkeley: University of California Press, 1972.

Kedourie, Elie. *Afghani and Abduh: An Essay on Religious Unbelief and Political Activism in Modern Islam*. London: Frank Cass, 1966.

Kedourie, Elie. *Democracy and Arab Political Culture*. Washington, DC: The Washington Institute for Near East Policy, 1992.

Kenny, L. M. "Al-Afghani on Types of Despotic Government," *Journal of the American Oriental Society*, 86:1 (January-March 1966), 19–27.

Kerr, Malcolm H. *Islamic Reform: The Political and Legal Theories of Muhammad 'Abduh and Rashid Rida*. Berkeley: University of California Press, 1966.

Khadduri, Majid and Liebesny, Herbert J. (eds). *Law in the Middle East, vol. 1: Origin and Development of Islamic Law*. Washington, DC: The Middle East Institute, 1955.

Krämer, Gudrun. "Good Counsel to the King: The Islamist Opposition in Saudi Arabia, Jordan and Morocco," in Joseph Kostiner (ed.), *Middle East Monarchies: The Challenge of Modernity*, 257–288. Boulder, CO and London: Lynne Rienner Publishers, 2000.

Krämer, Gudrun. "Islamist Notions of Democracy," *Middle East Report*, 183 (July-August 1993), 2–8.

Kramer, Martin. "Where Islam and Democracy Part Ways," in Yehudah Mirsky and Matt Abrens (eds), *Democracy in the Middle East: Defining the Challenge*, 31–40. Washington, DC: The Washington Institute for Near East Policy, 1993.

Landau, Jacob M. *Parliaments and Parties in Egypt*. Tel Aviv: Israel Publishing House, 1953.

Landolt, Laura K. and Kubicek Paul, "Opportunities and Constraints: Comparing Tunisia and Egypt to the Coloured Revolutions," *Democratization*, 21:6 (2014), 984–1006.

Lauzière, Henri. "The Construction of Salafiyya: Reconsidering Salafism from the Perspective of Conceptual History," *International Journal of Middle Eastern Studies*, 42:3 (August 2010), 369–389.

Leavitt, Donald M. "Darwinism in the Arab World: The Lewis Affair at the Syrian Protestant College," *The Muslim World*, 71:2 (April 1981), 85–98.

Lewis, Bernard. "A Historical Overview: Islam and Liberal Democracy," *Journal of Democracy*, 7:2 (April 1996), 52–63.

Lewis, Bernard. *The Muslim Discovery of Europe*. New York and London: W.W. Norton & Company, 1982.

Lombardi, Clark B. "Constitutional Provisions Making Sharia 'A' or 'The' Chief Source of Legislation: Where Do They Come from? What Do They Mean? Do They Matter?" *University of Washington School of Law, Legal Studies Research Paper*, 2014–01 (2013), 732–774.

Manning, D. J. *Liberalism*. London: J. M. Dent, 1976.

March, Andrew. *Islam and Liberal Citizenship: The Search for an Overlapping Consensus*. Oxford: Oxford University Press, 2009.

Marty, Martin E. and Appleby, R. Scott (eds). *Fundamentalisms Comprehended, Fundamentalism Project, vol. 5*. Chicago, IL and London: University of Chicago Press, 1995.

Marzouki, Nadia. "From Resistance to Governance: The Category of Civility in the Political Theory of Tunisian Islamists," in Nouri Gana (ed.), *The Making of the Tunisian Revolution: Contexts, Architects, Prospects*, 207–223. Edinburgh: Edinburgh University Press, 2013.

Milton-Edwards, Beverley. *Islamic Fundamentalism since 1945*. London and New York: Routledge, 2004.

Mitchell, Richard P. *The Society of the Muslim Brothers*. New York, Oxford and Toronto: Oxford University Press, 1993.

Moghadam, Valentine M. "What is Democracy? Promises and Perils of the Arab Spring," *Current Sociology*, 61:4 (2013), 393–408.

Moore, James. "That Evolution Destroyed Darwin's Faith in Christianity—Until He Reconverted on His Deathbed," in Ronald N. Numbers (ed.), *Galileo Goes to Jail and Other Myths about Science and Religion*, 142–151. Cambridge, MA: Harvard University Press, 2009.

Moore, Randy. "Creationism in the Biology Classroom: What Do Teachers Teach and How Do They Teach It?" *The American Biology Teacher*, 70:2 (February 2008), 79–84.

Moore, Randy. "Creationism in the United States (part 1)", *The American Biology Teacher*, 60:7 (September 1998), 486–498.

Moore, Randy. "Creationism in the United States (part 2)", *The American Biology Teacher*, 60:8 (October 1998), 568–577.

Morgan, Michael Hamilton. *Lost History: The Enduring Legacy of Muslim Scientists, Thinkers and Artists*. Washington DC: National Geographic, 2007.

Moussalli, Ahmad S. *Moderate and Radical Islamic Fundamentalism: The Quest for Modernity, Legitimacy, and the Islamic State*. Gainesville: University Press of Florida, 1999.

Moussalli, Ahmad S. *The Islamic Quest for Democracy, Pluralism and Human Rights*. Gainesville: University Press of Florida, 2001.

Najjar, Fauzi M. "Islamic Fundamentalism and the Intellectuals: The Case of Nasr Hamid Abu Zayd," *British Journal of Middle Eastern Studies*, 27:2 (November 2000), 177–200.

Najjar, Fauzi M. "The Debate on Islam and Secularism in Egypt," *Arab Studies Quarterly*, 18:2 (Spring 1996), 1–21.

Nasr, Vali. "The Rise of 'Muslim Democracy'," *Journal of Democracy*, 16:2 (April 2005), 13–27.

Numbers, Robert L. "Creationism in 20th-Century America," *Science*, 218:5 (November 1982), 538–544.

Numbers, Robert L. *The Creationists*. Berkeley, Los Angeles and London: University of California Press, 1993.

Nyazee, Imran Ahsan Khan. *Theories of Islamic Law: The Methodology of Ijtihād*. Islamabad: Islamic Research Institute and International Institute of Islamic Thought, 1994.

Opwis, Felicitas. *Maslaha and the Purpose of the Law: Islamic Discourses and Legal Change from the 4th/10th to 8th/14th Century*. Leiden and Boston, MA: Brill, 2010.

Opwis, Felicitas. "The Construction of Madhhab Authority: Ibn Taymiyya's Interpretation of Juristic Preference (Istihsan)," *Islamic Law and Society*, 15:2 (2009), 219–249.

Opwis, Felicitas. "Maslaha in Contemporary Islamic Legal Theory," *Islamic Law and Society*, 12:2 (2005), 182–223.

Parker, Theodore. *A Discourse of the Transient and Permanent in Christianity*, published by Electronic Texts in American Studies, University of Nebraska, January 16, 2007, accessed October 27, 2014: http://digitalcommons.unl.edu/etas/14.

Parray, Tauseef Ahmad, "'Islamic Democracy' or Democracy in Islam: Some Key Operational Democratic Concepts and Notions," *World Journal of Islamic History and Civilization*, 2:2 (2012), 66–86.

Parray, Tauseef Ahmad, "The Legal Methodology of 'Fiqh al-Aqalliyyat' and its Critics: An Analytical Study," *Journal of Muslim Minority Affairs*, 32:1 (March 2012), 88–107.

Paulson, Steve. *Atoms and Eden: Conversations on Religion & Science*. Oxford and New York: Oxford University Press, 2010.

Pew Research Center, "Egyptians Embrace Revolt Leaders, Religious Parties and Military, As Well," *Global Attitudes Project*, April 25, 2011, accessed September 1, 2015: http://p ewglobal.org/files/2011/04/Pew-Global-Attitudes-Egypt-Report-FINAL-April-25-2011.pdf.

Piscatori, James. *Islam in a World of Nation-State*. Cambridge: Cambridge University Press, 1986.

Piscatori, James. *Islam, Islamists, and the Electoral Principle in the Middle East*. Leiden: ISIM, 2000.

Polka, Sagi. "The Centric Stream in Egypt and Its Role in the Discourse Surrounding the Shaping of the Country's Cultural Identity," *Middle Eastern Studies*, 39:3 (July 2003), 39–64.

Popper, Karl R. *The Open Society and Its Enemies*. London: Routledge, 1969, first published 1945.

Redondi, Pietro. *Galileo Heretic*, translated by Raymond Rosenthal. Princeton, NJ: Princeton University Press, 1987.

Riedler, Florian. *Opposition and Legitimacy in the Ottoman Empire*. London: Routledge, 2011.

Riexinger, Martin. "Responses of South Asian Muslims to the Theory of Evolution," *Die Welt des Islams*, 49:2 (2009), 212–247.

Rosenthal, Erwin. "Some Reflections on the Separation of Religion and Politics in Modern Islam," *Islamic Studies*, 3:3 (September 1964), 249–284.

Ryad, Umar. *Islamic Reformism and Christianity: A Critical Reading of the Works of Muhammad Rashid Rida and His Associates (1898–1935)*. Leiden: Brill, 2009.

Sandeen, Ernest R. *The Roots of Fundamentalism: British and American Millenarianism 1800–1930*. Chicago: University of Chicago Press, 1970.

Scott, Eugenie C. "Antievolution and Creationism in the United States," *Annual Review of Anthropology*, 26 (1997), 263–289.

Scott, Rachel M. "The Role of 'Ulama' in an Islamic Order: The Early Thought of Muhammad al-Ghazali (1916–1996)," *The Maghreb Review*, 32:2–3 (2007), 149–178.

Sepkoski, David. "Evolutionary Paleontology," in Michael Ruse (ed.), *The Cambridge Encyclopedia of Darwin and Evolutionary Thought*, 353–360. Cambridge: Cambridge University Press, 2013.

Sfeir, George N. "Basic Freedoms in a Fractured Legal Culture: Egypt and the Case of Nasr Hamid Abu Zayd," *The Middle East Journal*, 52:3 (Summer 1998), 402–414.

Shavit, Uriya. *Islamism and the West: From "Cultural Attack" to "Missionary Migrant"*. London and New York: Routledge, 2014.

Shavit, Uriya. *Shari'a and Muslim Minorities: The Wasati and Salafi Approaches to Fiqh al-Aqalliyyat al-Muslima*. Oxford: Oxford University Press, 2015.

Shaw, Stanford J. and Shaw, Ezel Kural. *History of the Ottoman Empire and Modern Turkey, vol 2*. Cambridge: Cambridge University Press, 1977.

Silberstein, Laurence J. (ed.). *Jewish Fundamentalism in Comparative Perspective: Religion, Ideology and the Crisis of Modernity*. New York: New York University, 1993.

Skovgaard-Petersen, Jakob. "Yusuf al-Qaradawi and al-Azhar," in Bettina Gräf and Jakob Skovgaard-Petersen (eds), *Global Mufti: The Phenomenon of Yusuf al-Qaradawi*, 27–53. London: Hurst & Company, 2009.

Smith, Charles D. "The Crisis of Orientation: The Shift of Intellectuals to Islamic Subjects in the 1930's," *International Journal of Middle East Studies*, 4:4 (1973), 382–410.

Solberg, Anne Ross. *The Mahdi Wears Armani: An Analysis of the Harun Yahya Enterprise*. Stockholm: Södertörns högskola, 2013.

Şükrü, Hanioğlu M. *A Brief History of the Late Ottoman Empire*. Princeton: Princeton University Press, 2008.

Tamimi, Azzam S. *Rachid al-Ghannouchi: A Democrat within Islamism*. Oxford: Oxford University Press, 2001.

Tamimi, Azzam S. "The Renaissance of Islam," *Daedalus*, 132:3 (July 2003), 51–58.

Tammam, Husam. "Yusuf Qaradawi and the Muslim Brothers: The Nature of a Special Relationship," in Bettina Gräf and Jakob Skovgaard-Petersen (eds), *Global Mufti: The Phenomenon of Yusuf al-Qaradawi*, 55–84. London: Hurst & Company, 2009.

Tibi, Bassam. "Islamist Parties and Democracy: Why They Can't be Democratic," *Journal of Democracy*, 19:3 (July 2008), 43–48.

Tibi, Bassam. "The Worldview of Sunni Arab Fundamentalists," in Martin E. Marty and R. Scott Appleby (eds), *Fundamentalisms and Society: Reclaiming the Sciences, the Family and Education—The Fundamentalist Project, vol. 2*, 73–102. Chicago and London: The University of Chicago Press, 1993.

Toprak, Binnaz. "Islam and Democracy in Turkey," *Turkish Studies*, 6:2 (June 2005), 167–186.

Torelli, Stefano Maria. "The 'AKP Model' and Tunisia's al-Nahda: From Convergence to Competition?" *Insight Turkey*, 14:3 (2012), 65–83.

Toynbee, Arnold. *Civilization on Trial*. London, New York and Toronto: Oxford University Press, 1948.

Villarreal, Judith A. "God and Darwin in the Classroom: The Creation/Evolution Controversy," *Chicago-Kent Law Review*, 64:1 (January 1988), 335–374.

Voll, John O. "Fundamentalism in the Sunni Arab World: Egypt and the Sudan," in Martin E. Marty and R. Scott Appleby (eds), *Fundamentalisms Observed*, part of the Fundamentalism Project, vol. 1, 345–402. Chicago and London: University of Chicago Press, 1991.

Von Kügelgen, Anke. "A Call for Rationalism: 'Arab Averroists' in the Twentieth Century," *Alif: Journal of Comparative Poetics*, no. 16 (January 1996), 97–132.

Weismann, Itzchak. *Abd al-Rahman al-Kawakibi: Islamic Reform and Arab Revival*. London: Oneworld Publications, 2015.

Whittingham, Martin. *Al-Ghazali and the Qur'an: One Book, Many Meanings*. London and New York: Routledge, 2007.

Wright, Conrad. *Three Prophets of Religious Liberalism: Channing, Emerson, Parker*. Boston: Beacon Press, 1961.

Yavuz, Hakan M. *Secularism and Muslim Democracy in Turkey*. Cambridge: Cambridge University Press, 2009.

Ziada, Nikula. *Tunis fi 'Ahd al-Himayya 1881–1934*. n.p.: 1963.

Ziadat, Adel A. "Early Reception of Einstein's Relativity in the Arab Periodical Press," *Annals of Science*, 51:1 (1994), 17–35.

Ziadat, Adel A. *Western Science in the Arab World: The Impact of Darwinism, 1860–1930*. London: Palgrave Macmillan, 1986.

INDEX